MEMOIRS OF THE LIFE OF
SIR SAMUEL ROMILLY

The Development of Industrial Society Series

MEMOIRS OF THE LIFE OF SIR SAMUEL ROMILLY

with a Selection from His Correspondence

Edited by His Sons

Volume 1

IRISH UNIVERSITY PRESS
Shannon Ireland

First edition London 1840
Second edition London 1840

This I U P reprint is a photolithographic facsimile of the second edition and is unabridged, retaining the original printer's imprint.

ISBN 0 7165 1784 1 Three volumes
ISBN 0 7165 1785 X Volume 1
ISBN 0 7165 1786 8 Volume 2
ISBN 0 7165 2062 1 Volume 3

T M MacGlinchey Publisher

Irish University Press Shannon Ireland

PRINTED IN THE REPUBLIC OF IRELAND BY
ROBERT HOGG PRINTER TO IRISH UNIVERSITY PRESS

The Development of Industrial Society Series

This series comprises reprints of contemporary documents and commentaries on the social, political and economic upheavals in nineteenth-century England.

England, as the first industrial nation, was also the first country to experience the tremendous social and cultural impact consequent on the alienation of people in industrialized countries from their rural ancestry. The Industrial Revolution which had begun to intensify in the mid-eighteenth century, spread swiftly from England to Europe and America. Its effects have been far-reaching: the growth of cities with their urgent social and physical problems; greater social mobility; mass education; increasingly complex administration requirements in both local and central government; the growth of democracy and the development of new theories in economics; agricultural reform and the transformation of a way of life.

While it would be pretentious to claim for a series such as this an in-depth coverage of all these aspects of the new society, the works selected range in content from *The Hungry Forties* (1904), a collection of letters by ordinary working people describing their living conditions and the effects of mechanization on their day-to-day lives, to such analytical studies as Leone Levi's *History of British Commerce* (1880) and *Wages and Earnings of the Working Classes* (1885); M. T. Sadler's *The Law of Population* (1830); John Wade's radical documentation of government corruption, *The Extraordinary Black Book* (1831); C. Edward Lester's trenchant social investigation, *The Glory and Shame of England* (1866); and many other influential books and pamphlets.

The editor's intention has been to make available important contemporary accounts, studies and records, written or compiled by men and women of integrity and scholarship whose reactions to the growth of a new kind of society are valid touchstones for today's reader. Each title (and the particular edition used) has been chosen on a twofold basis (1) its intrinsic worth as a record or commentary, and (2) its contribution to the development of an industrial society. It is hoped that this collection will help to increase our understanding of a people and an epoch.

The Editor
Irish University Press

Painted by Sir T. Lawrence, P.R.A. *Engraved by E. Finden.*

London, John Murray, Albemarle Street, April, 1840.

MEMOIRS

OF

THE LIFE

OF

SIR SAMUEL ROMILLY,

WRITTEN BY HIMSELF;

WITH A SELECTION FROM

HIS CORRESPONDENCE.

EDITED BY HIS SONS.

IN THREE VOLUMES.

VOL. I.

Second Edition.

LONDON:
JOHN MURRAY, ALBEMARLE STREET.
MDCCCXL.

LONDON:
Printed by A. SPOTTISWOODE,
New-Street-Square.

PREFACE.

THE publication of the "Memoirs of Sir Samuel Romilly edited by his Sons" requires some explanation of what is included under this title, and of the motives which have led to this undertaking.

From the great mass of papers left by Sir S. Romilly, those have been selected which furnish, in some measure, a connected history of his life. They begin with a narrative, in two parts, of the events of his earliest years, from 1757 to the close of 1789. The former of these bears date 1796, two years previous to his marriage: it appears to have been carefully revised and corrected, and a fair copy was made of it, of which no other instance is to be found amongst these papers. The latter part, dated in 1813, seems to have been more hastily written; the rough draft, consisting of loose sheets, is the only copy; and the alterations and corrections which are to be found in it appear to have been made when it was originally written. With the exception of two passages, both parts have been published entire.

This narrative is followed by a series of letters written to his brother-in-law, the Rev. Mr. Roget, who was then residing at Lausanne: they commence in 1780, and continue till the death of Mr. Roget in 1783. Besides many domestic details, most of which are omitted, these letters contain an account of the principal events which took place in England during those years, and much criticism on the books he was then reading. Such of them have been selected as present the most faithful picture of his mind and disposition at that period of his life.

No original materials exist from which alone it would have been possible to continue the history of Sir Samuel Romilly's life during the sixteen years which elapsed from 1789 to the beginning of 1806. This interval has been filled up with a selection from such letters, either from his correspondents or himself, as seemed best calculated to supply this deficiency. To this correspondence has been added the diary of a visit to Paris in 1802, and an unfinished narrative of certain events belonging to the history of his life which took place in 1805.

The next and principal part of this work is a journal of his parliamentary life, extending from the beginning of the year 1806 to the close of it in 1818. The original manuscript is contained in three small quarto volumes. Except a few references to subsequent passages, and some pages inserted in the middle of the second volume, containing letters relating to the Bristol election, no addition appears to have been made to any part of it after it was first written; and, except two lines which are effaced in the second volume, no passage is erased, and very few corrections are to be found, throughout this manuscript. The Editors have added several notes, some to furnish explanations and references, and some for the purpose of introducing at the proper dates a few contemporaneous letters: all the other notes and the marginal abstracts which appear here, together with a copious index, exist in the original. A few passages have been omitted, but no attempt has been made to remove any of those marks of haste which show the manner in which this journal was written from day to day, as the occasion prompted.

Four papers, which are entitled "Letters to C.," to which is prefixed a separate explanatory introduction, constitute the last portion of these Memoirs.

Such is a short account of the papers which compose this work. The reader must not expect to find in them any connected history of the times in which they were written, and scarcely any but an incidental reference to the great events which were then taking place on the continent of Europe. But to record public events did not enter into the views with which these Memoirs were written, neither does it constitute any part of those with which they are published. It should be borne in mind, throughout, that to give such a history of Sir Samuel Romilly's life, as will illustrate his character, by describing his feelings and opinions as far as the production of original documents will accomplish it, is the exclusive object of this work. The Editors have accordingly strictly confined themselves to the task of selection and arrangement. They have sedulously abstained from comment or remark; and, with the exception of the few notes and references, not a word will be found in these volumes which has not been written by their father, or by one of his correspondents. They have, however, availed themselves, although very sparingly*, of the power of suppression; but in no case has any passage been omitted which would have given a different colour to the observations in the text.

Some passages will be found in the parliamentary diary in which the conduct of various persons is animadverted upon; but wherever these have been retained they have been considered to relate exclusively to public character or public conduct, and to be such as the terms in which they are expressed, and the object for which they were written, entitled the Editors to publish, and would not have justified them in suppressing.

There are, however, many deficiencies in these Memoirs which, consistently with the plan adopted, the Editors are unable to supply. Of one part, and that a most material one, of their father's life, they regret to say that no account is to be found in these pages. Of his labours in the study of the law, of his gradual rise and ultimate success in his profession, to which he owed the opportunities of doing all that is here recorded, these pages contain scarcely any mention. Although abundant materials remain which testify the intensity of his labours in his profession, he has left none which show the

* The passages omitted from the parliamentary journal amount, in the whole, to eight pages, of which five are a mere catalogue of places passed through in travelling.

mode by which he rose, or the eminence which he reached. The Editors have not sought for information to supply this omission, being anxious that his character should appear as it is displayed by himself. If, in truth, they had departed from this course, it would have been, not to record his triumphs in his profession, or to relate the influence of his eloquence, but to describe some few of those scenes which live in the memories of them all, when, in the intervals of relaxation from his labours and in the midst of his children, he sympathised with their pursuits, partook of their enjoyments, added by his gaiety to their mirth, and to each, in his different way, was scarcely less a companion than a father. This gratification, however, they have not ventured to allow themselves; and, as they neither pretend to write his life, nor affect to possess the impartiality which should belong to those who undertake that task, they have deemed it necessary, with whatever reluctance, to confine themselves strictly to the course they had laid down for their conduct, and to which alone they felt themselves to be equal. The portrait they present must, they are aware, be in many respects unfinished, and in some scarcely more than an outline; but many considerations, amongst which the following have had the greatest weight, have induced them to offer it, imperfect as it is, to the observation of the public:—

In a codicil to Sir Samuel Romilly's will, after stating that he had prepared materials for a work on Criminal Law*, he proceeds to say, "What I

* The papers here referred to are mentioned subsequently in a note to the introduction to the Letters to C., Vol. III. p. 372.

have written is not by any means in a state fit for publication; but I should be glad if some friend of mine would look over it; and if he thought that there were any extracts or detached parts of it which it might be useful to publish, either as furnishing good observations, or affording hints which might be serviceable to others who may treat on the subject, that so much of them should be printed with my name. That such a publication may be injurious to my reputation as an author or a lawyer I am quite indifferent about; if it can be any way useful, that is all I desire."

Every perusal of their father's manuscripts impressed the Editors with the belief that the publication of another portion of them, that which forms the principal part of these volumes, would, though in a different way, fulfil the spirit of his wishes, and accomplish the objects he had in view, without diminishing or impeding any benefit which might flow from a compliance with the request he had expressed. And they further felt a conviction that, although he perhaps did not contemplate the possibility of these Memoirs being known to others than his children and their descendants, yet that, if he had believed that a more extended knowledge of them could in any way tend to the advancement of human happiness, he would, had it been possible to consult his wishes, have consented to their publication.

Strongly as the Editors felt this conviction, they distrusted their own judgment in a case where they felt personally so deep an interest, and would probably have refrained from acting upon it, if they had not been supported by other authority; but their opinions were confirmed and enforced by those of the late Mr. Dumont, the earliest of the friends who survived their father, and who, after an attentive consideration of these papers, urged their publication in the following manner, in a letter * intended to be addressed to the friend to whom Sir Samuel Romilly had entrusted the care of his children, and who, as far as it was possible for any one to do so, has supplied to them the place of their father.

"I propose, my dear Whishaw, to set down the principal observations which have occurred to me in reading the memoirs of the friend whose virtuous intentions we wish to fulfil, and whose objects we desire to accomplish, by devoting to the public good those writings which breathe, in a peculiar manner, the spirit of patriotism and benevolence.

"The private memoirs being written only for himself and his family, and he never having thought of publishing them, it may be asked if his friends have the right to do so; that is, if they would be authorised by him thus to reveal his inmost thoughts, and to display the privacies of life, the very secrecy of which endears them to us? Should I wish it, were I in his place? and I, who knew him so well, who was thoroughly acquainted with his most intimate disposition, can I

* This letter was, in fact, never sent, but was found amongst Mr. Dumont's papers after his death. The passage in the text is a translation of that portion of it which relates to the private memoirs and the parliamentary journal; the rest of the letter refers to other manuscripts of Sir Samuel Romilly, which are not of an autobiographical character.

believe that he would approve of their publication? I believe — to answer my own question — that, always true, always seeking in the public good for the sources of his actions, he would say, 'If my friends think that this publication can injure no one, and that it may be of public utility, I resign myself to their judgment, and sacrifice my own inclination.' I think also that it must have occurred to him, as to every one who writes his own life, that these recollections might be one day published either by his friends, or from some accidental cause; and this appears to me the more probable from the habitual reserve which is preserved towards the persons mentioned in them.

"There is, I think, no other work of this kind which could produce the same moral effects upon a youthful mind. On one side we see great talents, great reputation, and ample fortune; and, on the other, an obscure origin, scarcely any education, years lost,—and all these disadvantages overcome by unwearied application, and by efforts constantly directed towards the same end. It is a lesson composed entirely of facts, worth more than volumes of moral sentiments; to which none of those pretences, by which young people commonly reconcile to themselves their own nothingness, can be suggested as an answer. Nor does the example stop here. During twenty years, no one enjoyed happiness surpassing his, and this of a kind to be described by him alone who felt it. Although his natural disposition was not without a tinge of melancholy, this had ceased at the moment of his marriage, and left only that serious turn of mind which gave weight to all his thoughts. I, who knew him from the age of two-and-twenty, could describe how vividly his flexible imagination dwelt on the pleasures derived from the beauties of nature, from literature, from the fine arts, and from the society of his friends; and how he made all these enjoyments keep their proper place in the disposal of his time. But never did I see in him any trace of those habits of despondency which produce discontent with one's self and with the world. A charm, too, is spread over the whole work, and it leaves in the mind a feeling of affection for the author; and this because he displays himself without pretension, and because the picture he draws relates only to those moral feelings, those private virtues, which every one can imitate, and to that domestic life, the happiness of which, as it is derived from the purest and most amiable feelings, creates jealousy in the breast of no one. Mere men of the world will probably disbelieve it: in their eyes it will appear a romance, but one that will not offend them; and, by the middling ranks, the most numerous class of society, these Memoirs will be read with the same feeling as that which dictated their composition.

"As to the Memoirs of his Parliamentary life, I should have still fewer doubts about them. I know that he wrote them only for his private use; but, at the same time, the only objection that he could have made to their publication is derived from their imperfect state, the consequence of the little care he was able to bestow upon them. But it appears to me that we are able to appreciate the force of this objection. If these Memoirs present a very interesting summary; if they will be read (and as far as I can myself judge this will be the case) with very great pleasure; if they contain a parliamentary history, instructive in the highest degree with regard to the course of public affairs, to the incidents which determine their issue, to the difficulties which lie in the way of all reforms, and to the precautions necessary to ensure success; if they contain abundance of novel and striking observations on many parts of civil and penal legislation; if, as I believe, all this is true, then I think that the publication of these Memoirs, although in some respects and on certain subjects they be but mere sketches, will confer an essential benefit on the public.

"Above all, it appears to me that no one ever saw a more perfect model of all that ought to contitute a public man in the character of a member of parliament. And all this appears by a simple statement, with no pretension, no exaggeration, no display of feeling, not a word of satire, not an expression which denotes a man hurt by his want of success, but, on the contrary, representing him never discouraged, always ready to renew his defeated projects, and always entertaining the hope that reason would one day triumph.

"To me, these Memoirs appear a precious monument: and when I reflect that this laborious undertaking was the work of a man always occupied to the utmost extent, who gave up to it, as well as to all his legislative labours, that time from whence he might have derived very considerable professional advantages, it seems to me that it cannot fail to produce a lasting effect upon those who know how to profit by a great example, and to reflect upon what may be done with life by him who chooses to employ it."

It is not for the purpose of recording praise of their father, or of deprecating criticism on these papers, which it would ill become his sons to attempt, that they have inserted this letter, but because the writer's intimacy with him, prolonged without interruption from youth to the last concluding scenes of his life, gives a weight and authority to the opinion here expressed, which scarcely leave them the liberty of choice.

In addition to these, the weightiest considerations, they have felt that, if they shrank from this task, it might be performed at some distant period, when those to whom the perusal of this work would afford the highest gratification had passed away, and when none remained either to correct accidental errors, or to bear witness to the accuracy of its author.

If the following pages can furnish any useful example or convey any useful instruction, and thus contribute to the honour of their father's memory, their end will be answered. It is, in truth, with the view of promoting the objects to which he devoted his life, in obedience to the spirit which dictated the latest wish recorded by himself, and under the conviction that these objects and this wish will, by these means, be to some extent accomplished, that his sons now give these papers to the world.

THE following statement respecting that portion of Sir Samuel Romilly's papers which, not being of an autobiographical nature, forms no part of the present publication, is inserted by the Editors, at the request of their father's executor, Mr. Whishaw.

"In a codicil to Sir Samuel Romilly's will, dated Oct. 1818, there is the following passage: —

"'I have for some time past employed what leisure I have had in preparing materials for a work on Criminal Law, and have written some observations, and collected facts upon different heads, which would enter into such a work. What I have written is not by any means in a state fit for publication; but I should be glad if some friend of mine would look over it; and if he thought that there were any extracts or detached parts of it which it might be useful to publish, either as furnishing good observations, or affording hints which might be serviceable to others who may treat on the subject, that so much of them should be printed with my name. That such a publication may be injurious to my reputation as an author or a lawyer I am quite indifferent about; if it can be any way useful, that is all I desire. If my friend, Mr. Whishaw, would look over the papers with this view, and decide what should be done with respect to them, I should be highly gratified; they could not possibly be in better hands. If it were not to suit him to undertake such a task, perhaps my friend Mr. Brougham, who finds time for any thing that has a tendency to the advancement of human happiness, would be able, notwithstanding his numerous occupations, to perform this office of friendship.'

"In compliance with these directions, Mr. Whishaw carefully examined the papers in question, and, on full consideration, was of opinion that, under all the circumstances of the case, the publication of them was no longer a matter of importance, and, unless accompanied or preceded by a more general publication, was, on the whole, not advisable. The amendment of the Criminal Law had made great progress in public opinion, had engaged the attention of Parliament and the executive government, and several of the proposed measures had been anticipated by the legislature. He willingly admits that his peculiar habits, and aversion to publicity, may have contributed to this opinion. But on consulting others in whom he had confidence, and especially his excellent friend Sir James Mackintosh, then chairman of the Parliamentary committee on the amendment of the Criminal Law, his opinion was confirmed by their judgment. He intimated this to the Editors; and delivered up to them all their father's manuscripts at that time in his possession, including those which form the principal part of the following work, and respecting which no other directions had been left, but that they 'should be preserved for his children.' The papers on Criminal Law were then in the hands of Lord Brougham; but these also were subsequently returned to the family, with expressions of great kindness and approbation. To that distinguished individual Mr. W. gladly avails himself of the present occasion to record the deep sense of gratitude he, in common with every member of Sir S. Romilly's family, entertains for the repeated tributes paid by his Lordship, in his writings and in his speeches, to the talents and virtues of their departed friend."

CONTENTS

OF

THE FIRST VOLUME.

NARRATIVE OF THE EARLY LIFE OF SIR SAMUEL ROMILLY.

1757—1778.

1778—1789.

LETTERS TO THE REV. JOHN ROGET.

1780—1783.

LETTERS FROM THE COUNT DE MIRABEAU AND OTHERS.

1783—1787.

CORRESPONDENCE WITH M. DUMONT AND OTHERS.

1788—1789.

MEMOIRS

OF

SIR SAMUEL ROMILLY.

NARRATIVE OF HIS EARLY LIFE WRITTEN BY HIMSELF IN 1796.

1757—1778.

August 16. 1796.

I SIT down to write my life; the life of one who never achieved any thing memorable, who will probably leave no posterity, and the memory of whom is therefore likely to survive him only till the last of a few remaining and affectionate friends shall have followed him to the grave. A subject so uninteresting will hardly awaken the curiosity of any one into whose hands this writing may chance to fall, and I may almost be assured of having no reader but myself. In truth, it is for myself that I write, for myself alone; for my own instruction, and my own amusement. In old age, if I should live to be old, I may find a pleasure, congenial to that season of life, in retracing the actions and sentiments of my youth and of my manhood, less imperfectly than by the aid of an impaired and decaying memory, and as it were in living again with relations and with friends long deceased.

If I had the inclination, I have not the means of speaking of many of my ancestors. The first of them that I have ever heard of is my great-grandfather; and of him I know little more than that he had a pretty good landed estate at Montpellier, in the south of France, where he resided. He was a Protestant, but living under the religious tyranny of Louis XIV., and in a part of France where persecution raged with the greatest fury, he found it prudent to dissemble his faith, and it was only in the privacy of his own family that he ventured to worship God in the way which he judged would find favour in His sight. His only son, my grandfather, he educated in his own religious principles, and so deeply did the young man imbibe them that, when he was about seventeen years of age*, he made a journey to Geneva for the sole purpose of there receiving the sacrament. It was a journey which had most important consequences to his posterity, and to which I owe that I was not born under the despotism of the French monarchy, and that I have not fallen a victim to the more cruel despotism which succeeded it. At Geneva my grandfather met with the celebrated Saurin, who happened to be on a visit there. The reputation of that extraordinary man was then at the highest. He was revered as an apostle; and his eloquence and his authority could not fail to make a forcible impression on a young mind deeply tinctured with that religious fervour, which persecution generally inspires. The result of a few conversations was a fixed determination in my grandfather to abandon

* In 1701: he was born in 1684.

for ever his native country, his connexions, his friends, his affectionate parents, and the inheritance which awaited him; and to trust to his own industry for a subsistence amidst strangers and in a foreign land, but in the enjoyment of civil and religious liberty. Instead of returning to Montpellier, he set out for London; and it was not till he had landed in England, that he apprized his father of the irrevocable resolution which he had formed. He, at first, met with much more prosperity in the country, which he had thus adopted, than he could have had reason to expect. His father endeavoured to alleviate the hardships of his exile by remitting him money; and, after he had been a few years in England, he set up with a tolerable capital at Hoxton, in the neighbourhood of London, in the business of a wax-bleacher. He soon afterwards married Judith de Monsallier *, the daughter of another French refugee, and he became the father of a very numerous family. His generosity, his piety, his affection for his wife, his tenderness towards his children, and their reciprocal fondness and veneration for him, are topics on which I have often heard my father and my aunts enlarge with the most lively emotion. His generosity, indeed, was such, that it led him into expences, which the profits of his business alone would have ill enabled him to support; but he had a better resource in the remit-

* She was one of four children of Francis de Monsallier: the other three were also daughters; Lucy, married to Solomon Pages; Anne Marie Picart, married to a person of the name of De Laferty; and Elizabeth, married to *** Fludyer. See the will of Francis de Monsallier, dated 5th May, 1725. When he died does not appear, but there is a codicil to his will, dated 13th Oct. 1726.

tances, which he was seldom long without receiving from his father.

This resource, however, at last failed, and a sad reverse of fortune ensued. His father died: a distant relation (but the next heir who was a Catholic) took possession of the estate, and my grandfather was reduced to a very scanty income for the subsistence of his large family; difficulties were soon multiplied upon him, and bankruptcy and poverty were the consequences. His gentle spirit sunk under these calamities, and he died at the age of forty-nine of a broken heart, leaving behind him a widow, four sons, and four daughters, and most of them wholly unprovided for.* To them, though they were all of an age to discern the full extent of the melancholy prospect before them, all misfortunes appeared light in comparison with the loss of such a parent; and the youngest of them, whose name was Joseph, abandoning himself to grief and despair, was within a few months buried in the grave, which had recently closed upon his father.

Of the three remaining sons, Stephen, Isaac, and Peter, my father was the youngest. He was born in the year 1712, and had been bound by my grandfather an apprentice to a jeweller, of the name of Lafosse, who lived in Broad Street, in the City.

During his apprenticeship he contracted a great intimacy with one of his fellow-apprentices of the name of Garnault, who was, like himself, the son of

* He died in 1733. His four daughters were Ann, afterwards married to **** Gibbons; Catherine, who married **** Hunter, and Martha and Margaret who were never married.

a Protestant refugee. This lad had a sister to whom my father was introduced, and his acquaintance with her soon grew up into a mutual passion. The brother long encouraged it; but afterwards, either from a change in his own prospects in life, founded on a hope which he conceived that a rich uncle would leave him his estate, or from mere caprice, he began to look on my father with coolness, disapproved the visits to his sister, and at last desired that they might be discontinued. She had no money, indeed, but she had rich relations, and they too were averse to her marrying a young man without fortune, and with no other expectations than what industry, honesty, youth, and good health could enable him to form. The passion, however, which, under the sanction of her nearest relations, she had indulged, had taken too strong possession of her mind to be dismissed just as they should dictate; but what she could do she did, she submitted to their authority, resigned all hopes of marrying my father, and gave herself up to a despair which destroyed her health, and endangered her life.

My father soon afterwards quitted the kingdom, and went to reside at Paris. There he continued for a considerable time, working as a journeyman in his business; and having saved out of his little earnings a small sum of money, he employed it in making an excursion into the south of France. Montpellier was amongst the places which he visited; and he did not fail to take a view of the family estate, now in the possession of strangers and irrecoverably lost, since it could be redeemed only by falsehood and apostacy.

* * * * * *[1]

His children were his greatest delight; and yet of the six eldest of those children, five died in infancy. The sixth, a girl, lived indeed a few years longer, but she lived only till she had taken stronger hold of his affections, and then was torn from him like the rest. The death of this favourite child was considered by my father as the greatest calamity of his life. Her extraordinary perfections, my father's doting love of her, his habit of waking her in the morning by playing on a flute at the side of her bed, his anxious solicitude during her illness, and the violence of his grief at the loss of her, have been often described to me. I was not born[2] myself till several years after her death.

Naturally, my father was of the most cheerful and happy disposition, always in good humour, always kind and indulgent, always, even in the worst circumstances, disposed to expect the best, enjoying all the good he met with in life, and consoling himself under adversity with the hope that it would not be of long duration. Of extreme sensibility, and quick in expressing what he felt, he was subject to violent transports of anger; but they were always short and transient, and left not the least trace of resentment behind, not even where a real

[1] In this part of the MS. there is a considerable erasure. The writer had no doubt proceeded to give an account of his father's marriage, and of the circumstances connected with that event; but dissatisfied, as it would seem, with what he had written, he expunged several pages. This chasm in the narrative he never afterwards filled up; and, the papers he has left do not afford any materials from which to supply the deficiency, beyond the fact that Miss Garnault's family at length consented to her union with Mr. Romilly's father, which accordingly took place. — Ed.

[2] He was born on the 1st of March, 1757. — Ed.

injury had been done him: warm and persevering in his friendship, he can hardly be said to have ever entertained an enmity. He was very religious, but his religion was without austerity: and, though he did not fail to read prayers in the midst of his family every Sunday, he attached much less importance to the forms of religion than to the substance of it; and the substance he thought consisted in doing good to our fellow-creatures. His charity far exceeded the means of his fortune, and he sometimes indulged it to a degree which cold discretion might tax with imprudence. At a time when he had but a slender income, and a numerous family, it happened that he frequently observed in a street in his neighbourhood a woman lying at a door in rags and dirt, half naked, and apparently in extreme distress, yet generally intoxicated: she had a female infant by her side, who was crying for bread, but to whose cries she seemed insensible. My father's imagination was forcibly struck by this spectacle of wretchedness and depravity. He pictured to himself, in strong colours, the fate to which the wretched child seemed devoted, and he determined if possible to save her. He applied to the woman, who, without difficulty, parted with the child, of which she did not pretend to be the mother. He clothed her, maintained her for several years, had her taught to read and work, and when she had grown up to a proper age, provided for her the place of a servant, and had the satisfaction to see her in that situation living for many years with reputation and comfort.

There was one occurrence, and that a very important one, in his life, in which he acted with such unexampled disinterestedness, and made so extraordinary a sacrifice of his happiness to what he conceived to be his duty, that it is with great reluctance that I deny myself the satisfaction of relating it; but it is unfortunately connected with transactions, the memory of which might give great pain to persons now living, and who perhaps may survive me. My father, therefore, I am sure, would be sorry that it should be remembered, and I suppress what would add so largely to his praise from a pious respect for his benevolence.

He used often to talk to his children of the pleasure of doing good, and of the rewards which virtue found in itself; and from his lips that doctrine came to us, not as a dry and illusive precept, but as a heart-felt truth, and as the fruit of the happiest experience.

All my father's favourite amusements were such as his home only could afford him. He was fond of reading, and he had formed for himself a small, but a tolerably well chosen, library. He was an admirer of the fine arts, but pictures being too costly for his purchase, he limited himself to prints; and in the latter part of his life, as he grew richer, indulging himself in this innocent luxury to a degree perhaps of extravagance, he had at last a very large and valuable collection. He took pleasure in gardening, and he hired a small garden, in which he passed in the summer most of the few leisure hours which his business afforded him. But I am anticipating a subsequent period.

The loss of so many children filled my father

with consternation. He began to ascribe it to the unwholesomeness of a constant town residence, and he determined to take a small lodging in the country, where his family might, during the summer months, breathe a purer air than that of London. He accordingly hired some rooms at Marylebone, which was then a small village about a mile distant from town, though it has now, for many years, by the increase of new buildings, been united to, and become a part of the metropolis. My father had reason to congratulate himself upon the success of this experiment, for all the children which he afterwards had lived to years of maturity. They were only three; my brother Thomas, my sister Catherine, and myself.

We were brought up principally by a very kind and pious female relation of my mother's, a Mrs. Margaret Facquier, who had lived in our family ever since my mother's marriage. She taught us to read, and to read with intelligence; though the books in which we were taught were ill suited to our age. The Bible, the Spectator, and an English translation of Telemachus, are those which I recollect our having in most frequent use. But this kind relation had too bad a state of health to attend to us constantly. During the last forty years of her life, it seldom happened that many weeks passed without her being confined to her bed, or at least to her room. The care of us, upon these occasions, devolved on a female servant of the name of Mary Evans, who was ill qualified to give us instruction or to cultivate our understandings; but whose tender and affectionate nature, whose sensibility at the sufferings of others, and earnest desire to relieve them to the utmost extent of her little means, could hardly fail to improve the hearts of those who were under her care.

Perhaps there hardly ever existed three persons more affectionate, more kind, more compassionate, and whose sentiments and whose example were better calculated to inspire every soft and generous affection, than these two excellent women and our most excellent father. It was under the influence of these examples that we passed our earliest years; as for my mother, she was incapable, from the bad state of her health, of taking any part in our education.

The servant whom I have mentioned was to me in the place of a mother. I loved her to adoration. I remember, when quite a child, kissing, unperceived by her, the clothes which she wore; and when she once entertained a design of quitting our family and going to live with her own relations, receiving the news as that of the greatest misfortune that could befal me, and going up into my room in an agony of affliction, and imploring God upon my knees to avert so terrible a calamity.

It is commonly said to be the happy privilege of youth to feel no misfortunes but the present, to be careless of the future, and forgetful of the past. That happy privilege I cannot recollect having ever enjoyed. In my earliest infancy, my imagination was alarmed and my fears awakened by stories of devils, witches, and apparitions; and they had a much greater effect upon me than is even usual with children; at least I judge so, from their effect being of a more than usual duration. The images of terror, with which those tales abound, infested my imagination very long after I had discarded all belief in the tales themselves, and in the notions on which they are built; and even now, although I have been accustomed for many years to pass my evenings and my nights in solitude, and without even a servant sleeping in my chambers, I must, with some shame, confess that they are sometimes very unwelcome intruders upon my thoughts. I often recollect, and never without shuddering, a story which, in my earliest childhood,(for my memory hardly reaches beyond it,) I overheard, as I lay in bed, related by an old woman who was employed about our house, of a servant murdering his master; and particularly that part of it where the murderer, with a knife in his hand, had crept, in the dead of night, to the side of the bed in which his master lay asleep, and when, as from a momentary compunction, he was hesitating before he executed his bloody purpose, he on a sudden heard a deep hollow voice whispering close to his ear in a commanding tone, "that he should accomplish his design!"

But it was not merely such extravagant stories that disturbed my peace; as dreadful an impression was made on me by relations of murders and acts of cruelty. The prints, which I found in the lives of the martyrs and the Newgate Calendar, have cost me many sleepless nights. My dreams too were disturbed by the hideous images which haunted my imagination by day. I thought myself present at executions, murders, and scenes of blood; and I have often lain in bed agitated by my terrors, equally afraid of remaining awake in the dark, and of falling asleep to encounter the horrors of my dreams. Often have I in my evening prayers to God besought him, with the utmost fervour, to suffer me to pass the night undisturbed by horrid dreams.

I had other apprehensions, and some of a kind which are commonly reserved for maturer years. I was oppressed with a constant terror of death, not indeed for myself, but for my father, whose life was certainly much dearer to me than my own. I never looked on his countenance, on which care and affliction had deeply imprinted premature marks of old age, without reflecting that there could not be many years of his excellent life still to come. If he returned home later than usual, though but half an hour, a thousand accidents presented themselves to my mind; and, when put to bed, I lay sleepless and in the most tormenting anxiety till I heard him knock. This state of mind became so habitual to me, that an uneasiness and a foreboding of some misfortune came upon me regularly about half an hour before the usual time of his return, and went on increasing till the moment of his arrival. So far, indeed, was I from endeavouring to overcome this weakness, that I willingly encouraged it, from a strange idea which I had conceived, that by dreading misfortunes I prevented them, and that the calamity, which I feared would, whenever it happened, come upon me quite unawares. I took a pleasure therefore in indulging my terrors, and reproached myself if ever I felt a moment of security.

The idea of my father's approaching death pursued me even in the midst of scenes which seemed most likely to dispel such gloomy reflections. I remember once accompanying him to the theatre on a night when Garrick acted. The play was Zara, and it was followed by the farce of Lethe. The inimitable and various powers of acting, which were displayed by that admirable performer in both those pieces, could not for a moment drive from my mind the dismal idea which haunted me. In the aged Lusignan I saw what my father in a few years would be, tottering on the brink of the grave; and when in the farce the old man desires to drink the waters of Lethe that he may forget how old he is, I thought that the same idea must naturally present itself to my father; that he must see as clearly as I did that his death could not be at the distance of many years; and that, notwithstanding his apparent cheerfulness, that idea must often prey upon his mind, and poison his happiness more even than it did mine. I looked at his countenance as he was sitting by me, persuaded myself that I observed a change in his features, conjectured that the same painful reflections had occurred to him as had to me, repented of having entered the theatre, and returned from it as sad and as dejected as I could have done from a funeral.

The anxiety which I constantly felt about my father strengthened in me the natural inclination which I always had for a life of peace and tranquillity; and gave me such an aversion, and even a terror of every kind of tumult and disturbance, as I can hardly describe. It was not often that my father took us to any public amusements: it did however sometimes happen; and my mother, whenever her health would allow of it, was of the party. My father, as I have already observed, was of a temper warm and impatient of injury, and his solicitude for the beloved objects which he had under his charge made him resent, with an unnecessary degree of warmth and violence, the incivility of those who happened to crowd upon us, or in any way to incommode us. The dread of such quarrels, and of what might be the consequence of them to him, always depressed my spirits when in any place of public resort; and the greatest pleasure I reaped from those kind of amusements was the satisfaction with which, upon our return home, I reflected that he was safe, as if there had been some mighty danger which he had escaped.

My infancy and my childhood, though they were thus clouded, did not however pass without many gleams of sunshine. My spirits were often high, even to a degree of tumult and intoxication, and my imagination was not always employed upon melancholy subjects. My imagination, indeed, was the faculty which I most exercised, and it was often very busily employed when those about me were little aware of it. During the winter months, we were always very regular on Sundays in our morning and evening attendance at church. My father had a pew in one of the French chapels, which had been established when the Protestant refugees first emigrated into England, and he required us to attend alternately there and at the parish church. It was a kind of homage which he paid to the faith of his ancestors, and it was a means of rendering the French language familiar to us: but nothing was ever worse calculated to inspire the mind of a child with respect for religion than such a kind of religious worship. Most of the descendants of the refugees were born and bred in England, and desired nothing less than to preserve the memory of their origin; and their chapels were therefore ill attended. A large uncouth room, the avenues to which were narrow courts and dirty alleys, and which, when you entered it, presented to the view only irregular unpainted pews and dusty plastered walls; a congregation consisting principally of some strange-looking old women scattered here and there, one or two in a pew; and a clergyman reading the service and preaching in a monotonous tone of voice, and in a language not familiar to me, was not likely either to impress my mind with much religious awe, or to attract my attention to the doctrines which were delivered. In truth, I did not even attempt to attend to them; my mind was wandering to other subjects, and disporting itself in much gayer scenes than those before me, and little of religion was mixed in my reveries.

But it is time to say something of my education, if the little instruction I ever received from masters deserves to be so called. My brother and myself were sent, when we were very young, to a day-school in our neighbourhood, of which the sole recommendation seems to have been, that it had once been kept by a French refugee, and that the sons of many refugees were still scholars at it. All the learning which it afforded we were to receive; but the utmost that our master professed to teach was reading, writing, arithmetic, French, and Latin, and the last was rather inserted in his bill of fare by way of ornament, and to give a dignity and character to the school, than that there was any capacity of teaching it either in our master or in any of his ushers. I doubt whether any one of them was capable of construing a single sentence of the easiest Latin prose. Our master was ignorant, severe, and brutal: my brother and myself, however, escaped the effects of those bad qualities, by the help of others which he possessed; for towards his scholars he was unequal and partial, and we were both among his favourites. The severity with which he treated many of the other boys, however, often excited my indignation and aversion; and I often burned with shame at not being among the victims of his injustice. He had very bad health, and his disorder gave an edge to his ill-humour, and kept it in constant activity. Many a poor boy have I seen overwhelmed with stripes, because our master had a sleepless night, or felt the symptoms of a returning rheumatism. Young as I then was, I was struck with the bad effects of this severe treatment. There were some boys who were always in scrapes, continually playing truant and continually punished with increasing severity. Their faults, and the mischievousness of their dispositions, seemed to increase in proportion to the severity with which they were treated. The observation, however, could not, by daily experience, force itself upon the mind of so thorough-bred a schoolmaster as Mr. Flack. He would as soon have doubted that food is the proper remedy for hunger, as that blows and stripes are the only genuine promoters of goodness, and incentives to virtue. From the nature of the school may be conjectured what was, in general, the description of the scholars. They consisted, principally, of the sons of all the barbers, bakers, and butchers, in the neighbourhood; and the superior gentility of my father's trade was, I believe, the contemptible motive for the favour which we experienced. At this miserable seminary we continued for several years, and the only acquisitions that we made at it were writing, arithmetic, and the rules of the French grammar. The more familiar use of that language we acquired at home; it being a rule established by my father, that French should be spoken in the family on a Sunday morning, the only time which a constant attendance to business allowed him to pass with us.

My father was particularly desirous that I should learn Latin, and Latin was among the things which my master professed to teach me; but, after the account which I have given of my instructors, it is unnecessary to say that I made no proficiency in it. The motive with my father for wishing me to learn it was a desire, which he entertained, that I should enter into the profession of the law; as he destined my brother to succeed himself in his business. But those plans, which he had formed in his own mind, were formed in perfect subordination to what might be our own choice; it being a fixed opinion of his, that few men succeed in any profession which they have not themselves chosen. He endeavoured, however, by his conversation, to give me a favourable opinion of the way of life of a lawyer, an attorney I should say, for his ideas certainly soared no higher. But, unfortunately for the success of his plan, there was one attorney, and only one, among his acquaintance, a certain Mr. Liddel, who lived in Threadneedle Street, in the City, and was, I believe, a man eminent enough in his line. He was a shortish fat man with a ruddy countenance, which always shone as if besmeared with grease; a large wig which sat loose from his head; his eyes constantly half shut and drowsy; all his motions slow and deliberate; and his words slabbered out as if he had not exertion enough to articulate. His dark and gloomy house was filled with dusty papers and voluminous parchment deeds; and in his meagre library I did not see a single volume which I should not have been deterred by its external appearance from opening. The idea of a lawyer and of Mr. Liddel were so identified in my mind, that I looked upon the profession with disgust, and entreated my father to think of any way of life for me but that; and, accordingly, all thoughts of my being an attorney were given up as well by my father as myself.

But my father was not long without forming other schemes for me. Sir Samuel Fludyer, and his brother Sir Thomas, who were at the head of a great commercial house in the city, were his cousins-german; two of his brothers *, my uncles,

* Stephen and Isaac.

had been partners in the house, and he began to entertain hopes of my arriving in time at the same situation. The Fludyers had begun their career in very narrow circumstances; but, by extraordinary industry, activity, enterprise, and good fortune, they had acquired inordinate wealth, and were every day increasing it by the profits of a most extensive commerce. Sir Samuel was an alderman of the city of London, and a member of Parliament.* He had been created a Baronet, and had served the office of Lord Mayor in a year very memorable in the history of city honours; for it was that in which the King, upon his marriage, made a visit to the corporation, and dined in Guildhall. Notwithstanding, however, the great elevation at which fortune had placed these opulent relations above my father, they always maintained a very friendly intercourse with him, and professed, perhaps sincerely, a great desire to serve him. Sir Samuel, too, was my god-father; and the humble situation of a clerk in his counting-house might, if I had pleased him by my conduct, have led to a very brilliant fortune. My father therefore determined to fit me for that situation, and it was resolved that I should learn the art, or science (I know not which it should be called) of keeping merchants' accounts. A master was accordingly provided for me. I was equipped with a set of journals, waste books, bill books, ledgers, and I know not what; and I passed some weeks in making careful entries of ideal transactions, keeping a register of the times when fictitious bills of exchange would

* For Chippenham.

become due, and posting up imaginary accounts. I should have lost more time than I did in this ridiculous employment, if my instructor, Mr. Johnson, as he was called, (but whose name was perhaps as fictitious as those of my correspondents at Amsterdam, at Smyrna, and in both the Indies, and to whose merits my father had been introduced only by an advertisement in a newspaper,) had not suddenly decamped to avoid his creditors. Events, which soon afterwards happened, made it unnecessary to look out for a new professor of the mercantile science. Sir Samuel Fludyer died of an apoplexy; Sir Thomas did not long survive him; and all the prospects of riches and honours, which we thought opening upon me, were shut out for ever.

Other plans were now to be thought of, and my father talked at one time of placing me as an apprentice with a jeweller and silversmith in Cheapside. Neither this, however, nor any other scheme was carried into execution. What prevented them I do not recollect; but at the age of fourteen, when I had left school, I remained at home without any certain destination, and my father began to employ me in his business, at first because I had no other occupation, and afterwards with a view to its being carried on by me and my brother when he should decline it.

A short time before his marriage, my father had set up for himself as a jeweller; and by his diligence and honesty in his dealings, and the taste and merit of his workmanship, he had so much extended his business, and had acquired in it such celebrity, that, for several years, about the period of which I am now speaking, its returns were not less than twenty thousand pounds a year. With all this, however, he had not acquired much riches by it. He had contented himself with very moderate profits, and that not at the beginning only, and as a means of establishing his name, but when his reputation was at the highest, and he was obliged to decline much of the business that was offered him. His easy and unsuspecting nature, too, had induced him to give credit incautiously, and his losses had been considerable. The business itself, however, if properly and skilfully managed, would afford very ample profits, was capable of being much enlarged, and might be considered as a very good provision both for me and for my brother.

My new employment was merely to keep my father's accounts, and sometimes to see and receive orders from his customers. In this occupation about two years of my life were spent. It was an occupation which never pleased me but in one respect; it imposed little restraint upon me, and left me many hours of leisure. These I employed in reading, which had been for some time my principal amusement. I read, without system or object, just such books as fell in my way, such as my father's library afforded, and such as several circulating libraries, to which I subscribed in succession, could supply. Ancient history, English poetry, and works of criticism, were, however, my favourite subjects; and poetry soon began to predominate over them all. After a few attempts, I found myself, to my unspeakable joy, possessed of a tolerable faculty of rhyming, which I mistook for a talent for poetry. I wrote eclogues, songs, and satires, made translations of Boileau, and attempted imitations of Spenser. My feeble verses, and puerile images were received with the most flattering applause by my family, and afforded supreme delight to myself. I was soon persuaded that I possessed no inconsiderable share of genius. My father's business became every day more unpleasant to me, and I lamented that I had not been educated for some profession connected with literature. I considered that it was not yet too late for me, with an abundance of zeal, to make a very great progress. I determined, therefore, when I was between fifteen and sixteen years of age, to apply myself seriously to learning Latin, of which I, at that time, knew little more than some of the most familiar rules of grammar. Having made myself tolerably master of the grammar, I was fortunate enough to meet with a very good scholar in a Scotchman of the name of Paterson, who kept a school, in Bury Street, St. James's, and who became my instructor. From him I every day received a lesson, which consisted in his correcting my Latin exercises, and hearing me construe a few pages of some Latin author. But the hour I passed with him was a very small portion of the time which I every day dedicated to this new study. I consumed the greatest part of my time in poring over Cæsar, Livy, and Cicero; in consulting, at every difficulty, the translations of those authors which I had procured; and in making translations of my own, first from Latin into English, and then back again into Latin.

In the course of three or four years, during which

I thus applied myself, I had read every prose writer of the ages of pure Latinity, except those who have treated merely of technical subjects, such as Varro, Columella, and Celsus. I had gone three times through the whole of Livy, Sallust, and Tacitus: I had read all Cicero, with the exception, I believe, only of his Academic questions, and his treatises *De Finibus*, and *De Divinatione*. I had studied the most celebrated of his orations, his *Lælius*, his *Cato Major*, his treatise *De Oratore*, and his Letters, and had translated a great part of them. Terence, Virgil, Horace, Ovid, and Juvenal, I had read again and again. From Ovid and from Virgil I made many translations in verse, for so I ought to call them, rather than poetical translations. At the time, however, they appeared to me to have such merit, that I remember reading with triumph, first Dryden's translation, and then my own, to my good-natured relations, who concurred with me in thinking that I had left poor Dryden at a most humiliating distance; a proof certainly, not of the merit of my verses, but of the badness of my judgment, the excess of my vanity, and the blind partiality of my friends.

In ranging through such a variety of authors and studying their works, I did not imagine that I was doing any thing extraordinary. With great simplicity, I supposed that a similar course of reading entered into the plan of education adopted at our public schools and Universities. Greek I attempted, but with no success; and, after seriously considering the difficulties which the language presented, and the little probability there was at my time of life of my ever becoming completely master of it, or even of my making in it any tolerable progress, without sacrificing a large portion of time which might be more usefully employed, I renounced the hope of ever reading the Greek writers in the original. I determined, however, to read them ; and I went through the most considerable of the Greek historians, orators, and philosophers, in the Latin versions, which generally accompany the original text.

My reading had been so various, that I had acquired some slight knowledge of a good many sciences. Travels had been one of my favourite subjects ; and, as I seldom read either travels or history without maps before me, I had acquired a tolerable stock of geographical knowledge. I had read, too, a good deal of natural history, and had attended several courses of lectures on natural philosophy, given by Martin, the optician in Fleet Street, by Ferguson, and by Walker.

My father's taste for pictures and prints could hardly fail of being communicated to his children. I found a great source of amusement in turning over the prints he was possessed of, became a great admirer of pictures, never omitted an opportunity of seeing a good collection, knew the peculiar style of almost every master, and attended the lectures on painting, architecture, and anatomy, which were given at the Royal Academy.

Such were my pursuits and my amusements ; but these were not my only amusements. My father's house furnished me with others most congenial to my disposition. Several happy changes had by this time taken place in our family. As my mother advanced in age her constitution was strengthened, and she at last recovered a good state of health. Our family had been increased and enlivened by two female cousins, the children of my uncle Isaac, who had been left orphans in their infancy by the premature and almost sudden death of both their parents within a few days of each other. Immediately after that melancholy event had happened, Sir Samuel Fludyer took the eldest under his guardianship, and Sir Thomas the youngest; but a few years only passed before death reduced them both to a second orphanage. Their sprightly society and amiable dispositions contributed most essentially to the happiness of us all.

The eldest, particularly, added to the utmost sweetness of temper, extraordinary accomplishments and uncommon beauty. Her charms were really most captivating, and both my brother and myself felt the effects of them. Mine, however, was the love of a child, and soon yielded to my brother's more earnest passion, which increased and strengthened with time, and was many years afterwards rewarded by marriage. They have ever since lived happy in each other and in their children, surrounded at this moment by eight of them, and having never for a single instant had their harmony interrupted.

Among other changes, a very considerable one had taken place in my father's circumstances. A very rich relation of my mother's, a Mr. de la Haize, had died, and had left us very large legacies. To me and to my brother 2000*l.* a-piece, to my sister

3000*l.*, to my father, my mother, and Mrs. Facquier, legacies of about the same amount for their lives, with remainder to my brother, my sister, and myself, and to each of us a share of the residue of his fortune equally with the rest of his legatees. The whole property bequeathed to us amounted together to about 14,000*l.* or 15,000*l.* Blessed be his memory for it! But for this legacy, the portion of my life which is already past must have been spent in a manner the most irksome and painful, and my present condition would probably have been wretched and desperate. I should have engaged in business; I should probably have failed of success in it; and I should at this moment have been without fortune, without credit, and without the means of acquiring either, and, what would have been most painful to me, my nearest relations would have been without resources.

Upon receiving so large an accession to his fortune, my father removed out of his country lodgings into a house, still however at Marylebone; though, by the increase of the new buildings, it had ceased to be the country, and was merely the outskirts of London. There our whole family now resided throughout the year, what had been our town-house being appropriated entirely to business. Our new house was in High Street, and, to judge from its external appearance, its narrow form, its two small windows on a floor, and the little square piece of ground behind it, which was dignified with the name of a garden, one would have supposed that very scanty and very homely, indeed, must have been this our comparative opulence and luxury. But those who had mingled in our family, and had hearts to feel in what real happiness consists, would have formed a very different judgment. They would have found a lively, youthful, and accomplished society, blest with every enjoyment that an endearing home can afford; a society united by a similarity of tastes, dispositions, and affections, as well as by the strongest ties of blood. They would have admired our lively, varied, and innocent pleasures; our summer rides and walks in the cheerful country, which was close to us; our winter-evening occupations of drawing, while one of us read aloud some interesting book, or the eldest of my cousins played and sung to us with exquisite taste and expression; the little banquets with which we celebrated the anniversary of my father's wedding, and of the birth of every member of our happy society; and the dances with which, in spite of the smallness of our rooms, we were frequently indulged. I cannot recollect the days, happily I may say the years, which thus passed away, without the most lively emotion. I love to transport myself in idea into our little parlour with its green paper, and the beautiful prints of Vivares, Bartolozzi, and Strange, from the pictures of Claude, Caracci, Raphael, and Corregio, with which its walls were elegantly adorned; and to call again to mind the familiar and affectionate society of young and old intermixed, which was gathered round the fire; and even the Italian greyhound, the cat, and the spaniel, which lay in perfect harmony basking before it. I delight to see the door open, that I may recognise the friendly countenances of the servants, and above all, of the old nurse, to whom we were all endeared, because it was while she attended my mother that her health had so much improved.

But yet with such means of happiness, and in the midst of enjoyments so well suited to my temper and disposition, I was not completely happy. The melancholy to which I had from my childhood been subject, at intervals oppressed me; and my happiness was often poisoned by the reflection, that at some time or other it must end.

The dislike which I had conceived for my father's business every day increased, and I earnestly wished for some other employment. My indulgent father readily yielded to my wishes, and, after some consideration, it was determined that I should enter into some department of the law. The Commons were first thought of; but it was afterwards judged, by the friends whom my father consulted, that a more advantageous situation for me would be the office of the Six Clerks in Chancery. This was accordingly decided on; and, at the age of sixteen, I was articled to Mr. William Michael Lally, one of the sworn clerks in Chancery, for a period of five years. The prejudice which Mr. Liddel had inspired me with against all lawyers had been before this time removed; but if any vestige of it had remained it must have yielded to the temper and manners of Mr. Lally. A strong natural understanding, improved by much general reading, and much knowledge of the world, a high sense of honour, the purest integrity, a very brilliant fancy, great talents for conversation, an extraordinary flow of spirits, and a most convivial disposition, were the predominant characteristics of this amiable and estimable man.

I had not, it was not possible indeed that I should have, any accurate idea of the business of a sworn clerk in Chancery till I had adopted it for my profession. His business lies in a very narrow compass: it consists almost entirely in making copies of bills, answers, and other pleadings in Chancery; in receiving notices of motions to be made in suits, and the service of orders pronounced by the court, and transmitting them to the solicitors of the different suitors; and in occasional attendance upon the Court of Chancery at the hearing of causes, and upon the masters in Chancery when they are proceeding upon matters referred to them. Except these attendances, all the business of a clerk in court is transacted at a public office in Chancery Lane. Mr. Lally acted, as indeed did most of the other clerks, as a solicitor in Chancery as well as a clerk in court; and his business of a solicitor procured me much more attendance upon the court, and in the masters' offices, than I should have otherwise had. In these occupations I found no amusement, and took little interest; but they still left me a great deal of leisure. The office was open only during certain hours of the day. In the time of vacation, and in one season of the year for three months together, no attendance was required. The paternal house still continued to be my home, and I still had the means of pursuing, with little intermission, my favourite studies and amusements. I had soon laid out the plan of my future life, which was to follow my profession just as far as was necessary for my subsistence, and to aspire to fame by my literary pursuits. For a few years I still cultivated the talent for poetry which I supposed myself to possess. But insensibly, as my judgment improved, my self-admiration abated; I even grew dissatisfied with what I wrote, and before I had attained my nineteenth year I had the sense, and I may say the good taste, to wean myself entirely from the habit of versifying. I did not, however, relinquish the pleasing hope, for such it was to me, of becoming a very distinguished author. I began, therefore, to exercise myself in prose compositions; and, judging translations to be the most useful exercise for forming a style, I rendered into English the finest models of writing that the Latin language afforded; almost all the speeches in Livy, very copious extracts from Tacitus, the whole of Sallust, and many of the finest passages in Cicero. With the same view of improving my style, I read and studied the best English writers, Addison, Swift, Bolingbroke, Robertson, and Hume, noting down every peculiar propriety and happiness of expression which I met with, and which I was conscious that I should not have used myself.

While I was pursuing these studies with unremitting zeal, I formed an acquaintance which has had great influence on all the subsequent events of my life. It was that of Mr. John Roget, a clergyman and a native of Geneva, who had then lately left that city, and had been elected minister of the French chapel we attended. It was no longer the gloomy building which I have described. Out of the permanent funds of the church a new chapel had been erected upon a different spot; small indeed, and suited to the congregation, but neat and cheerful. The difference between the old and the new edifice was not greater than between the newly elected preacher and his predecessor. Instead of the stammering monotony, and the learned, but dry and tedious, dissertations of Monsieur Coderc, we heard, from Roget, sermons composed with taste and eloquence, and delivered with great propriety and animation. He was, indeed, possessed of the genuine sources of eloquence; an ardent mind, a rich imagination, and exquisite sensibility. Immediately upon his arrival in England, he became acquainted with our family, and that acquaintance soon grew into very great intimacy with us all. He took pleasure in talking with me about my studies; used to give me great encouragement to persevere in them; and often pronounced of the talents, which he supposed me to possess, predictions that have never been fulfilled, but which, as is often the case with prophecies of another kind, had a strong tendency to bring about their own accomplishment.

Roget was an admirer of the writings of his countryman Rousseau, and he made me acquainted with them. With what astonishment and delight did I first read them! I seemed transported into a new world. His seducing eloquence so captivated my reason, that I was blind to all his errors. I imbibed all his doctrines, adopted all his opinions, and embraced his system of morality with the fervour of a convert to some new religion. That enthusiasm has long since evaporated; and though I am not even now so cold and insensible, as to be able under any circumstances to read his writings with an even and languid pulse, and unmoistened eyes, yet I am never tempted to exclaim, *Malo cum Platone errare, quàm cum aliis vera sentire,*—a motto which I once seriously inscribed in the first page of *Emile*. But though the writings of Rousseau contain many errors on the most important subjects, they may yet be read with great advantage. There is, perhaps, no writer so capable of inspiring a young mind with an ardent love of virtue, a fixed hatred of oppression, and a contempt for all false glory, as Rousseau; and I ascribe, in a great degree, to the irrational admiration of him, which I once entertained, those dispositions of mind, from which I have derived my greatest happiness throughout life.

In our family, Roget found a society well suited to his taste. His visits to us became frequent; his conversation was uncommonly interesting, and he had soon secured the friendship of us all. My sister he inspired with warmer sentiments than those of friendship. On his part, he was by no means insensible to her merits, but he forbore for some time to offer his addresses to her. He had no property but the very moderate income which his church afforded him; my sister's fortune, though not large in itself, was comparatively large, and her expectations were supposed to be much greater, for my father, from his assiduity, the long time he had been in business, his extensive dealings, and his moderate expenses, was reputed to be possessed of great wealth. Roget's intimate friends endeavoured to dissuade him from making a proposal, which, they said, they foresaw would be unfavourably received; they were, however, as much mistaken with respect to my father's disposition as with respect to his fortune. Upon the first mention of Roget's addresses, my father declared, that, if they had my sister's approbation, they had his; he had long before resolved never to resist, or even to check, his daughter's inclinations. With respect to Roget, however, it was not a case in which my father was merely not to oppose; he could not but approve a marriage so well calculated to render a beloved child happy; and it was, soon afterwards, solemnized * to the great satisfaction of all our family.

There was one person, indeed, who, though not of our family by blood, was from long intimacy and mutual affection considered almost as a part of it, to whom this event gave as much pain as it did satisfaction to all the rest. This was a young man of the name of Randolph Greenway. He had been an apprentice to my father, and as such had lived with us. He had afterwards travelled together with my brother, upon a tour of seven or eight months, on the continent; and, upon his return, an uncle, who was possessed of an estate of about 500*l.* a year in Oxfordshire, had died and left him his heir. Though no longer living under the same roof, we still continued in habits of the greatest intimacy: he was of all our parties, ac-

* On the 12th of February, 1778.

companied us in our rides, in our walks; and was always a welcome, and a happy guest at our house. He had conceived, unknown to us all, a warm affection for my sister: from the natural reserve of his temper, or for some other cause which I have never learned, he did not give the least intimation of his affection to any one; not even to her who was the object of it. The only expression that ever dropped from him, which bespoke any inclination to open his mind, was, during a visit, which after his uncle's death, my father and mother, together with my sister, made him at his house in the country. In answer to a compliment which my father paid him upon the appearance of his house, and the air of comfort which prevailed in it, he said, "Yes, sir, it wants nothing but a mistress." My father, either from not understanding his meaning, or from having determined not to control or influence in any manner his daughter's choice, remained silent; and poor Greenway construed that silence into disapprobation of what he supposed could not fail to be understood. My sister certainly felt no affection for him, but she highly esteemed him: his person was agreeable; his temper was even and amiable; and he had an intrinsic goodness of heart, a disinterestedness, a generosity, and a sense of honour, which it was impossible not to admire. Her heart, too, was at that time disengaged, and, but for the most fatal reserve on his part, he undoubtedly might have obtained for his wife the woman, without whom, as it afterwards appeared, it was impossible for him to live and to be happy. He remained, however, silent;

not an expression ever fell from him which could lead to a discovery of his secret, not even to my brother or myself, in our greatest intimacy. He was a witness to Roget's being introduced into our family; marked the progress which he made in our friendship; observed the first dawning of affection in my sister's breast; watched the sentiments, which she and Roget mutually entertained for each other, growing up into attachment, affection and the warmest passion; and still observed the most profound silence; and it was not till after the marriage had been resolved on, that any of us discovered the cause of that melancholy which had then long become apparent in him; nor should we, even then, have discovered it, but it would perhaps have passed with him in silence into that grave into which his misfortunes soon led him, but for the most accidental circumstance.

One night, my brother and myself supped with him, at the house of one of our friends. We stayed very late, and drank a good deal of wine; not enough, however, to produce a visible effect on any of us, but on poor Greenway. On him was produced an effect the most extraordinary: his spirits were not exhilarated, his reason was not clouded, or his articulation impeded; but the passions, which had long preyed upon his mind, heightened and inflamed, overcame at once the restraint which he had long imposed on them, and burst out in the most vehement expression. As we were walking home, he talked in vague terms of his wretchedness, till, unable to proceed, he sunk down on the steps of a door; and there, in a transport of passion, and in words, and with an accent that penetrated to the soul, expressed the cause and extent of his misery; and in a spirit of prophecy, which was but too truly fulfilled, exclaimed, that he should never, never again know what it was to be happy.

Immediately after the intended marriage of my sister was made public, he entered into the Oxfordshire militia, which was then encamped, in the hope that the bustle and novelty of a military life might efface those recollections which were incompatible with his peace of mind. But all was in vain. A deep melancholy settled and preyed upon his mind. Calamities the most dreadful, which in the course of a few years afterwards happened in his own family, increased this load of affliction. His mother became disordered in her mind; one of his sisters was affected with all the symptoms of a consumption; and his brother became the subject of a public prosecution. This last misfortune struck a blow to his peace of mind, from which he never recovered. I saw him, immediately after the news of it had reached him, suffering tortures of the mind which I have never witnessed before or since. He soon afterwards set out upon a journey into France, in the hope that a change of place, and of objects, might relieve the anguish which he suffered; but it was to no purpose. Nothing could dissipate, for a single moment, the gloom which hung upon him. He had no sooner arrived in any town than he was impatient to leave it; and he hurried from place to place, more dejected every day, and more declining in his health, till, upon his arrival at Calais, on his return, he was too ill to proceed any farther. His companion in his travels * immediately wrote to me to apprize me of his situation; and with all possible expedition I set out to join him. I trembled lest he should not have made a will, for I knew the distressed state of his sisters, and that, if he were to die intestate, all his estates would descend to the very brother who had shortened his days. I arrived; but too late for every thing but to witness his last agonies. He turned upon me his dying eyes, attempted to speak, but was unable, and shortly after expired. The recollection of the situation in which he left his family aggravated his sufferings. He had twice attempted to make his will, but found it impossible. In the delirium of the fever which consumed him, he often exclaimed, when disturbed by the noise of a hammering in the court-yard of the inn where he lay, that he heard they were preparing the rack for him. Unhappy man! the torments of his sensible and affectionate mind were more poignant even than those of the rack which he dreaded; and yet he, whose destiny it was thus exquisitely to suffer, had employed his whole life in serving his friends, in acts of kindness, humanity, and generosity, and had never done an injury to any one, or entertained a sentiment but of virtue and benevolence. His body was conveyed to Canterbury, and now lies buried in the churchyard of the cathedral.

The worst evils to his family, which on his deathbed he anticipated, soon befell them. The brother enjoyed the estate, and left the youngest of his sisters (though her conduct had always been irre-

* Mr. Byrne, the engraver.

proachable) in a condition so wretched and destitute, that, but for the charity of one[1] of his friends, who maintained her, she would have perished through misery and hunger.

The melancholy fate of poor Greenway has led me much beyond the period to which I had brought down the account of myself. I wished to conclude his story before I proceeded with my own; and I have spared myself the frequent renewal of affliction, by crowding into a few pages the miseries and the daily sufferings of several years. From the time of my sister's marriage, nay, from the time when it was first in contemplation, he knew no happiness; but he lingered through seven tedious years, before his sorrows laid him in the grave. He lived long enough to see the instability of human happiness; and to witness the cruel misfortunes which overwhelmed those whom he had considered as completely blessed.

But let me not anticipate other calamities; let me rather postpone them as long as possible, and forget awhile that they are fast approaching, to live over again and enjoy completely the too short period of pure and unmixed happiness, which followed my sister's marriage. I had always loved her with the tenderest affection. I had conceived for Roget the sincerest friendship, and their union increased and enlivened these sentiments. I passed most of my leisure hours with them, enjoying the small but well selected society which frequented

[1] In an account book kept by him, during this period, and down to 1792, there are frequent entries of small sums paid by him to Miss Greenway. — Ed.

their house, and enjoying still more their conversation when alone.

I shall never forget the charms of our little frugal suppers, at which none but us three were present; but where we never were at a loss for topics that went to the hearts of all of us: where each spoke without the least reserve, nay, where each thought aloud, and was not only happy in himself, but happy from the happiness of those most dear to him. Our happiness, indeed, was such that it could hardly be increased; but, if not increased, we might, at least, reckon upon its duration; the sources of our enjoyment were in ourselves, not dependant upon the gifts of fortune, and not subject to the tyranny of opinion. We were young; myself, indeed, but just of age: and many years, in the enjoyment of the purest friendship and affection, seemed to be in store for us. Vain, however, were these expectations! our happiness was as transient as it was pure.

NARRATIVE OF HIS EARLY LIFE, CONTINUED BY HIMSELF IN 1813.

1778—1789.

Tanhurst[1], August 28. 1813.

After an interval of seventeen years I am about to resume the task of writing my life; a task undertaken in very different circumstances, and with very different views, from those with which I now resume it. When I began to set down the few events of my unimportant history, I was living in great privacy; I was unmarried, and it seemed in a very high degree probable that I should always remain so. My life was wasting away with few very lively enjoyments, and without the prospect that my existence could ever have much influence on the happiness of others; or that I should leave behind me any trace by which, twenty years after I was dead, it could be known that ever I had lived. But since that period, and within the last few years, I have been in situations that were more conspicuous; and though it has never been my good fortune to render any important service, either to my fellow-creatures or to my country, yet, for a short period of time, at least, some degree of public attention has been fixed on me. It is, however, with no view to the public that I am induced to preserve any memorial of my life; but wholly from

[1] A country house, in Surrey, on the side of Leith Hill. — Ed.

private considerations. It is in my domestic life that the most important changes have taken place. For the last fifteen years, my happiness has been the constant study of the most excellent of wives; a woman in whom a strong understanding, the noblest and most elevated sentiments, and the most courageous virtue, are united to the warmest affection, and to the utmost delicacy of mind and tenderness of heart; and all these intellectual perfections are graced and adorned by the most splendid beauty that human eyes ever beheld. She has borne to me seven children, who are living; and in all of whom I persuade myself that I discover the promise of their, one day, proving themselves not unworthy of such a mother. Some of them are of so tender an age that I can hardly hope that I shall live till their education is finished, and much less that I shall have the happiness to see them established in life; and of some it is not improbable that I may be taken from them while they are yet of such tender years that, as they advance in life, they may retain but little recollection of their father. To these, and even to my dear wife, if, as I devoutly wish, she should many years survive me, it may be a source of great satisfaction to turn over these pages; to learn or to recollect what I was, what I have done, with whom I have lived, and to whom I have been known. Such is the information that these pages will afford, and they will, I fear, afford nothing more. Of instruction there is but little that they can supply: what to shun or what to pursue, is that of which a life, so little chequered with events as mine, can hardly present any very striking lessons. I have been in no trying situations; the force of my character has never been called forth; I have fallen into no very egregious faults, and I have had the good fortune to escape those situations which generally lead to them; but, from the pious affection which may have been instilled into my children's minds, they may set a considerable value, and take a lively interest in facts which, to the rest of mankind, must appear altogether insipid and indifferent. It is, therefore, to enjoy conversation with my children, at a time when I shall be incapable of conversing with any one; and to live with them, as it were, long after I shall have descended into the grave, that I proceed with this narrative of my life. It is surrounded by these children in their happy infant state; cheered with the little sallies of their wit; exhilarated with their spirits; become youthful, as it were, by their youth; and transported at sometimes discovering in them the dawnings of their mother's virtues; it is in the repose of a short period of leisure after unusual fatigues in my profession; it is in a fine season, in the midst of a beautiful country, with some of the richest and most luxuriant scenes of nature spread before me: it is in the midst of all these sources of enjoyment and of happiness, that I sit down to this pleasing employment.

Writing of times so long past, my memory may sometimes fail me (for till within the last seven years I have never kept any journal, but while I was travelling); it can be, however, only in trifles that it can fail; and even as to matters the most trifling, I shall endeavour most strictly and religiously to adhere to truth.

When my former narrative broke off, I think (for I have it not at this moment before me) I was serving Mr. Lally as his articled clerk. I had never, during my clerkship, thought very seriously of engaging in the line of the profession for which that noviciate was intended to qualify me. To distinguish myself in some literary career was the chimerical hope which I had long indulged; and I had once even supposed that I might become illustrious as a poet; but this delusion was not of long duration. The important moment, however, had arrived when it was necessary to come to a decision, upon the prudence or folly of which my future fate was to depend. The encouragement I had received from Roget had very strongly inclined me not only to continue in the profession, but to look up to a superior rank in it; and, although I had yet taken no step whatever towards such an object, I could not, now that it was requisite to decide, persuade myself to decide against it. With the exception, however, of Roget, I believe most of my friends thought it a hazardous and imprudent step; Mr. Lally deemed it so in a very high degree. He did not, indeed, undervalue my talents, though I believe he did not rate them very high; but he thought my diffidence invincible, and such as must alone oppose an insurmountable bar to my success. He had, however, the generosity not to urge his objections with the force with which he felt them. He thought himself interested in my decision, since, being desirous himself of retiring from business, it was of him that I should naturally purchase a seat in the Six Clerks' office, for it is by purchase only that these situations are obtained. Others of my friends thought that, whatever my talents might be, and even if my modesty could be overcome, yet my delicate health was hardly equal to the laborious course of study which I was about to undertake; and I had very kind intimations of this from many of my friends; but I do not recollect that I had a direct remonstrance on the folly of what I was doing from any one. My good-natured father (too good-natured perhaps in this instance) hardly interposed his advice; he left every thing to my own decision; and that decision was to renounce the Six Clerks' office for ever, and, as the only other course that was left me, to aspire to a higher fortune. What principally influenced this decision was, that it enabled me to leave in my father's hands my little fortune (the 2000*l.* legacy), and the share of the residue (perhaps 700*l.* or 800*l.* more) which M. De la Haize had left me; and which I knew it would be very inconvenient to him that I should call for; but which would have been indispensably necessary, if I had purchased a sworn clerk's seat, 2000*l.* being about the price which it would cost. This consideration, I am sure, had no weight with my father, in his acquiescing in my resolution; but it was decisive with me in forming it; and it is not the only instance of my life in which a decision, which was to have most important consequences, has been taken principally to avoid a present inconvenience.

Even with a view, however, to my father's pecuniary circumstances, the determination I took was hardly to be justified: because, however inconvenient to him the immediate payment of the money might have been, yet it would have secured to me, without the possibility of risk, an income much larger than I had then occasion for; and with which I might, in the course of a few years, have replaced as large or a larger sum in his hands. The course of life I was entering upon, on the contrary, insured expense; and postponed all prospect of profit certainly for five years, and probably for a much longer period. At a later season of my life, after a success at the bar which my wildest and most sanguine dreams had never painted to me; when I was gaining an income of 8000*l.* or 9000*l.* a year; I have often reflected how all that prosperity had arisen out of the pecuniary difficulties and confined circumstances of my father. There was another circumstance, which, though a trifling one, I ought to mention; for it certainly had some, though I cannot at this distance of time recollect how great an influence over the judgment which I exercised. The works of Thomas had fallen into my hands: I had read with admiration his *Eloge* of Daguesseau; and the career of glory, which he represents that illustrious magistrate to have run, had excited to a very great degree my ardour and my ambition, and opened to my imagination new paths of glory.

I had completed my twenty-first year before my resolution was taken, and at this late period of life I entered myself of the Society of Gray's Inn;

took there a very pleasant set of chambers, which overlooked the gardens; arranged my little collection of books about me, and began with great ardour the painful study of the law. My good friend, Mr. Lally, advised me to become the pupil of some Chancery draftsman for a couple of years; and, for the first year, to confine myself merely to reading under his direction and with his assistance. This advice I followed, and placed myself under the guidance of Mr. Spranger. I was the only pupil he ever had; and, indeed, his drawing business was hardly sufficient to give employment, even to a single pupil. I did not, however, repent of the step I had taken. I passed all my mornings and part of most of my evenings at his house. He had a very good library, which I had the use of; he directed my reading; he explained what I did not understand; he removed many of the difficulties I met with; and, what was of no small advantage to me, I formed a lasting friendship with this very kind-hearted and excellent man, who was universally esteemed, and who had a high character in the profession.

As I read, I formed a common-place book; which has been of great use to me, even to the present day. It is, indeed, the only way in which law reports can be read with much advantage.

It was not, however, to law alone that I confined my studies. I endeavoured to acquire much general knowledge. I read a great deal of history; I went on improving myself in the classics; I translated, composed, and endeavoured (though I confess with a success little proportioned to the pains I took) to form for myself a correct and an elegant style; I translated the whole of Sallust, and a great part of Livy, Tacitus, and Cicero; I wrote political essays, and often sent them without my name to the newspapers, and was not a little gratified to find them always inserted; above all, I was anxious to acquire a great facility of elocution, which I thought indispensably necessary for my success. Instead, however, of resorting to any of those debating societies which were at this time much frequented, I adopted a very useful expedient, which I found suggested in Quinctilian; that of expressing to myself, in the best language I could, whatever I had been reading; of using the arguments I had met with in Tacitus or Livy, and making with them speeches of my own, not uttered, but composed and existing only in thought. Occasionally, too, I attended the two Houses of Parliament; and used myself to recite in thought, or to answer the speeches I had heard there. That I might lose no time, I generally reserved these exercises for the time of my walking or riding; and, before long, I had so well acquired the habit of it, that I could think these compositions as I was passing through the most crowded streets.

The very close application with which I pursued my studies proved at last injurious to my health. There were other causes, too, which tended to impair it. Among the principal of these was the great anxiety I long felt for my sister and her husband. The happiness they enjoyed upon their marriage was as pure, and as complete, as is ever the portion of human beings; but it was of very short duration. They were blessed with one sweet child to increase that happiness; but not long after the joyful event of his birth, in the spring of 1779, and just when I had projected to pass the approaching summer with them in a lodging they had taken at Fulham, and when we had begun to carry our project into execution, Roget was seized with an inflammation of the lungs, attended with a violent spitting of blood, and with other symptoms so alarming, that his life appeared to be in the most imminent danger. As the only chance of saving him, his physician recommended that he should be removed to his native air; and he, soon afterwards set out for Geneva. But he set out in such a state, and the violence of his disease so much increased upon the journey, that it soon appeared very doubtful whether he would ever be able to reach the end of it. A situation more distressing than my sister's can hardly be imagined. Separated for the first time completely from her family, in a foreign country, amongst strangers, without even an attendant; exposed to all the inconveniences of wretched inns, and destitute of all medical assistance in which she could place any confidence, she was doomed to watch the progress of a terrible disease, undermining and gaining every day upon the strength of a husband, on whom she doted with the fondest affection. Her letters during this journey, and after it had terminated, written with a simplicity and a resignation which were celestial, but in which it was impossible for her to conceal the torment of mind which she suffered and the constant alarms she entertained, pierced me to the heart; and the dread of what she probably had still to undergo preyed continually on my mind.

Roget arrived, at last, with my sister at Geneva; but it seemed as if he had arrived only to die there; and it was long, very long, before their prospects at all brightened, and before they ventured to flatter themselves with any hopes.

The declining state of my own health induced me to take medical advice. My stomach was particularly disordered, and my physician advised me to try the waters of Bath; and accordingly, in the spring of 1780, I passed six weeks at that place. There happened, soon after I arrived there, to be an auction of a law library, at which I bought many books. With this supply I continued my studies, and probably too closely: I drank too much of the water; I was advised by an apothecary there to try the bath: I followed that advice, but I went into the bath when it was too hot, I stayed in it too long, and in a short time, by these various means, I found myself in a much worse state than that in which I had left town. The disorder in my stomach was all I had then to complain of; but now I was disordered throughout my whole frame. I was incapable of walking half a mile without excessive fatigue. Any exertion either of mind or body produced the most distressing palpitation of my heart. My nights were sleepless, my days restless and agitated. My apprehensions for the future were the most gloomy. Having heard at Bath of persons who had never recovered from the relaxed and nervous habit into which an intemperate use of the hot bath had reduced them, I persuaded myself that such was my destination. I imagined that my whole life (and I feared it might be a long one) would drag on in my then state, useless to all mankind and burdensome to myself; and I entertained strong apprehensions that my disorder might end in madness.

Under the pressure of all these real and imaginary ills, I returned to town. Sir William Watson, my physician, endeavoured to repair all the mischief I had been doing. He made me use the cold bath, and drink the chalybeate waters of Islington: and he recommended me for a time to relinquish all study; but this recommendation was unnecessary, for my constant restlessness and uneasiness made it impossible for me to fix my attention upon any thing.

Gradually I got better; but my health had not made any considerable progress, when I was obliged to undergo bodily fatigues which threw me back again, and left me in a very deplorable state. In the beginning of June broke out that most extraordinary insurrection, excited by Lord George Gordon, which has hardly any parallel in our history. In a moment of profound peace and of perfect security, the metropolis found itself on a sudden abandoned, as it were, to the plunder and the fury of a bigoted and frantic populace. The prisons were broken open and burned; and their inhabitants — debtors, men accused of crimes, and convicted felons—indiscriminately turned loose upon the public, and received into the first ranks of their deliverers to assist in further acts of devastation.

One night, the flames were seen ascending from nine or ten different conflagrations, kindled by these unresisted insurgents. The Inns of Court were marked out as objects of destruction; and Gray's Inn, in which many Catholics resided, was particularly obnoxious. Government, which had acted with extraordinary irresolution at first, took at last very vigorous measures to put a stop to these disgraceful outrages. In the mean time, however, it had become necessary for every man to trust to himself for his security; and the barristers and students of the different Inns of Court determined to arm themselves in their own defence. The state of my health rendered me quite unequal to so great an exertion. I was ashamed, however, of being ill at such a season. I did therefore as others did; was up a whole night under arms, and stood as sentinel for several hours at the gate in Holborn.

This fatigue, and the excessive heat of the weather, threw me back into a worse state of health than ever. I was so relaxed that I could hardly stand; I had, from mere weakness, continual pains in all my limbs. My nights were restless; and if the continual agitation of my fibres would have permitted me to sleep, the pulsation of my heart, which was continually sensible to me, and which was visible through my clothes when I was dressed, would have prevented me. I hurried out of town to try the effect of sea air; found myself worse, and hastened back again. Very slow indeed was my recovery. Throughout the whole of the following winter I was incapable of walking more than a mile at a time. My studies I was obliged almost entirely to lay aside. I read little but for my amusement, and rather by way of diverting my thoughts from my malady, and from the melancholy prospect that I had before me, than with any view to my improvement. It was at this time, and with this object, that I began to read Italian; and I certainly found considerable entertainment in the novelties which the literature of Italy presented to me.

My constitution seemed so much altered, I felt so sensibly and so very disagreeably every change of the atmosphere, and this had lasted so long, that I continued strongly possessed with the idea that my health was irrecoverably lost; that for the rest of my days I should be a wretched valetudinarian; and that the bright prospects of success in my profession, in which I had sometimes indulged, were shut out from me for ever. Such I continued throughout the winter, and during the following spring. Fortunately for me, an occasion presented itself, early in the summer, which tempted me to go abroad.

When Roget's deplorable state of health compelled him and my sister to quit this country, they had been obliged to leave their child, an infant then not a year old, behind them. They had intended to be absent but for a few months; but they were soon convinced that a return to this country, if ever to be ventured on, could not, without the greatest danger, be undertaken for several years; and, with this sad conviction, they had naturally become very impatient to have their child restored to them. My most affectionate father had grown dotingly fond of his little grandson; and though he would reluctantly resign him to the hands of my poor sister, who in a foreign country, and with a sick husband, stood in great need of such a consolation, yet he would not consent to commit his little charge to the care only of strangers, or of a servant, for so long a journey. I offered, therefore, to convey him, and deliver him into the hands of his parents; and this offer was very thankfully, on all sides, accepted.

His nursery maid was of course to go with him, and, as the best mode of conveyance for such a party, and the most economical too (which was a consideration very important to be attended to), we put ourselves under the care of one of those Swiss *voituriers*, who were at that time in the habit of convoying parties of six or eight persons to any part of Switzerland. Our party consisted of seven: a Mr. Bird, who was going to Turin; a Mr. Barde, a Genevese; a young man of the name of Broughton; a little effeminate Englishman, whose name I do not recollect; the nursery maid, the child, and myself.* It was a time of war, and we were therefore obliged to pass through the Low Countries; and, as is necessary in this mode of travelling, which is performed with the same horses, we made short and easy journeys of not more than thirty or forty miles a day, which gave us an opportunity of seeing all the objects of curiosity that lay upon our road.

The improvement of my health and spirits as I proceeded, the great variety of places we passed through, and the novelty of every thing I saw, made

* We set out June 16. 1781.

it to me a most delightful journey. I shall never forget the impression I received on first landing at Ostend; and, afterwards, upon entering the magnificent city of Ghent: every human creature, every building, every object of superstition, almost every thing that I beheld, attracted my notice, and excited and gratified my curiosity.

We pursued our course through Brussels, Namur, Longwy, Metz, Nancy, Plombières, and Besançon, to Lausanne, where I delivered safely their little boy to Roget and my sister.

I found Roget much better than I had expected; obliged, indeed, to live by the strictest rule, and compelled to make his health the subject of his continual care and attention, but well enough to enjoy the society of a few friends, and to amuse himself with literary pursuits. He had formed the project of writing a history of the American war, and it served to employ very agreeably many hours of the few last years of his life; but he did not live long enough to complete the work, or even to make any considerable progress in it. His friendship for me, and the favourable opinion he had entertained of my talents, had been greatly increased by absence, and by the numerous and long letters which had, during that absence, passed between us. My success at the bar he considered as certain; and, knowing what that success leads to in England, he spoke of my future destination with a degree of exultation and enthusiasm, which rekindled those hopes that had for some time been nearly extinguished in my mind. The recollection of one of these conversations, which took place as we were walking upon the terrace of his garden one fine summer night, when not a cloud appeared upon the atmosphere to intercept the effulgence of the stars scattered over every part of the heavens, has since a thousand times occurred to me, and is now as fresh in my memory as if it had been an event of yesterday. Scarcely any thing, indeed, that I saw, or heard, or read, during the six weeks that I passed in this delightful retirement, have I since forgotten.

The situation was one of the most beautiful that imagination could paint. It was about a mile from Lausanne, and at a considerable eminence above it, commanding a most extensive view of that enchanting country, with the lake of Geneva stretching out to its whole extent, and bounded by the lofty and rude mountains of Savoy. Never could there be a clearer refutation of the common saying, that the most beautiful objects by familiarity tire upon the sight, than what I here experienced. The window of my room commanded this sublime prospect: every day I gazed upon it with fresh rapture; and the last time that I beheld it, its beauty kindled in me the same pious admiration as the first.

From Lausanne I proceeded to Geneva, where I made a stay of only about a month; but, during that short residence, I saw so great a variety of persons, and I saw so much of them, that I derived as much profit as I could under other circumstances from a much longer residence. It was in the midst of those political contests which, soon afterwards, ended so fatally for that republic. I lived with Chauvet, who was deeply engaged with the popular party, and was one of those who, upon the aristocratical faction becoming triumphant, was banished the republic. Duroveray, formerly attorney-general of the republic, a man of great talents, but unfit from his unconciliatory manners to be the leader of a party; Clavière, afterwards for a short time, and at a very unhappy season, minister of finance in France, possessed of considerable abilities, and a man of unbounded ambition, though wholly deficient in courage to gratify it; and Reybaz, of a better judgment, of more extensive knowledge, and of more solid talents, but equally wanting in courage; were amongst the foremost of those who conducted the measures of the popular party. Politics, though they served to bring out the characters of individuals, and display all the variety of dispositions incident to mankind, had, in some respects, considerably hurt the society of Geneva. Politics had engrossed what before was given to literature. The society of Geneva must, indeed, judging of it even under all the disadvantages in which I saw it, have been at one time highly interesting. It had the liveliness of French conversation without its frivolity, and the good sense of England, with a refined literary taste formed by an intimate and familiar acquaintance with the writings of Rousseau and Voltaire, to which we have no pretensions.

I was very desirous, while I thus passed through foreign countries, to inform myself as well as I could of their laws, particularly their criminal law, and their mode of administering justice. While I was at Geneva, an opportunity presented itself of learning the manner of conducting criminal trials there, which few travellers have had the good fortune to meet with. The proceedings, as in most other parts of the Continent, are secret; and none but the prisoner, his counsel, and two friends named by him to assist him, are permitted to be present when the cause is pleaded. It happened, before I arrived here, that a burglary had been committed by a gang of Savoyards, of whom three were seized, and the rest, three more in number, had made their escape. A criminal trial of any kind was, at this time, in this little republic, of very rare occurrence, and always excited an interest proportioned to its novelty. The advocates of the highest reputation were accustomed to afford their gratuitous assistance to the accused, and to conduct their defence with as much care and zeal as the wealthiest and most liberal client could desire. I was acquainted with one of the advocates upon this occasion; and he suggested to one of the prisoners, who was a stranger in Geneva, to name me to assist him. Before I was admitted to be his assistant, I was obliged to take an oath before one of the syndics (the chief magistrates of the republic), that I would not give, or suffer to be taken, copies of any papers in the cause; and that I would return to the court, immediately after the cause should be ended, all the copies or extracts which I might have made for my own use. All the prisoners were found guilty; but their sentences varied according to the degree of evidence which had appeared against each. One, a lad of sixteen, was sentenced to be whipt, and then to be sent to the galleys for twenty years (the French Government having some time since agreed to take all the criminals of the republic to work in their galleys). Another was condemned to be present while his companion was whipt, and then to be banished the territory of the republic for life; and the doom of the third was merely banishment. As to the three accomplices, who had escaped, they were sentenced to be whipt in effigy; which was executed by the pictures of men being whipt, with the names of the offenders inscribed under them, being carried round the city.

During this residence at Geneva, I formed a friendship with a young man about my own age, of the name of Dumont, who was then studying for the church, and was soon after admitted one of its ministers. Roget, who had been long acquainted with him, had spoken to each of us in such favourable terms of the other that we were desirous of becoming friends before we had met; and a personal acquaintance, improved by a little tour we made together to the glaciers of Savoy, and round the lake of Geneva by the Tête Noire, Martigny, Bex, and Vevey, was soon matured into a very intimate and firm friendship, which remains to this day, increased and strengthened by the number of years during which it has lasted. His vigorous understanding, his extensive knowledge, and his splendid eloquence, qualified him to have acted the noblest part in public life; while the brilliancy of his wit, the cheerfulness of his humour, and the charms of his conversation, have made him the delight of every private society in which he has lived: but his most valuable qualities are, his strict integrity, his zeal to serve those whom he is attached to, and his most affectionate disposition.

While I was in this enchanting country, I made several little excursions to see and admire its beauties; amongst others to the Lac de Joux, to Evian, and the rocks of Meillerie; and one, which more than all the rest made a deep impression on me, to the summit of the Dent d'Oche, a very high mountain of Savoy on the southern bank of the lake of Geneva. The ascent is very difficult, and for that reason, perhaps, it is seldom visited by strangers; but the prospect it affords is the most beautiful and the most sublime that ever I beheld: the lake of Geneva stretched out to its whole extent with the rich country of the Pays de Vaud and its numerous towns, on the one side, and the Alps of Savoy on the other, like a vast sea of mountains, terminated by the distant Mont Blanc, towering far above the rest. It was after this expedition that, crossing the lake, I again paid a short visit to Lausanne, and took leave of my sister and of Roget. The precarious state of his health, and the prospect of the renewal of my own studies, and of the occupations which I hoped might follow them, made both of us apprehensive, of what proved but too true, that we were bidding each other an everlasting farewell.

Upon quitting this country, I made a party with

three other persons* to visit the Grande Chartreuse, intending from thence to get the best way I could to Lyons, and to return home by way of Paris, which I was desirous of seeing. I have since often regretted that I did not extend my travels, and allow myself to visit at least some of the cities in the northern part of Italy. Perhaps, however, I did well to resist the temptation which this opportunity held out to me. The prolongation, for a few months more, of this interruption of all regular habits of study might have had very serious consequences to me, and have disappointed all my future schemes. Our road to the Grande Chartreuse lay through a very beautiful country; and we had an opportunity of visiting Chambery, the capital of Savoy. The wild and romantic scenery of the Chartreuse has been often celebrated. I saw it to some disadvantage; for though it was early in September, we had so deep a fall of snow, and which lasted so long, that the roads became impassable, and for three days we were obliged to prolong our stay with the hospitable fathers against our will. Amongst the travellers collected together, there were two young French officers; one of whom was going to Lyons, and I joined his company. We proceeded together on mules to Grenoble, and there hired a cabriolet, which conveyed us to Lyons. At that place we parted: and I proceeded to Paris in the *diligence* or *messagerie*, a large carriage containing eight inside passengers; not a very convenient

* M. Juventin, pasteur of Geneva; M. de Végobre, an advocate there; and Mr. Shore, a young Englishman, who was at Geneva for his education.

or a very elegant conveyance, but one which was well suited to my humble circumstances, and in which much more is to be learnt of the manners of a people, than by being shut up in a commodious English carriage, and travelling post. Arrived at Paris, I left my luggage at the *Bureau des diligences;* and set off on foot to inquire my way through the street for an hotel at the other end of the town, to which I had got a direction. It was in the Rue de Richelieu, and in a very pleasant situation, the back windows looking upon the gardens of the Palais Royal; for a garden it then was, though the Duke of Orleans, to the great indignation of the Parisians, was preparing to cover it with buildings. At Paris I saw all that common travellers see, the theatres, the palaces, the public buildings, collections of pictures, and other objects of curiosity. I saw, too, the court in all its splendour; and I was present at the Royal Chapel at Versailles when high mass was celebrated before the king.

An event happened while I was there which showed Paris to great advantage; this was the birth of a Dauphin, after the Queen had been married several years without having had a son. Great public rejoicings took place. The theatres were thrown open to the people with gratuitous representations; and at the *Comédie Française* they were indulged with the adventures of Henry IV., their good and favourite King. There were public illuminations too, but these were commanded; and I felt no small surprise when I read placarded in the corners of the streets the mandate by which the loyal people of Paris were ordered to shut up their shops, and to illuminate their houses for three successive nights, and the officers of the police were enjoined to see the order executed. The illumination corresponded with its cause; and in many a house I observed one solitary lamp at each window glimmering, not in token of joy, but in reluctant obedience to the pleasure of the government. The public buildings, however, were splendid; and in most of the large squares were orchestras and bands of music, which played to the dancing of the people. The Place de Grève was (as I thought unfortunately) chosen as the favourite scene of these amusements. The Hôtel de Ville was resplendent with lamps. Fire-works were played off before it; and to the music of four different orchestras were as many parties of dirty and ragged creatures dancing, with as much life and gaiety as if they were in a theatre devoted only to mirth and joy. For myself, I confess that my cheerfulness was not a little damped by the squalid appearance of the dancers; by the soldiers ranged on every side; by the sudden appearance, from time to time, of the horse patrol (*maréchaussée*) silently and unexpectedly making their way through the thickest of the crowd; and by the recollection that the ground on which I stood was the common place of execution, which had been so often wet with blood, and had so often witnessed the lengthened agonies of tortured wretches expiring in flames, or upon the wheel.

The King went to Notre Dame in great state to return thanks to God for the birth of his son. The scene was a very splendid one, and the crowds which pressed on every side to see the royal procession pass, were immense. Only eight years afterwards I was present at a ceremony accompanied with the same military pomp, and beheld with the same eager curiosity by many of the same spectators, but which was of a very different kind; it was when, in the same church, the colours of the National Guard of Paris received the benediction of the archbishop, and when a patriotic sermon was preached on the occasion by the Abbé Fauchet.

I saw at Paris a great variety of persons; artists, advocates, and authors. Amongst these were D'Alembert and Diderot, the most celebrated of all the writers then remaining in France. D'Alembert was in a very infirm state of health, and not disposed to enter much into conversation with a person so shy and so unused to society as I was. Diderot, on the contrary, was all warmth and eagerness, and talked to me with as little reserve as if I had been long and intimately acquainted with him. Rousseau, politics, and religion, were the principal topics of his conversation. The *Confessions* of Rousseau were, at that time, expected shortly to appear; and it was manifest, from the bitterness with which Diderot spoke of the work and of its author, that he dreaded its appearance. On the subject of religion he made no disguise; or rather he was ostentatious of a total disbelief in the existence of a God. He talked very eagerly upon politics, and inveighed with great warmth against the tyranny of the French government. He told me that he had long meditated a work upon the death of Charles the First; that he had studied the trial of that prince; and that his intention was to have tried him over again, and to have sent him to the scaffold if he had found him guilty, but that he had at last relinquished the design. In England he would have executed it, but he had not the courage to do so in France.

D'Alembert, as I have observed, was more cautious; he contented himself with observing what an effect philosophy had in his own time produced on the minds of the people. The birth of the Dauphin afforded him an example. He was old enough, he said, to remember when such an event had made the whole nation drunk with joy *; but now they regarded with great indifference the birth of another master.

I must not quit the subject of my abode at Paris without the mention of two acquaintances I formed there, for to them I owed the most agreeable hours I passed in that celebrated city. The one was a person of my own name, a watchmaker, who then lived in the Place Dauphine, a Genevese, of the age of seventy, but who had all the gaiety and vivacity of youth. He was a man of very great merit in his business, had seen a great deal of the world, and was not without a considerable portion of literature. All the articles upon the subject of his own art, which are to be found in the *Encyclopédie*, were his. He conceived himself to be under obligations to my family, on account of the great kindness which his son had received during his

* This was in 1729. "On était dans une ivresse de joie."

residence in London at the hands of my father. The son had been elected a minister of one of the French Protestant churches in London; but ill health forced him to return to Geneva, where he died about a year before I arrived there. He was the author of two articles in the *Encyclopédie*, "Toleration" and "Virtue," which had very great celebrity. These, and two volumes of sermons, which were published after his death, attest the merits of that extraordinary man. He was the delight of the societies in which he lived, and his good-natured repartees were in every body's recollection at Geneva when I visited it. Nothing could exceed the zeal of this good old M. Romilly to serve me while I was at Paris, or the attentions which were paid me by his family, particularly his son-in-law and his daughter, M. et Mad^e de Corancez. It was to them I was indebted for my introduction to D'Alembert and Diderot, and for all the society I knew at Paris; which was confined, however, to the *bourgeoisie*, and to the descriptions of persons I have before enumerated.

The other valuable acquaintance which I have said that I formed at Paris was that of Mad^e Delessert, one of the most benevolent and amiable of women. She was from Switzerland; was, as long as Rousseau saw any body, one of his best friends; and it is to her that were addressed the charming Letters on Botany which, since his death, have been published. She had a large collection of other letters from him, of some of which she permitted me to take copies. At her country house at Passy, in her society, and in that of her amiable daughter, then a girl of fifteen, of a very agreeable person and of a very cultivated understanding, I spent most usefully the time I passed at Paris. There is nothing, indeed, by which I have through life more profited than by the just observations, the good opinion, and the sincere and gentle encouragement of amiable and sensible women.

I returned to London by way of Lisle and Ostend, still travelling in public carriages, having greatly benefited in every respect by my short travels. My health particularly was very much improved; though I still occasionally, during the winter, felt the effects of my former maladies. I was able, however, to resume my studies with great ardour, and I prosecuted them with considerable success. Soon after my return, I published, in *The Morning Chronicle*, a tolerably detailed account of the late political events at Geneva, which I had written while I was there.

There was a young man of my own age, a student and an inhabitant of Gray's Inn, with whom I, about this time, formed a great degree of intimacy. His great talents, and his learning as a classical scholar, as an English antiquary, and as a profound lawyer, must, if he had lived, have raised him to very great eminence in his profession; though his honest and independent spirit would, probably, to him have barred all access to its highest offices. This was John Baynes. He was a native of the West Riding of Yorkshire; had received his early education at Richmond in that county; and had afterwards very much distinguished himself both in mathematics and in the classics in the University of Cambridge, where he became a fellow of Trinity College. A man more high-spirited, more generous, more humane, more disposed to protect the feeble against the oppression of the powerful and the great, never adorned the annals of England. His premature death, which happened five or six years after the time I am speaking of, I have always considered as a very great public loss. To our profession, particularly, the loss of such a man, and in such a state of the profession as that in which it happened, was the greatest that it could suffer. The intimacy which I formed with this excellent man soon ripened into the firmest friendship. We prosecuted our studies together; we communicated to each other, and compared the notes which we took during our attendance in the courts. We used to meet at night at each other's chambers to read some of the classics, particularly Tacitus, in whom we both took great delight; and we formed a little society, to which we admitted only two other persons, Holroyd and Christian, for arguing points of law upon questions which we suggested in turn. One argued on each side as counsel, the other two acted the part of judges, and were obliged to give at length the reasons of their decisions; an exercise which was, certainly, very useful to us all.

On the last day of Easter Term, 1783, I was called to the bar. It was my intention to have gone a circuit, but this I was obliged to postpone till the ensuing spring.

Roget, whose health had continued very precarious from the time when I left him, had, early in the present summer, a fresh attack of his disorder, which in a few weeks proved fatal to him. His death happened at a most unfortunate time for my poor sister, for it was when she had been brought to bed only six weeks of her daughter. Never did any woman adore a husband with more passionate fondness than she did hers; never had anxiety surpassed that with which she had been tortured during the different periods of his long disease; and never was affliction greater than that which she now endured. My father and all our family were very impatient that she should return to us from the strange land in which her melancholy lot had been cast. But with two children, and one of so very tender an age, and with no companion but her maid, it was an alarming journey to undertake. My brother was married, and was entirely occupied by his business. There was no person who could, without the greatest inconvenience, attend her on such a journey but myself, and I therefore undertook it; it was only losing one circuit, and it was rendering a very essential service to all those whom I most loved and valued.

Baynes was desirous of seeing Paris, and agreed to be my companion so far on my journey. It was not the most direct road to Lausanne; but it was that by which I was likely to find the best opportunities of conveyance. We, accordingly, proceeded to Paris together; and his good spirits and agreeable society rendered it a very pleasant journey. At Paris I staid only a week, and had little more than time to renew my acquaintance with the connexions I had formed there, particularly with M. Romilly and Mad[e] and M[lle] Delessert. Baynes had a letter of introduction to Dr. Franklin, who was then residing at Passy, and I had the great satisfaction of accompanying him in his visit. Dr. Franklin was indulgent enough to converse a good deal with us, whom he observed to be young men very desirous of improving by his conversation. Of all the celebrated persons whom, in my life, I have chanced to see, Dr. Franklin, both from his appearance and his conversation, seemed to me the most remarkable. His venerable patriarchal appearance, the simplicity of his manner and language, and the novelty of his observations, at least the novelty of them at that time to me, impressed me with an opinion of him as of one of the most extraordinary men that ever existed. The American Constitutions were then very recently published. I remember his reading us some passages out of them, and expressing some surprise that the French government had permitted the publication of them in France. They certainly produced a very great sensation at Paris, the effects of which were probably felt many years afterwards. Diderot was at this time dead; and D'Alembert was in so infirm a state that I thought he would gladly enough dispense with a visit from me.

From Paris I travelled by the direct road to Geneva, in company with a M. Gautier, a Genevese, with whom I had, some years before, made acquaintance in London, a very worthy and friendly man. He, afterwards, married M[lle] Delessert; and with him and his incomparable wife I constantly maintained a correspondence by letters. I made but a short stay at Geneva; few of my best friends were then remaining there. The revolution which had taken place had afforded a complete triumph to the aristocratical party; but it had been effected by the interference of France, and by the terror of its arms. I shall never forget the burning indignation which I felt as I looked down upon a French regiment, which was mounting guard in the place of Bel-air, under the windows of my hotel, and as I heard the noise of its military music, which seemed, as it were, to insult the ancient liberties of the republic.

At Lausanne, I met with the Abbé Raynal; but I saw him with no admiration either of his talents or his character. Having read the eloquent passages in his celebrated work with delight, I had formed the highest expectations of him; but those expectations were sadly disappointed. I was filled at this time with horror at West Indian slavery and at the Slave Trade, and Raynal's philosophical history of the two Indies had served to enliven these sentiments; but when I came to talk on these subjects with him, he appeared to me so cold and so indifferent about them, that I conceived a very unfavourable opinion of him.* His conversation was certainly so inferior to his celebrated work, as to give much countenance to the report,

* I brought with me from Lausanne, on my former visit to it, a little tract on West Indian Slavery, which the Marquis de Condorcet had had printed there, and had written under the pretended name of Schwartz, a Swiss clergyman. I translated it into English; but upon offering it to a bookseller, I found that he would not undertake the printing. I laid it aside, therefore; and it never appeared.

which has been very common, that the most splendid passages in it were not his own.

My return to England with my sister and her two children was but a melancholy journey. We put ourselves under the care of a Swiss *voiturier;* and, for the sake, I think, of avoiding any of the places through which my sister had passed with her husband when she left her country, and which she thought would be attended with remembrances too painful for her to endure, we made rather a circuitous journey. We passed through Soleure, Berne, Basle, Louvain, Malines, Antwerp, Breda, and Rotterdam, to Helvoetsluys, whence we crossed to Harwich. At Helvoetsluys we arrived just after the packet had sailed; and as four days would elapse before the next, and we were unwilling to venture in any other vessel, I took advantage of this delay to make a little excursion to the Hague, and I returned time enough to accompany my sister in her passage across the sea.

Thus was my first long vacation passed. By Michaelmas term I had returned to business, or rather to attend the courts, and to receive such business as accident might throw in my way. I had endeavoured to draw Chancery pleadings before I was called to the bar, as an introduction to business when I should be called. In that way, however, the occupation I got under the bar was very inconsiderable; but soon after I was admitted to the bar, I was employed to draw pleadings in several cases. This species of employment went on very gradually increasing for several years; during which, though I was occupied in the way of my profession, I had scarcely once occasion to open my lips in court.

In the spring of 1784, I first went upon the circuit. All circuits were indifferent to me, for I had no friends or connexions on any one of them ; and my choice fell upon the Midland, because there appeared to be fewer men of considerable talents or of high character as advocates upon it than upon any other, and consequently a greater opening for me than elsewhere. It was, besides, shorter than some other circuits, and would, therefore, take me for a less time from the Court of Chancery; and, what was no unimportant consideration, my travelling expenses upon it would be less. The circuit did not, indeed, when I joined it, appear to be overstocked with talent. At the head of it, in point of rank, though with very little business, was Serjeant Hill; a lawyer of very profound and extensive learning, but with a very small portion of judgment, and without the faculty of making his great knowledge useful. On any subject on which you consulted him, he would pour forth the treasures of his legal science without order or discrimination. He seemed to be of the order of lawyers of Lord Coke's time, and he was the last of that race. For modern law he had supreme contempt; and I have heard him observe, that the greatest service that could be rendered the country would be to repeal all the statutes, and burn all the reports which were of a later date than the Revolution. Next to him in rank, but far before him in business, and, indeed, completely at the head of the circuit, stood * * * * ; who, without talents, without learning, without any one qualification for his

Fac-Similes of the Han

Lond

It would seem, my dear Roget, by your last Letter that
on which I am to enter only to draw from you such prai
been mine, must have been fully gratified by your Silen
more offensive to Modesty even than a panegyric upon
however I assure you, I had no such wish, & that what I
but realize the partial hopes & Expectations of my friends
but in myself I have a much less indulgent Censor, &, in this
weight with my own. I have taught myself however a ve
in my Situation which is not to suffer my Happiness to de
myself to employ all the Talents & all the authority I may

If you should see an Ask

-writing of Sir Samuel Romilly.

-n. 7 Jan: 1783.

you thought I had affected doubt of succeeding in the way of Life
s as might encourage me in my pursuit. That Object, had it
, which, introduced as it is, is a greater Encouragement to me, & is
lents which your Indulgence might have supposed me to possess
rote to you was but a faithful transcript of what I felt. Could I
here could be no doubt of my success almost beyond my wishes
rh aps alone, I cannot suffer their Judgment to have equal
y useful Lesson of practical Philosophy to make myself easy
pend upon my Success. Should my wishes be gratified I promise
equire for the public good.

-me in any thing I hope

profession, had, by the mere friendship, or rather companionship, of Mr. Justice * * *, obtained the favour of a silk gown; and by a forward manner, and the absence of commanding abilities in others, had got to be employed in almost every cause. The merits of a horse he understood perfectly well; and when in these, as sometimes happened, consisted the merits of a cause, he acquitted himself admirably; but in other cases nothing could be more injudicious than his conduct. In spite, however, of his defects, and notwithstanding the obvious effects of his mismanagement, he continued for many years, while I was upon the circuit, in possession of a very large portion of business. The other men in business on the circuit were Dayrell, Balguy, Parker Coke, Clarke, White, Gally, and Sutton (afterwards Lord Manners, and Chancellor of Ireland); none of them very much distinguished as lawyers, or as advocates. There were, besides, some young men without business, and who seemed to have little prospect of ever obtaining it; George Isted, Rastal, Aufrere, Skrine, Gough, Shipston, Tom Smith, and some others whose names I may probably have forgotten. The society of the circuit was not very much to my mind, but I formed in it a friendship with several men whom I highly valued. Of these, however, Gally and Sutton were the principal; the others joined the circuit some years after I had entered upon it. At different places we had provincial counsel, who joined us. The most remarkable of these was Old Wheler (so we always called him), who lived in the neighbourhood of Coventry; an honest, sensible, frank, good-natured, talkative old lawyer. He had been upon the circuit forty years when I first joined it, and was attending the assizes at the time of the rebellion of 1745. It was some years later, and when I attended the Coventry and Warwick Quarter Sessions, that I became very intimate with this cheerful, open-hearted, kind old man; but I was so much delighted with his conversation and society, that I cannot, upon the first mention of the lawyers whom I found upon the circuit, refuse myself the pleasure of speaking of him. He had read nothing but law, he had lived only among lawyers, and all the pleasant stories he had to tell were of the lawyers whom he remembered in his youth. His stories, indeed, were repeated by him again and again; but they were told with such good humour, and had so much intrinsic merit, that I always listened to them with pleasure. Among some peculiarities which he had, was a very great dislike to parsons and to noblemen. He often remarked, that it would have given him the greatest joy if his daughter and his only child had married a lawyer; but he had the mortification (a singular one, undoubtedly, but such it appeared to him) of seeing, before he died, his two grandsons the presumptive heirs of two different peerages.

Soon after my return from this, my first circuit, I lost my dear and excellent father. He died * in his seventy-third year, of a palsy which had affected him several weeks before it proved fatal. Happily, he suffered no pain, and was never sensible

* On the 29th of August, 1784.

of the nature of his disease. A few years before, I had persuaded myself that he was likely to live to a much more advanced period. His faculties were then all unimpaired, his natural cheerfulness unclouded, and his activity unabated. I remember his once observing that he had grown an old man to others without seeming so to himself; and his telling us of a pleasant mistake he had made, when, being announced at some house, and one of the servants having, from the top of the stairs, called out "that the old gentleman was desired to walk up," he had drawn aside, altogether forgetting himself, in order to let the venerable person, whoever he might be, who he supposed was meant, pass him: and he, probably, would have lived to a very great age, if in his latter days he had enjoyed that serenity of mind to which his virtues so justly entitled him; but, alas! they were harassed with perpetual anxiety. The expensive stock in trade, necessary to the carrying on of his business, had obliged him to raise money by procuring the discount of bills, which were from time to time renewed. As he was known to be a man of the strictest integrity, and was supposed to be very wealthy, he had for a considerable time found no difficulty in procuring his bills to be discounted; but when, in the latter end of the American war, there was a great stagnation of credit, he, in common with others, found himself involved in difficulties, and he became exceedingly alarmed for the consequences. These alarms had damped his natural cheerfulness, had greatly agitated his mind, and may be truly said to have brought upon him, though he was then of the age of seventy, a premature old age.

When I was called to the bar, it became necessary for me to have a servant, one who should be always in chambers to receive briefs, cases, and instructions for pleadings, if any should chance to be brought for me, and who should attend me upon the circuit, in the various characters of clerk, valet, and groom. It was a singular choice that I made of a man to serve me in these capacities. I have mentioned, I think, in the early part of my life, a female servant, to whom the care of myself, my brother, and my sister was intrusted, one Mary Evans, as simple-hearted, honest, and affectionate a creature as ever existed. Before she left my father's house, she had become strongly infected with methodism; and, not long after she left it, she married a pious journeyman shoemaker, of the name of Bickers, as fervent a methodist as herself. The poor man began to grow infirm; he had become incapable of working assiduously at his trade, and consequently incapable of supporting himself, and of supporting her. I could not endure the idea of seeing a woman, whom in my infancy I had revered almost as a mother, and who had loved me as her son, reduced to distress; and I could not afford to maintain her husband and to pay the wages of a servant besides. I determined, therefore, unpromising as the project seemed, to try whether I could not make shift with him as a servant. I certainly suffered, during several years, for my good nature. He could ride, and he could stand behind my chair at dinner, but this was almost all that he could do; and though I, sometimes, employed him to copy papers for me, he wrote very ill, and made a thousand faults of spelling. The want of proper attendance, however, was far less disagreeable to me than the jokes which he excited on the circuit. His appearance was singular and puritanical; and the first day he was seen on the circuit, he was named by the young men upon it, "the Quaker," an appellation by which he was always afterwards known. It is not easy to give an idea of the great familiarity which existed amongst the young men who went the circuit, of the strong disposition to turn things into ridicule which prevailed, and how very formidable that ridicule was. To all his defects, Bickers added that of sometimes getting drunk; and he has often made me pass very unpleasant hours under the apprehension that, half elevated with liquor, and half inspired with the spirit of methodism which possessed him, he would say or do something which would afford an inexhaustible fund of mirth to the whole circuit. All this, however, I submitted to, from the motives which I have already mentioned; and, in spite of his increasing defects and infirmities, and notwithstanding the disagreeable hours which he made me pass, he continued my servant till the day of his death, (a period, I think, of about seven years,) though I was obliged, at last, to take a temporary servant to attend me on the circuits. With all his defects, he had some excellent qualities. He knew that it could not be for the services he rendered me that I continued him in my service, and he was all gratitude for my kindness. In every way that it was possible far him he showed his zeal and his attachment to me; and I shall not soon forget the earnestness with which he once ventured to offer me his advice upon what appeared to him to be a matter of no small moment. I had, sometimes, employed him to copy papers which I had amused myself with writing upon abuses existing in the administration of justice, and upon the necessity of certain reforms. He had seen with great regret the little progress I had made in my profession, and particularly upon the circuit, and had observed those whom he thought much my inferiors in talents far before me in business; and, putting these matters together in his head, he entertained no doubt that he had, at last, discovered the cause of what had long puzzled him. The business of a barrister depends on the good opinion of attorneys; and attorneys never could think well of any man who was troubling his head about reforming abuses when he ought to be profiting by them. All this he, one day, took the liberty of representing to me with very great humility. I endeavoured to calm his apprehensions, and told him that what I wrote was seen only by himself and by me; but this, no doubt, did not satisfy him.

But it is time for me to mention the acquaintance which I formed with some celebrated men. It was in the latter end of the year 1784 that I first met the Count de Mirabeau, and it was to D'Ivernois that I owed his acquaintance. His extraordinary talents, the disorders of his tumultuous youth, the excesses he had committed, the law-suits in which he had been engaged, the harsh treatment he had experienced from his father, his imprisonment in the dungeon of Vincennes, and the eloquent work he had written with the indignant feelings which so unjust an imprisonment inspired, had already given him considerable celebrity in Europe; but it was a celebrity greatly inferior to that which he afterwards acquired. He brought with him to this country a short tract, which he had written against the Order of the Cincinnati lately established in America, which it was his object to publish here. He was desirous that an English translation of it should appear at the same time with the original. He read his manuscript to me; and, seeing that I was very much struck with the eloquence of it, he proposed to me to become his translator, telling me that he knew that it was impossible to expect any thing tolerable from a translator who was to be paid. I thought the translation would be a useful exercise for me; I had sufficient leisure on my hands, and I undertook it. The Count was difficult enough to please; he was sufficiently impressed with the beauties of the original. He went over every part of the translation with me; observed on every passage in which justice was not done to the thought, or the force of the expression was lost; and made many very useful criticisms. During this occupation, we had occasion to see one another often, and became very intimate; and, as he had read much, had seen a great deal of the world, was acquainted with all the most distinguished persons who at that time adorned either the royal court or the republic of letters in France, had a great knowledge of French and Italian literature, and possessed a very good taste, his conversation was extremely interesting, and not a little instructive. I had such frequent opportunities of seeing him at this time, and afterwards at a much more important period of his life, that I think his character was well known to me. I doubt whether it has been as well known to the world, and I am convinced that great injustice has been done him. This, indeed, is not surprising, when one considers that, from the first moment of his entering upon the career of an author, he had been altogether indifferent how numerous or how powerful might be the enemies he should provoke. His vanity was, certainly, excessive; but I have no doubt that, in his public conduct as well as in his writings, he was desirous of doing good, that his ambition was of the noblest kind, and that he proposed to himself the noblest ends. He was, however, like many of his countrymen, who were active in the calamitous revolution which afterwards took place, not sufficiently scrupulous about the means by which those ends were to be accomplished. He, indeed, in some degree, professed this; and more than once I have heard him say that there were occasions upon which "*la petite morale était ennemie de la grande.*" It is not surprising that with such maxims as these in his mouth, unguarded in his expressions, and careless of his reputation, he should have afforded room for the circulation of many stories to his disadvantage. Violent, impetuous, conscious of the superiority of his talents, and the declared enemy and denouncer of every species of tyranny and oppression, he could not fail to shock the prejudices, to oppose the interests, to excite the jealousy, and to wound the pride of many descriptions of persons. A mode of refuting his works, open to the basest and vilest of mankind, was to represent him as a monster of vice and profligacy. A scandal once set on foot is strengthened and propagated by many who have no malice against the object of it. Men delight to talk of what is extraordinary; and what more extraordinary than a person so admirable for his talents, and so contemptible for his conduct, professing in his writings principles so excellent, and in all the offices of public and private life putting in practice those which are so detestable? I, indeed, possessed demonstrative evidence of the falsehood of some of the anecdotes which, by men of high character, were related to his prejudice.

While he was in London, he lost a great part of his linen, and a manuscript copy of the correspondence between Voltaire and D'Alembert, which was at that time unpublished, but has since appeared in Beaumarchais' edition. A person of the name of Hardy, who served him in the capacity of amanuensis, having abruptly left him, although his wages remained unpaid, suspicion naturally fell on him, and the Count obtained a warrant against him; and after some time he was apprehended and tried at the Old Bailey. The evidence was very slight, and the man was properly acquitted; but nothing at all discreditable to Mirabeau appeared upon the trial. On the contrary, Baron Perryn, who tried the prisoner (Mr. Justice Buller being at the same time upon the bench), declared, that though the prisoner ought certainly to be acquitted, no blame whatever was to be imputed to the prosecution. Lord Minto, then Sir Gilbert Elliot, who had been at the same school with Mirabeau, and was the greatest friend he had in England, Baynes, and myself, were present at the trial, and had been consulted by Mirabeau upon all the steps he had taken upon the occasion. When the trial was over, Lord Minto said that it would be extremely important to have an accurate account of what had passed upon the trial inserted in some of the newspapers, to prevent any misrepresentation of it, which he thought might be apprehended from Mirabeau's enemies; for it had been observed that some of them, and particularly Linguet, had taken a great interest in the affair, and had been present watching every thing that passed, as well upon the trial as previously upon the examination of the prisoner before the magistrate who committed him. At Lord Minto's suggestion, therefore, he, together with Baynes and myself, went immediately from the Court to Baynes's chambers; and there drew up a very full account of the trial, which was the next day published in one of the newspapers. I have the paper still in my possession, and it contains a most scrupulously exact account of every thing that passed. What was my astonishment, therefore, some years afterwards, when Mirabeau had, by his conduct in the National Assembly of

France, drawn the attention of all Europe upon him, to hear, as I did, that Mr. Justice Buller had stated * in different companies, that Mirabeau had had the villany, because his servant demanded his wages of him, and threatened him with an arrest, to charge him with a felony, for which there was so little foundation that it was proved upon the trial that Mirabeau had never been possessed of so many shirts as he had accused his servant of stealing! That Mr. Justice Buller deliberately circulated these untruths, knowing them to be such, I do not believe. He had a very imperfect recollection of the trial, although he had himself presided at it; he fancied what he stated; he did not give himself the trouble of looking back to his notes, and it did not seem to him to be very important that he should be scrupulously exact respecting a man who had already so bad a reputation, and who would not be the better or the worse for what was thought of him in England. It is in this way, only, that I am able to account for what appears so extraordinary, but upon which it is hardly possible that I can have made any mistake.

Mirabeau's indifference as to the enemies he made was shown in various instances during his residence in England. In his notes upon his *Cincinnati*, he attacked Sir Joseph Banks for his conduct as President of the Royal Society; and he arraigned the judgment of the Court of King's Bench, in the celebrated case of the Dean of

* I heard this from persons who told me they were present when Mr. Justice Buller made these statements.

St. Asaph. In private company he was positive and intolerant in his opinions. One remarkable instance of this appeared at a dinner, at which I was present, at Mr. Brand Hollis's. Among the company were John Wilkes, General Miranda, and Mirabeau. The conversation turned upon the English criminal law, its severity, and the frequency of public executions. Wilkes defended the system with much wit and good-humour, but with very bad arguments. He thought the happiest results followed from the severity of our penal law. It accustomed men to a contempt of death, though it never held out to them any very cruel spectacle; and he thought that much of the courage of Englishmen, and of their humanity too, might be traced to the nature of our capital punishments, and to their being so often exhibited to the people. Mirabeau was not satisfied with having the best of the argument, and with triumphantly refuting his opponent; he was determined to crush him with his eloquence. He declaimed with vehemence, talked of Wilkes's profound immorality, and with a man less cool, less indifferent about the truth, and less skilled in avoiding any personal quarrel than Wilkes, the dispute would probably have been attended with very serious consequences.

Mirabeau seemed to provoke and to take a pleasure in these sort of controversies with celebrated men; and he wrote a letter to me while I was on the circuit in 1785, in which he gave me a very detailed account of a dispute which he supposed himself to have had with Gibbon, the historian, at

Lord Lansdowne's table, and in which he expressed himself with so much violence, that he seems in some degree to admit that he was to blame. The most extraordinary circumstance, however, is, that he certainly never had any such dispute with Gibbon; and that, at the time, when he supposed it to have taken place, Gibbon was actually residing at Lausanne. How the mistake happened, and who it was that he took for Gibbon, I never discovered, but of the fact there can be no doubt, for I have still the letter in my possession.[1]

I have dwelt too long, perhaps, on this extraordinary man, especially as I shall have occasion to mention him again, and probably more than once. My acquaintance with him may have had considerable influence on the subsequent events of my life, though I am unable to say with any certainty whether it really had such an influence. He introduced me to Benjamin Vaughan, and Benjamin Vaughan made me acquainted with Lord Lansdowne. Mirabeau, too, was loud in his praises of me to that nobleman; he had formed high expectations of me; he was anxious that I should act a distinguished part in the country; and he was impatient to see me in Parliament, as the only theatre upon which that part could be acted. In all this he was actuated by the most disinterested motives, and by the purest friendship for me.[2]

Lord Lansdowne's acquaintance with me was entirely at his own request. He begged that I

[1] See *infrà*, "Letters from Mirabeau" in 1785. — Ed.
[2] Ibid.

would call on him to give him some information respecting my friend Dumont, who at that time was the pastor of a protestant church at Petersburgh, and whom he had some thoughts of engaging to come into this country to undertake the education of his younger son, Henry, the present Marquis of Lansdowne. I accordingly waited on his Lordship, and was received by him in the most flattering manner. From that time he anxiously cultivated my acquaintance and my friendship; and to that friendship I owe it that I ever knew the affectionate wife who has been the author of all my happiness. What procured me so kind a reception by Lord Lansdowne was less the praises of Mirabeau, than a small tract which I had written on a subject which at that time very much interested the public. The trial of the Dean of St. Asaph had revived and given a more lively interest to the question, often before discussed, 'what was the proper province of the jury in matters of libel'; Upon this question I had drawn up a paper, which I called *A Fragment on the Rights and Duties of Juries* [1], or by some such title, and which I had sent anonymously to the Constitutional Society, that Society having warmly entered into the controversy, and being, indeed, deeply interested in the trial out of which it arose, since the dialogue, written by Sir William Jones, which the Dean was prosecuted for publishing in Welsh, had been originally printed in English by the Society itself. The only object of this Society, which consisted

[1] The accurate title of the tract is, *A Fragment on the Constitutional Power and Duties of Juries*. — Ed.

of a few men of great talents, but of which the greater number were well meaning but foolish persons, was to publish and circulate gratuitously political tracts which might inform the people upon the true principles of the constitution. These tracts, as Burke has somewhere observed, were never as charitably read as they were charitably published. The Society received my paper with great applause, and ordered many copies of it to be printed and distributed. Baynes, Vaughan, and a very few more of my friends knew the paper to be mine, and Vaughan mentioned it as such to Lord Lansdowne, who conceived from it a very favourable opinion of me, and became, in consequence, desirous of my acquaintance.* His Lordship loaded me with civilities, and seemed to take, and I have no doubt did sincerely take, a great interest in my success. The projects, however, which Mirabeau had conceived for me, were not at this time at all in question. If, indeed, they had been, I should not have hesitated to decline them, as, if I am not mistaken, I very fully stated to Baynes, in a letter which I wrote to him from the circuit, in answer to one[1], in which he stated to me all that Mirabeau had been dreaming about for my advantage. Some years afterwards, indeed, Lord Lansdowne did offer me a seat in Parliament, and

* I was not the only person whose supposed talents had procured him Lord Lansdowne's friendship. That admirable criticism on *Blackstone's Commentaries*, which was published under the title of *A Fragment on Government*, procured for its author, my most excellent friend, Jeremy Bentham, an introduction to Lord Lansdowne of the same kind, and in consequence of it his warm friendship.

[1] See *infrà*, "Letters from Mirabeau" in 1785.—Ed.

strongly pressed me to accept it, with an assurance that I was to be at perfect liberty to vote and act as I should think proper. This was at a time when I had got a tolerable share of business at the bar, when I seemed certain of gaining a competence in my profession, and when, in point of fortune, I should have risked very little by going into Parliament. It was that which, above all things, I should have rejoiced in, if I could have gone into the House of Commons perfectly independent, and not with the consciousness that I was placed there by an individual whose opinions might, on some important subjects, be very different from my own. Even with all these disadvantages, the offer was at that time so tempting, that I confess I hesitated: it was not, however, for long: I had the good sense and the honesty to decline it, and I have ever since applauded my determination.

But whatever distant views Lord Lansdowne might have had, he had no wish, at this time, to see me in the House of Commons; and I believe he did not imagine that I should ever be a successful speaker there. He was very desirous, however, that I should distinguish myself in my profession; and he was, at the same time, anxious that I should write some work which might attract the atention of the public. Madan had recently published his '*Thoughts on Executive Justice;*' a small tract, in which, by a mistaken application of the maxim, 'that the certainty of punishment is more efficacious than its severity for the prevention of crimes,' he absurdly insisted on the expediency of rigidly enforcing, in every instance, our penal code, sanguinary and barbarous as it is: the certainty of punishment he strongly recommended, but intimated no wish to see any part of its severity relaxed. The work was, in truth, a strong and vehement censure upon the judges and the ministers for their mode of administering the law, and for the frequency of the pardons which they granted. It was very much read, and certainly was followed by the sacrifice of many lives, by the useless sacrifice of them; for though some of the judges, and the government, for a time, adopted his reasoning, it was but for a short time that they adopted it; and, indeed, a long perseverance in such a sanguinary system was impossible. Lord Ellenborough, who seems to consider himself as bound to defend the conduct of all judges, whether living or dead, has lately, in the House of Lords, in his usual way of unqualified and vehement assertion, declared that it was false that this book had any effect, whatever, upon either judges or ministers. To this assertion I have only to oppose these plain facts: in the year 1783, the year before the work was published, there were executed in London only 51 malefactors; in 1785, the year after it was published, there were executed 97: and it was recently after the publication of this book that was exhibited a spectacle unseen in London for a long course of years before, the execution of nearly 20 criminals at a time. Lord Lansdowne, amongst others, was dazzled and imposed upon by this writer's reasoning; and he even recommended me to write something on the same subject. This, of course, induced me to look into the book; but I was so much shocked at the folly and inhumanity of it, that, instead of enforcing the same arguments, I sat down to refute them; and I soon afterwards produced a little tract, which I published without my name, as *Observations on a late Publication, entitled, 'Thoughts on Executive Justice;'* and I added to it a letter of Dr. Franklin's to Benjamin Vaughan, on the same subject. A few of my friends, — Baynes, Vaughan, Lord Lansdowne, Dr. Jebb, Wilberforce, and Sir Gilbert Elliot, knew that the work was mine, and highly approved it. I did not, however, publicly avow it, nor had I any encouragement to do so; for, though it was much commended in the Reviews, it had so little success with the public, that not more than a hundred copies of it were sold. I sent a copy to each of the judges; and I had great satisfaction in hearing Mr. Justice Willes, while he was on the circuit, speaking highly in its praise, and wondering who could be the author. To Lord Sydney, who was then Secretary of State for the Home Department, I also sent a copy; but it was not received, his servant having told the person by whom I sent it, that he had his Lordship's orders not to receive any letter or parcel without knowing whom it came from; a curious precaution to be used by a minister who is at the head of the police.

The little success of this pamphlet did not deter me from occupying my leisure hours in writing observations on different parts of our criminal law. Upon the circuit, too, I made the criminal law very much my study, and attended as often as I could in the Crown Court, and noted down all the most remarkable things that passed there; not merely the points of law that arose, but the effects which the different provisions of the law, the rules of evidence, and our forms of proceeding appeared to me to produce on the manners of the people, and on the administration of justice.

The society of the circuit had much improved within a few years after I first entered upon it, by the addition of several men for whom I entertained a very great regard. The principal of these were Ascough, Perceval, and Bramston. Ascough, though possessed of a large property, and though generous to a degree which amounted to a perfect contempt of money, followed the profession with as much ardour as if his subsistence had depended upon his success. He had read a great deal, always brought many books with him upon the circuit, and was possessed of much general knowledge, in which English lawyers are commonly so lamentably deficient. He was cheerful, warm, friendly, and was a great acquisition to the society of the circuit. So, too, was Perceval; with much less, and indeed with very little reading, of a conversation barren of instruction, and with strong and invincible prejudices on many subjects; yet, by his excellent temper, his engaging manners, and his sprightly conversation, he was the delight of all who knew him. I formed a strong and lasting friendship with both these men. Poor Ascough died of a consumption a short time after I was married; and Perceval, after he had, in a manner which my private friendship for him could never induce me to consider in a favourable point of view, obtained the situation of Prime Minister[1],

[1] See *infrà*, Parl. Diary, April, 1807. — Ed.

and quite to the moment of his tragical end, was desirous that our friendship should remain uninterrupted: I could not, however, continue in habits of private intimacy and intercourse with one whom in public I had every day to oppose. Bramston had the good humour and the friendly disposition of the other two, and his conversation was likewise very engaging. Many very happy hours have I passed in this society; particularly when we could contrive for a day to get away from the circuit, either at Matlock, or at our friend Digby's, at Meriden, in Warwickshire.

This sort of amusement, however, was for a considerable time the only profit that I derived from the circuit. Many of the barristers upon it had friends and connexions in some of the counties through which we passed, which served as an introduction of them to business; but for myself, I was without connexions every where: and at the end of my sixth or seventh circuit, I had made no progress. I had been, it is true, in a few causes; but all the briefs, I had had, were delivered to me by London attorneys, who had seen my face in London, and who happened to be strangers to the juniors on the circuit. They afforded me no opportunity of displaying any talents, if I had possessed them, and they led to nothing; I might have continued thus a mere spectator of the business done by others, quite to the end of the sixteen years which elapsed before I gave up every part of the circuit, if I had not resolved, though it was very inconvenient to me on account of the business which I began to get in London, to attend the

Quarter Sessions of some Midland County. There is, indeed, a course by which an unconnected man may be pretty sure to gain business, and which is not unfrequently practised. It is to gain an acquaintance with the attorneys at the different assize-towns, to show them great civility, to pay them great court, and to effect before them a display of wit, knowledge, and parts. But he who disdains such unworthy means may, if he do not attend the Quarter Sessions, pass his whole life in travelling round the circuit, and in daily attendances in court, without obtaining a single brief. When a man first makes his appearance in court, no attorney is disposed to try the experiment whether he has any talents; and when a man's face has become familiar by his having been long a silent spectator of the business done by others, his not being employed is supposed to proceed from his incapacity, and is alone considered as sufficient evidence that he must have been tried and rejected. It was an observation, indeed, which I heard Mr. Justice Heath make, "that there was no use in going a circuit without attending sessions," which determined me to try the experiment, and I fixed on Warwick as being the last place upon the commission, and therefore that part of it which I could attend with the least interruption of my business in Chancery, and as being also the place at which at that time the greatest number of causes were tried. At the sessions there is a much less attendance of counsel than at the assizes; and from the incapacity for business of many who do attend, every man is almost certain of being tried; and if he has any talents, of being a good deal employed. I found the experiment very successful: I had not attended many sessions before I was in all the business there; this naturally led to business at the assizes, and I had obtained a larger portion of it than any man upon the circuit, when my occupations in London forced me altogether to relinquish it: this, however, was at a period long subsequent to that to which I have brought down my narrative.

The increase of my business in town was so regular and considerable, as to make it evident that I ought principally to rely upon it, and that the circuit should be made a matter of very subordinate consideration. It was, indeed, more for the sake of cultivating the habit of addressing juries, of examining and cross-examining witnesses, and of exercising that presence of mind which is so essential to a *nisi prius* advocate, and which I thought might be of great use to me in the higher stations of the profession to which I began to aspire, than on account of the emolument I might derive from it, that I remained on the circuit.

In the summer of 1787, I suffered an irreparable loss by the death of my most excellent friend, Baynes. I had engaged to pass a part of the vacation with him at his father's in the neighbourhood of Skipton, in Yorkshire, and we were to have set out immediately, upon my return from the circuit; but, upon the circuit, I received the news of his illness, of the alarms which were entertained for him, and of his death. He had been applying himself to study with unusual assiduity; his business as a special pleader under the bar had much increased, and he had undergone extraordinary fatigues in it; and, during all this, he had determind to live with a very unusual degree of abstemiousness. He was attacked by a putrid fever, which baffled all the efforts of medicine, and in a very short time brought him to the grave. His loss was one of the greatest misfortunes which at that time could have befallen me, and it was a source of great affliction to me; but I shall ever account it one of the most fortunate occurrences, in my prosperous life, that, for six years before he died, I enjoyed his warm and generous friendship. In death, he bore testimony of his affection for me; he appointed me the executor of his will, and he left me a valuable part of his library, all his classics, and all his books upon law and legal antiquities. His friend Dr. Parr, at the instance of his father, wrote an inscription for his tomb, which is very happily characteristic of him.[1]

[1] The following is the inscription alluded to: — Ed.

JOANNI BAYNES, A.M.
COLLEGII S. TRINITATIS APUD CANTABRIGIENSIS SOCIO
JUVENI DISERTO ET SINE MALEDICTIS FACETO
VI INGENII AD EXCOGITANDUM ACUTA
ET FIRMA AD MEMORIAM MIRIFICE PRAEDITO
GRAECIS ET LATINIS LITERIS PENITUS IMBUTO
LEGUM ANGLICARUM INTERIORI
ET RECONDITA DISCIPLINA ERUDITO
LIBERTATIS CONSERVANDAE PERSTUDIOSO
PATRIAE BONORUMQUE CIVIUM AMANTISSIMO
SIMPLICI JUSTO ET PROPOSITI
ANIMOSE ET FORTITER TENACI
QUI VIXIT ANN. XXVIII. MENS. III. DIEB. XXVIII.
DECESSIT LONDINI PRIDIE NON. AUGUST.
ANNO SACRO
M.DCC.LXXX.VII.
GULIELMUS BAYNES
CONTRA VOTUM SUPERSTES
FILIO BENE MERENTI
H. M. P.

In the vacation of the following year, 1788, I made a third visit to Paris. My friend Dumont was my companion ; and my principal object was to amuse myself, and to see more of the society of that celebrated city than my former short visits had enabled me to do. As soon as the circuit was over, we set out together, and after a delightful journey through Normandy, by Dieppe and Rouen, we arrived at Paris. It was on a Saturday that we arrived ; and on the next day the ambassadors of Tippoo Saib were to be presented to the King at Versailles. We repaired thither ; and though we could only procure a place in one of the rooms through which the ambassadors passed, yet we had an opportunity of seeing all the splendour and gaiety of the court ; and its dazzling magnificence has often occurred to my imagination, when I have read of the horrible scenes which were, soon afterwards, acted on the same theatre.

We brought with us many letters of introduction, and particularly some from Lord Lansdowne ; we had both of us already acquaintances at Paris, and we saw a great number and a great variety of persons. Among the most remarkable were the Duke de la Rochefoucauld, M. de Malesherbes, M. de Lafayette, the Abbé Morellet, Chamfort, Dupont de Nemours, Condorcet, Mallet du Pan, the Count de Sarsfield, Jefferson the American ambasador, Etienne de St. Pierre, Target, and Mercier the author of the *Tableau de Paris*. Mirabeau, too, was, at this time, at Paris, publishing his great work on the Prussian

Monarchy. We saw him; I renewed my acquaintance with him; he was delighted with Dumont's wit and extraordinary talents; we became again very intimate, and passed many hours in his most captivating society. Amongst other objects of curiosity for travellers, we made, during our stay at Paris, a visit to Bicêtre. Mercier, Mallet du Pan, Dumont, and myself, were the whole party. I was much shocked and disgusted at what I saw, both in the hospital and the prison: I saw Mirabeau the next day, and mentioned to him the impression they had made on me; he exhorted me earnestly to put down my observations in writing, and to give them to him. I did so; and he soon afterwards translated them into French, and published them in the form of a pamphlet, under the title of *Lettre d'un Voyageur Anglais sur la Prison de Bicêtre;* and he added to them some observations on criminal law, which were very nearly a translation from the little tract I had published on Madan's *Thoughts on Executive Justice.* The work was suppressed by the police of Paris. The letter upon Bicêtre, after my return to London, I printed in a periodical publication called *The Repository*, which was published by Benjamin Vaughan, or under his auspices. I printed it as being a translation from Mirabeau, although it was in truth the original.

Amongst all the eminent persons we saw at Paris, there was none who impressed me with so much respect and attachment as the good and virtuous Malesherbes. There was a certain simplicity and warmth of heart in him, which, at the first moment, put those who approached him perfectly at their ease, and inspired them with the freedom of a long and intimate acquaintance. Of a man, who, soon afterwards, upon the trial of the unfortunate King, acted so magnanimous a part, it may be worth while to remember a circumstance, very trifling in itself, but yet which puts his affability and kindness of heart in a very amiable point of view. One day that I dined with him, the Count de Sarsfield, who was of the party, told me and Dumont that it would be well worth our while to go one day to some of the large *guinguettes* about Paris, and to observe the scenes that passed there, when they were filled, as they commonly were in the evenings, with persons of the lower orders. It happened that, in the neighbourhood of M. de Malesherbes, who lived beyond the Boulevards, there was one of the most celebrated and crowded of these places of entertainment; and the good-natured old man consented that, after dinner, the whole company should take a walk to it. Accordingly, in the evening, the party, which was a pretty large one, and consisted, amongst others, of M. de la Luzerne, M. de Lafayette, and Target the celebrated advocate, proceeded to the *guinguette*. The master of it, a man of very mean appearance and vulgar manners, was a tenant of M. de Malesherbes; and while they were conversing together with great familiarity and *bonhomie*, M. de Malesherbes, being desirous of surprising the poor fellow with the great name of one of his guests, and enjoying his admiration, asked him if he had ever happened to hear of a certain Marquis de Lafayette, pleasing himself with being able, when he had received for answer, as he expected, "to be sure he had, as had all the rest of the world," to point out to him the modest-looking gentleman, who was standing at his elbow; but, to his great disappointment, the man answered, "No, really I can't say I ever did. Pray, who was he?" His little disappointment, however, he took with that good nature which characterized every thing that he said or did, and he joined in the laugh against himself.

The state of public affairs, during this our visit to Paris, was highly interesting. The administration of the Archbishop of Sens had become extremely unpopular, and there were some trifling commotions in the streets. Crowds assembled on the Pont Neuf, and obliged all the passers-by to take off their hats, in token of respect, before the equestrian statue of Henry IV. In the coffee-houses of the Palais Royal, the freest conversations were indulged; and in the midst of the public ferment which prevailed, a change of ministry was announced, and M. Necker was recalled to the administration. He had not long returned to office before the King declared his determination to assemble the States General. Such an event, as may well be supposed, produced a very great effect, and was the subject of every conversation. The best and most virtuous men (and I place the Duke de la Rochefoucauld and M. de Malesherbes amongst the foremost of them) saw in it the beginning of a new era of happiness for France, and for all the civilized world. The ambitious rejoiced at the wide field that was opening to their aspiring hopes, and the men of letters began to entertain a higher opinion of their own importance than even they had before conceived. There was not, however, to be found a single individual, the most gloomy, the most timid, or the most enthusiastically sanguine, who foresaw any of the extraordinary events to which the assembling the States was to lead. Who, indeed, could, in that single measure, have discovered the seeds of what followed?—the abolition of the monarchy; the public execution of the king and queen; the destruction of the nobility; the annihilation of all religion; the erection of a petty but most sanguinary tyranny in almost every town of France; a succession of wars, all contributing to increase the martial glory of the nation; and, finally, the establishment of a military despotism, the subjugation of almost all the rest of Europe, and the nearest approach that is to be found in the history of modern times to universal empire!

Paris was at this time, from the different characters of the individuals we saw there, and the occasion which called these characters forth, as instructive to us as it was amusing. I should have been glad to have stayed longer, and to have enjoyed and profited more by it, but I was obliged to be back early in October, to attend the Coventry and Warwick Quarter Sessions; and to an object of such great importance to me as my success in my profession, I was disposed to make great sacrifices. We reluctantly, therefore, set out on our return, and yet I was near missing the object of it; for though we had allowed ourselves full time to perform our journey, when we arrived at Boulogne we found the wind adverse, and blowing so strongly that it was impossible to sail for England, either from that port or from Calais; and after staying at Boulogne nearly a week, we were still there on Saturday, at one o'clock in the day, when it was requisite that I should be in Court, at Coventry, by ten o'clock on the morning of the following Monday. This, however, by great good fortune, I was able to accomplish. We had a passage of only three hours; we proceeded the same night to Canterbury; and I arrived in London early enough on the next evening to obtain a place in a mail-coach, which conveyed me by nine o'clock the following morning to Coventry.

Some months after I had returned from Paris, I received a letter from the Count de Sarsfield, requesting me to send him some book which stated the rules and orders of proceeding in the English House of Commons. He thought it would be extremely useful to assist the States General in regulating their debates, and their modes of transacting business. There was no such book, and I could send him nothing that would answer his purpose. Hatsell omits the common rules which are known to every body, and which are just what the French would stand the most in need of; and he is very minute and very ample in precedents upon points which, to them, could not be of the smallest use. There was nothing to be done but to draw up a statement of the Rules of the House of Commons myself; and I very cheerfully set about it, though it was likely to occupy a good deal of my time. In truth, I thought it of extreme importance that the States should begin by making some regulations which might insure order and tranquillity in their proceedings. Dupont, who was one of the Secretaries of the Notables, and had a *procès verbal* of their proceedings, had mentioned to me the tumult which had often prevailed in that assembly, and which was sometimes carried to such a height that he was obliged to suspend his journal. It was once, he said, pleasantly proposed by one of the members to establish as a rule, that there should never be more than four members speaking at once. I gave myself great pains to make the paper I drew up as accurate as possible; and after I had finished it, I showed it to Sir Gilbert Elliot, who corrected it in some matters in which I had been mistaken, and who showed it likewise to Mr. Ley, the assistant clerk to the House of Commons. When it was as complete as I could make it, I sent it to the Count de Sarsfield. He received it most thankfully, and set about translating it into French. He died, however, before he had advanced far with the work; and from his hands the papers passed into those of Mirabeau. Mirabeau, fully sensible of the importance of the work, with all expedition, translated and published it. It never, however, was of the smallest use; and no regard whatever was paid to it by the National Assembly, as the States General were pleased, soon after their meeting, to call themselves. They met, having to form their rules and mode of proceeding. The leading members were little disposed to borrow any thing from England. They did not adopt these rules, and they hardly observed any others. Much of the violence which prevailed in the Assembly would have been allayed, and many rash measures unquestionably prevented, if their proceedings had been conducted with order and regularity. If one single rule had been adopted, namely, that every motion should be reduced into writing in the form of a proposition before it was put from the chair, instead of proceeding, as was their constant course, by first resolving the principle as they called it (*décréter le principe*), and leaving the drawing up what they had so resolved (or, as they called it, *la rédaction*,) for a subsequent operation, it is astonishing how great an influence it would have had on their debates and on their measures. When I was afterwards present, and witnessed their proceedings, I had often occasion to lament that the trouble I had taken had been of no avail.

I was among those who, in the early stages of the French Revolution, entertained the most sanguine expectations of the happy effects which were to result from it, not to France alone, but to the rest of the world; and I very early, I think some time about July, 1789, published a short pamphlet on the subject, under the title of *Thoughts on the probable Influence of the late Revolution in France upon other Countries*, or some such title.[1]

1 *Thoughts on the probable Influence of the French Revolution on Great Britain.* The year on the title-page is 1790.— Ed.

By the time that I was able to enjoy again the leisure of a long vacation, events in France had become so interesting, and the National Assembly, then sitting at Versailles, had become an object of such curiosity, that I could not resist the desire of being a near spectator of them. Accordingly I set out, on the first day after I was released from the circuit, for Paris. I arrived there shortly after the celebrated decrees of the 4th of August had been passed,—those decrees by which, in an evening sitting, and in a moment of enthusiasm, the Assembly had, by a string of hasty resolutions, abolished tithes and all feudal rights, without considering what consequences were to follow, or what compensations or precautions it might be expedient should accompany such important measures. As the rules which govern all other legislative assemblies had been neglected, no guards whatever had been put on the legislative powers which the Assembly exercised. It was not necessary that an alteration of the law should pass through various stages, so as to become the subject, or at least to afford the opportunity, of renewed consideration and debate. After some of the first resolutions had been passed, the rest were carried by acclamation the moment they were proposed; and I afterwards heard it lamented by several of the deputies, that they had not availed themselves of that fortunate moment of effervescence and enthusiasm to propose the abolition of other abuses, which it would then have been only necessary to have named in order to have destroyed. How unfortunate, I have heard it said, that no person happened to think of the Slave Trade!

At Versailles, I found Dumont and Duroveray living there together, and together conducting a periodical publication which gave an account of the proceedings of the National Assembly, and was entitled the *Courrier de Provence.* It passed with the public for Mirabeau's; and was a continuation of the Letters to his Constituents, which rendered them an account of his own conduct and of that of the other deputies. Duroveray and Dumont had gone to Paris early in the year, to endeavour to avail themselves of M. Necker being minister to procure for their common country, Geneva, an alteration of the law which France had guaranteed at the late fatal revolution in that republic. They had—and who could avoid it?—taken a great interest in the opening of the States, and the events that rapidly followed. Mirabeau was well aware of their talents, and was disposed to benefit by them. On several important occasions they assisted him; and the address of the Assembly to the King for the removal of the troops, an address which was adopted the moment that Mirabeau had proposed it, and which produced so great an effect in France, was entirely written by Dumont. The last of Mirabeau's letters to his constituents, one of the most eloquent compositions in the French language, was also Dumont's. Its extraordinary success suggested the idea of publishing a regular journal, under a different title, and not under Mirabeau's name, but which, from the great talents displayed in it, was generally supposed to be written by him; and he was too proud of the performance to deny it. Of course, I found

Dumont and Duroveray in great intimacy with Mirabeau. They were very well acquainted, too, with other members of the Assembly. I had a letter from Lord Lansdowne to Necker; I was acquainted with the Bishop of Chartres, a deputy to the States; and by these various means I saw a great number of the persons who were most distinguished as speakers in the Assembly. I was very frequent in my attendance there, and often heard Mounier, Barnave, Lally Tolendal, Thouret, Maury, Casales, and D'Epresmenil, who were some of the speakers at that time most looked up to by the different parties. I heard Robespierre; but he was then so obscure, and spoke with so little talent or success, that I have not the least recollection of his person. I met the Abbé Sieyes several times at the Bishop of Chartres'; he was the Bishop's *aumonier*, and a person of whose talents he entertained the highest opinion. Sieyes was of a morose disposition, said little in company, and appeared to have a full sense of his own superiority, and great contempt for the opinions of others. He was, however, when I saw him, greatly out of humour with the Assembly, and with every body who had concurred in its decree for the abolition of tithes, and seemed to augur very ill of the revolution. While I was at Versailles, he published his defence of tithes, with this motto prefixed to it—"Ils veulent être libres, et ils ne savent pas être justes." At the Bishop of Chartres', too, I sometimes met with Pétion, a man who appeared to me to have neither talents nor vices which could enable him to have so great and so unfortunate an influence on public affairs as he afterwards appeared to have. What struck me as most remarkable in the dispositions of the people that I saw, was the great desire that every body had to act a great part, and the jealousy which in consequence of this was entertained of those who were really eminent. It seemed as if all persons, from the highest to the lowest, whether deputies themselves, declaimers in the Palais Royal, orators in the coffee-houses, spectators in the gallery, or the populace about the door, looked upon themselves individually as of great consequence in the revolution. The man who kept the hotel at which I lodged at Paris, a certain M. Villars, was a private in the National Guard. Upon my returning home on the day of the benediction of their colours at Notre Dame, and telling him that I had been present at the ceremony, he said, "You saw me, Sir?" I was obliged to say that I really had not. He said, "Is that possible, Sir? You did not see me! Why I was in one of the first ranks—all Paris saw me." I have often since thought of my host's childish vanity. What he spoke was felt by thousands. The most important transactions were as nothing, but as they had relation to the figure which each little self-conceited hero acted in them. To attract the attention of all Paris, or of all France, was often the motive of conduct in matters which were attended with most momentous consequences.

The confidence which they felt in themselves, and their unwillingness to be informed by persons capable of giving them information, was not a little remarkable. I was dining one day at M. Necker's, at Versailles, at a great dinner, at which many of the deputies were present; amongst others, M. Mallouet, a man of considerable eminence. It was a day in which great tumult had prevailed in the National Assembly, and the Bishop of Langres, who was then the president, had rung his bell to command silence till he had broken it; but all had been in vain. The conversation turned upon this. Mallouet observed, that in the English House of Commons the greatest order prevailed, and that this was accomplished by dint of the great authority vested in the Speaker, who had power, if any member behaved disorderly, to impose silence on him by way of punishment for two months, or any other limited period of time. M. Necker turned round to me as the only Englishman present, and asked me if this was so. M. Mallouet had been so positive and bold in his assertion, that I thought the most polite way in which I could contradict him, was to say that I had never heard of it. But this only served to give that gentleman an opportunity of showing his great superiority over me. I might not, he said, have heard of it, but of the fact there was not the least doubt.

Mirabeau was acting a great part during the whole time that I was at Versailles; and it was not surprising that he was a little intoxicated by the applause and admiration which he received. He was certainly a very extraordinary man, with great defects undoubtedly, but with many very good qualities; possessed of great talents himself, and having a singular faculty of bringing forward and availing himself of the talents of others. He was a great plagiarist; but it was from avarice, not poverty, that he appropriated to himself the views and the eloquence of others. Whatever he found forcible or beautiful, he considered as a kind of common property which he might avail himself of, and which he ought to make the most of to promote the objects he had in view; and notwithstanding all that has been said against him, I am well convinced that both in his writings and in his speeches he had what he sincerely conceived to be the good of mankind for his object. He was vain, and he was inordinately ambitious; but his ambition was to act a noble part, and to establish the liberty of his country on the most solid foundations. He was very unjustly accused of having varied in his politics, and of having gone over to the court. From the beginning, and when he was the idol of the people, he always had it in view to establish a limited monarchy in France upon the model of the British Constitution. That at the time when the democratical leaders in France had far other projects in contemplation he was in secret correspondence with the court, and that he received money from the King, I think highly probable; and the gross immorality of such conduct I am not disposed to justify, or even to palliate. But those who believe that he suffered himself to be bribed to do what his own heart and judgment condemned, and that unbribed he would have acted a very different part, do him, in my opinion, and I had frequent opportunities of hearing his sentiments at the different periods when I was intimately acquainted with him, very great injustice.

I have already spoken of his relaxed morality, and of his vanity. In matters of indifference, aye, and sometimes in matters of importance too, the placing himself in an advantageous point of view to those whose applause or admiration he courted, far outweighed the interests of truth. Among many instances of this kind which came within my own observation, there was one so remarkable that I cannot forbear to mention it. In one of the early numbers of the *Courrier de Provence*, in which Mirabeau wrote himself, he represents Mounier as saying in the National Assembly that it was corruption which had destroyed England, and himself as very happily turning that extravagant hyperbole into ridicule, by exclaiming upon the important news so unexpectedly communicated to the Assembly of the destruction of England, and asking when and in what form that remarkable event had been brought about? The truth, however, is, that of all this not a single word was uttered in the Assembly. Neither Mounier nor any other person talked of the destruction of England; neither Mirabeau nor any other person made any such reply as he assumes to himself. The whole origin of this fiction was, that, while Mirabeau was writing his *Courrier de Provence*, exactly what he has stated passed in a private conversation, at which he was present. Brissot de Warville used the words which he has ascribed to Mounier, and Dumount those which he has claimed for himself. He thought the dialogue too good and too happily expressed to be lost; he made himself the hero of it, and placed the scene in the National Assembly; and this, though he well knew that Brissot, Dumont, Mounier, and all the members of the Assembly, could give evidence of the falsehood of his statement, and which, indeed, Mounier, took occasion formally to do in the justification of his own conduct, which he not long afterwards published.

Of all Mirabeau's extraordinary talents, his faculty of availing himself of the knowledge and abilities of others was perhaps the most extraordinary. As an author, he has published the works of others, and, with their permission, under his own name, and as if they were his own. The eight octavo volumes which he published on the Prussian Monarchy were entirely, as to every thing but the style, the work of M. de Mauvillon. His tracts upon finance were Clavière's; the substance of his work on the Cincinnati was to be found in an American pamphlet; his pamphlet on the opening of the Scheldt was Benjamin Vaughan's; and I once saw him very eager to undertake a great work on geography, of which he was totally ignorant, in the expectation that M. de Rochette, a geographer of great merit, and with whom he had contracted great intimacy, would supply him with all the materials for it. As an orator, he on many occasions delivered in the National Assembly speeches as his own, which had been composed for him by others; and so much confidence had he in the persons who thus contributed to establish his reputation, that he has sometimes, to my knowledge, read at the tribune of the Assembly speeches which he had not even cast his eyes upon before, and which were as new to himself as to his admiring audience.

I was again obliged to leave Paris by the end of September, that I might not lose the Quarter Sessions. I left it with a much less favourable opinion of the state of public affairs than that which I had entertained when I arrived there. I found the most exaggerated and extravagant notions of liberty entertained by many, and the most violent and bitter animosities prevailing, and all that disposition to violence on the part of the lower orders of the people, which, a few days afterwards, manifested itself in the insurrection that ended in bringing the Royal family to Paris.

CORRESPONDENCE.

LETTERS TO THE REV. JOHN ROGET, FROM 1780 TO 1783.

1780—1783.

Letter I.

Gray's Inn, June 6. 1780.

At last, then, my dear Roget, my mind may be somewhat at ease. The salutary air of Lausanne, and your great attention to your health, have, thank God, enabled you to write a letter which has given me the greatest joy. From the moment when I ought to have taken leave of you in the coach at Rochester, but could not, because I perceived I had not sufficient fortitude for the ceremony, to the instant that I received your letter from Lausanne, I have never thought of you without anxiety. I had no sooner read any of your letters from Geneva, than immediately the melancholy reflection rose in my mind, that you were ill; and that fourteen days had elapsed since my last news from you. But what was my anxiety when sometimes fourteen days were added to that, before we had another letter; and perhaps, from the delay of posts, even more. But I may flatter myself that, hereafter, the delay of receiving news from you will be no otherwise disagreeable, than as it will delay the pleasure of hearing that you continue to grow better. I will endeavour that my imagination shall be as active in magnifying to myself your increasing health and strength, as it was once busy, to my torment, in representing every circumstance that concerned you in too gloomy colours. Yes, my dear friend, the love of you and my dear sister will now be rewarded with uninterrupted felicity, I hope, in this life ; it is not presumptuous to say, I am sure it will in that to come.

The shameful means, by which, as I related to you in a former letter, names were procured to the petition for repealing the Catholic Act, did not give one any idea that the party could be either very formidable or numerous : but you know how dangerous an engine religion is, when employed upon the minds of the ignorant ; so dangerous, indeed, that it is formidable in any hands, however weak and contemptible. The Methodists, the followers of Wesley, and the sectaries of Whitfield, were the first, if not to raise, at least to join, the cry against Popery ; and it should seem, from the effects that have been produced, that no art has been left untried, which either could magnify the terrors of the people, by painting to their imagination in the most glaring colours all the horrors of Popery, or could infuse among them a mistaken zeal and a dangerous spirit of fanaticism. One way or other, 40,000 persons were prevailed on to sign the petition. Lord George Gordon, that he might give it greater weight, or rather, that he might by violence force it upon the House, advertised in the newspapers as president, and in the name of (what they style themselves) the Protestant Association, the day on which he purposed presenting the petition to the House, at the same time desiring the attendance of all the petitioners; and "as no hall is capable of containing 40,000 men" (such were the words of the advertisement), they were required to assemble in St. George's Fields, wearing blue cockades as a distinction by which they might know one another. The concourse of people on the appointed day, which was last Friday, was astonishing. You know how difficult it is to judge with accuracy of the numbers of a multitude assembled in an open field. By the largest computation I have heard, and which is certainly very much exaggerated, there were 100,000 in the fields; but, by the most moderate accounts, no less than 14,000 accompanied Lord George to the House of Commons.

When I arrived at Westminster, whither I went to hear a debate that was to come on in the House of Lords upon a motion of the Duke of Richmond, I found the large opening (which you may remember) between the Parliament House and Westminster Abbey, all the avenues of the House, and the adjoining streets, thronged with people wearing blue cockades. They seemed to consist, in a great measure, of the lowest rabble; men who, without doubt, not only had never heard any of the arguments for or against toleration, but who were utterly ignorant of the very purport of the petition. To give you one instance: a miserable fanatic who accosted me, not indeed with any friendly design, but to question me where my cockade was, which I very civilly informed him I had dropped out of my hat in the crowd, told me that the reign of the Romans had lasted too long — the object of the petition, you know, is only to repeal an Act [1] that passed the year before last. As I think there is much to be learned by studying human nature, even in its most humiliating and disgusting forms, I would fain have mingled in a circle which I saw assembled round a female preacher, who, by her gestures and actions, seemed to be well persuaded, or desirous of persuading others, that she was animated by some supernatural spirit; but I found it attended with some little danger: the want of a cockade was a sure indication of a want of the true faith, and I did not long remain unquestioned as to my religious principles. My joining, however, in the cry of "No Popery!" soon pacified my inquisitors, or rather, indeed, gained me their favour; for a very devout butcher insisted upon shaking hands with me as a token of his friendship. Upon my getting into the House of Lords, I found my Lord Mansfield, and five or six peers, who were all that were yet assembled, seemingly in great consternation from the news they had just received of Lord Stormont's being in great danger from the populace. That lord, however, soon made his appearance; he had been treated rudely, but not very outrageously, by the mob. Lord Hillsborough and several other

[1] There is a very good account of the object of this Act, and of the circumstances under which it was passed, in Burke's speech to the electors of Bristol.[a]

[a] This and the following notes, in the Correspondence, are inserted by the Editors.

peers came in soon after, with their hair dishevelled, having lost their bags in the scuffle they had to get into the House. Lord Bathurst, the late Chancellor, was pulled in by the attendants out of the hands of the populace. Several noblemen, among others Lord Sandwich, seeing the danger, had returned home; so that the House was rather thin. The Duke of Richmond, notwithstanding, rose to speak upon the motion he was about to make. He had proceeded in his speech for about an hour, though with frequent interruptions from the thundering of the mob at the doors of the House, and the shouting that was heard without, when one of the peers abruptly entered to inform the Lords that the populace had forced Lord Boston out of his coach, and that his life was thought to be in the greatest danger. Several lords immediately offered to go out and rescue him; but, by the assistance of the attendants and some of the people about the House, this was rendered unnecessary. Not long after, word was brought that Lord Ashburnham was in the same situation, surrounded by the mob and in great danger; at last, however, he was dragged into the House over the heads of the people, and apparently much hurt. The tumult becoming every moment more violent, it was found impossible to go on with any business; and at half-past eight the House adjourned. Thus far as to what I was myself a witness to.

At the House of Commons, the lobby was so much crowded with the petitioners, that the members could hardly get in; and none, it is said, were suffered to pass without giving in their names to

Lord George Gordon, and promising to vote for the repeal. As soon as the House sat upon business, the petition was taken into consideration; but certainly nothing could be done upon it then, for many members had been deterred from coming to the House, and those who were present were far from enjoying any freedom of debate. A motion was therefore made to defer the further consideration of it till the following Tuesday, and carried by a majority of 190 against 9. Lord George then came into the gallery over the lobby, and harangued the populace: he told them their petition was as good as rejected; that if they expected redress they must keep in a body, or meet day after day till the Catholic Act was repealed. Some of his friends, who stood behind him, besought him, with the greatest earnestness, not to excite the people to measures which must be destructive to themselves; but nothing could deter this frantic incendiary, till he was by violence forced back into the House. The clamours of the people were now become so loud, and there appeared among them symptoms of such a dangerous temper, that it was absolutely necessary to call up the Guards. This expedient was so far successful that the lobby and the avenues of the House were soon cleared; but, without doors, the fury of the populace was ungovernable. The Bishop of Lincoln, the Chancellor's brother, was torn out of his coach as he was going to the House; happily he escaped out of the hands of the mob, and took refuge in a house in Palace Yard; the mob, however, pursued him, broke the windows, and insisted so resolutely on being admitted to search for him, that it was impossible to keep them out any longer than while the Bishop changed his dress, and made his escape over the garden wall. The tumult continued till very late at night, when the mob divided into different parties and broke into three Romish chapels (two of which belonged to Ambassadors), tore down the altars, the organs, and decorations of the chapels, brought them out into the street and burned them. Not content with this, at the Sardinian Ambassador's, they carried the fire into the chapel: the inside was presently consumed, but fortunately no other damage was done.

It is well none of our patriots, except that madman, Lord George Gordon, promote these disturbances. The opposition, in general, are entirely against the object of the petition. I myself heard the Duke of Richmond declare, upon one of the occasions when he was interrupted in his speech, that 'he would ever oppose the repeal of the Act, that he was determined always to defend liberty of conscience in all sects of religion: those were his unalterable sentiments; no fears, no hopes, should ever make him change them; they were what he would not scruple to go out and declare to the multitudes who were assembled at the doors of the House, though they were twice 50,000.' Several of the rioters were taken, some in the very act of carrying fire into the chapel; these deluded wretches will be tried and executed without delay, for, the following day, the Lords voted unanimously, that an address should be presented to the King, to give directions for prosecuting with rigour the authors, abettors, and instruments of these outrages. Severity is a very dangerous instrument for suppressing religious fury. You know how often the guiltiest sufferers in such a cause are elevated into martyrs, and how a fanatical preacher may work upon his hearers to court a death, which is instantly to be rewarded with a crown of glory. And yet in the present circumstances there seems no other expedient. This rage of mistaken zeal is the more extraordinary, and the more to be dreaded, because it has no visible cause. The Catholics have not, of late, used any extraordinary pomp in their mass-houses, their numbers have not increased, nor have they in any respect made a bad use of the relaxations given them by the late Act. Stories, indeed, have, of late, been very artfully and very maliciously circulated of their making a number of proselytes; but not one instance of this that I can find is well authenticated. As to the hypocrites who excite these outrages, they affect the greatest moderation. In their advertisement, they requested the Protestants (for they pretend that none are Protestants but the petitioners) to behave with decency and order. What!—summon 40,000 fanatics to meet together, and expect them to be orderly! What is it but to invite hungry wretches to a banquet, and at the same time enjoin them not to eat? But the real intentions of these men are evident from some handbills they distributed, under the same pretext of inculcating moderation and the spirit of peace. In these they say that, as there was great reason to suspect that a number of Papists intended to mingle in disguise among the petitioners for the purpose of raising riots and disturbances, they entreated the Protestants not to return their insults or violence, but to secure the aggressors quietly, and give them up to the constables who should attend. Who does not see that the former part of this admonition was all that was intended to have any effect, and that when once the terrors of the people were set afloat, every purpose of it was answered?

On Sunday night the mob assembled again in Moorfields, broke into a mass-house that had lately been built there, and into some adjoining houses which were inhabited by Catholics, destroyed all the furniture, and every thing they could lay hands on, and at last set fire to the houses. Five were consumed besides the mass-house. Last night, they committed great outrages at the houses of several persons who had appeared as witnesses against those who were taken. Afterwards they broke all the windows and destroyed the furniture at the house of Sir George Saville, a man who bears an excellent character, who is one of the most active men in the opposition, and who was the very person who brought up the York petition to the Parliament; but all these merits it seems are cancelled by his having moved, two years ago, to give some privileges to an unfortunate class of men, who were unjustly the objects of very rigorous laws. I hope a sudden exertion of severity will put a stop to these enormities; but I confess I am not very sanguine in my hopes, for when a torrent of religious fury is once let loose, who shall say to it, "Thus far shalt thou go, and no farther?"

Though part of my paper remains unfilled, I

must here bid you good night, unless I postpone sending off this letter till another post, and I know you would be impatient to remain so long without hearing from your sincere friend,

Saml. Romilly.

Letter II.

Dear Roget, Gray's Inn, June 9. 1780.

I would not suffer a post to pass, after the alarming intelligence which my last letter contained, without writing to you; but it will be necessary first to inform you, that we are now quite at peace again, and that last night the most profound tranquillity reigned in every part of London. The evening of Tuesday, the day when I wrote to you last, was attended with the most violent outrages and excesses that can be imagined. I informed you, I believe, that the further consideration of the petition was referred to that day. Prodigious multitudes, wearing blue cockades, assembled, as before, in Palace Yard; but, on the first appearance of a crowd, guards, both foot and horse, were drawn up, and formed an avenue for the Members to pass to the House. But this martial appearance, far from intimidating the mob, only rendered them more insolent: they boldly paraded the streets with colours and music, and attempted to pass through the Park to Buckingham House; but were stopped by a very strong party of guards stationed there. The Lords, however, were suffered to go on to the House with no outrage, though they were followed by the hisses and reproaches of the people, till the arrival of Lord Sandwich. His chariot was stopped at the end of Parliament Street, where there happened not to be any guards, and the chariot doors were immediately torn open. At that instant three light horsemen rode up to his relief, but all the assistance they could give him was to make room for his carriage to turn round; this was accordingly effected, though with difficulty, and he drove back to the Admiralty with the utmost rapidity; but some of the most daring of the rioters seized the horses' bridles, and again stopped him. I expected that moment to have seen him torn in pieces; but, leaping quickly out of the chariot, he saved himself in a coffee-house, and a very strong party of guards immediately rode up and kept off the mob. About five o'clock, the rioters were become so outrageous, that there was no possibility of awing them but by reading the Riot Act, which (you know) gives a right to fire upon the mob if they do not disperse. Upon this a great part of the rioters quitted Palace Yard; but they only quitted it with an intention to wreak their fury upon the objects of their resentment in other parts of the town. One party went straight to the house of the justice of peace who had read the act, and entirely demolished it. Another, and a much stronger body, marched to Newgate, demanded the release of the persons who were confined there for burning the ambassadors' chapels; and, this demand not being complied with, broke open the doors, set at liberty all the felons and debtors, and set fire to the prison and to the keeper's house, which were both presently consumed. They then proceeded to the New Prison at Clerkenwell, and set free all the prisoners who were there in confinement. About one o'clock in the morning they attacked the house of Lord Mansfield; his Lordship had but just time to escape by a back door when they broke in. A bonfire was immediately made, in the street, of his furniture; and with merciless fury they threw into it all his books, and, among others, many manuscripts of inestimable value. At last, they set fire to the house, which was presently burned down to the ground. The soldiers, after having for a long time endured the insults of the populace, were at last obliged to fire. Eight or nine persons were killed, and several wounded. The same night, the house of Sir John Fielding was burned; and in different parts all over the town the houses of Catholics were pulled down or set on fire. Some of the mob at last insisted upon lights being put up at every window, in joy for the destruction of Newgate; the illumination accordingly was general. You can hardly represent to yourself so melancholy a sight as this appearance of involuntary rejoicing, and, at the same time, to behold the sky glowing on every side with the light of different conflagrations, as if the city had been taken by an enemy. The terror which these acts of violence spread throughout the town is not easy to be conceived. The next day, Wednesday, it was reported every where that, that night, the houses of the Secretaries of State, of every Bishop, of every Catholic, of every justice of the peace, and of all the King's tradesmen, were marked out for destruction. The Catholics, and many other persons, moved all their effects ; their neighbours as well as themselves, fled into the country, or waited, in the utmost horror, the approach of evening. The panic which had seized upon the people gave birth to a multitude of alarming reports ; at one time it was said that none of the soldiers would do their duty, but were all ready to join with the rioters ; at another, that there were insurrections as dangerous in the country, and that 30,000 colliers were upon their way to London to join the insurgents. The King and his Privy Council took the most effectual way to put a stop to the enormities which were being committed ; they ordered a great number of the regiments of the militia to march straight to London, and issued a proclamation commanding all persons to keep within their houses at night, and warning them of the ill consequences of neglecting this injunction, as the King was resolved to exert the military force to put an end to these rebellious and treasonable practices. Martial law was thus established, by which all persons taken, concerned in these riots, were liable to be tried by a court martial, and executed upon the spot ; but, as this proclamation was not universally known, and but few of the militia regiments arrived in town by Wednesday night, many daring outrages were still committed. Several houses were pulled down, the King's Bench prison thrown open, and about 700 prisoners released, and the prison set on fire and consumed. But the insolence and audaciousness of these men was not confined to night; in the middle of the day they made bonfires of the goods of several Papists openly in the streets; in some places they went in a large body, from house to house, exacting contributions, which they called mob-money. The excesses which these delirious wretches committed are inconceivable: among other houses, they threatened to pull down that of a Catholic, a distiller in Holborn; the man, to save his house, told the rioters that he would give them out liquor as long as they pleased; this stipulation was immediately concluded on, and spirituous liquors were accordingly handed out to the mob in large vessels; they drank to such a degree that numbers of them lay intoxicated in the middle of the way, and some died. But all this could not save the poor man's house, which was set fire to the following night. Last night, and to-day, every thing has been at peace: we have two encampments, one in St. James's Park, and another in Hyde Park; no man is suffered to wear a blue cockade in the streets, and we have no doubt that the rioters are entirely quelled. I have just received news that Lord George Gordon is taken; the person who told me saw him conducted through the Park by a party of light horse, under the care of the Usher of the Black Rod. I have not time to write more to you at present, but you may depend upon hearing from some of us by the next post.

Your affectionate brother,

SAML. ROMILLY.

Letter III.

Dear Roget, June 13. 1780.

I should not write to you again so soon, but for the sake of fulfilling the promise I made you in my last. Such a profound tranquillity reigns in London, that the late scenes of riot and confusion seem nothing but a dream. Indeed, the outrages which have been committed this week past were so unexpected and so unaccountable, that one would be inclined to believe one's senses had deceived one, did not the ruins of houses and other vestiges of the fury of the populace in all parts of the town make it evident that these calamities are but too real. In the account I have given you of these transactions, I mentioned no circumstance but what I was either an eyewitness of myself, or heard from authority which I had no reason to doubt. I could not disguise the truth, though I was afraid it would alarm you; much less would I be so cruel as to exaggerate the horror of my narration. It is really no exaggeration to say that, on Tuesday and Wednesday nights, London had the appearance of a city taken by storm. The fires blazing in different parts of the town, the terror and dismay of one part of the inhabitants, and the rage and licentiousness of the other, were equal to what one can imagine in such a catastrophe. There seems no probability that these monstrous excesses were concerted beforehand, or that they formed part of any regular plan to overturn the Government. They appear to me to have been only the accidental effects of the ungovernable fury and licentiousness of a mob, who gathered courage from their numbers, and who, having ventured on one daring act, found their only safety to lie in universal havoc and devastation. When once the rioters had gone so far as to burn down Newgate, one cannot be surprised at their entering on any enterprise, however daring; for, besides that they thought they might go on with impunity when they had left no prisons wherein to confine them, they gained as an accession to, or rather as leaders of their party, a set of criminals whose lives were already forfeited to their country. One of these wretches, who was to have been hanged the following day, appeared at my Lord Mansfield's on horseback, leading on the rioters. But religion has certainly been used, and too successfully, as an instrument to excite these feuds; not that I think any the wildest fanatics were concerned in breaking open the prisons, but they were certainly wrought up to a pitch of fury, which made them capable of any acts of violence against the Catholics, and ripe for any mischief that could be represented as serviceable to their religion. I can give you some proofs how grossly the people have been deceived and played upon by some designing villains. I have heard from three persons (all strangers to each other) who joined in conversation with the populace, that it was a current opinion among them that the King was a Papist. Some were sure of it: they pretended to know that he heard mass privately, and that his confessor had the direction of all political concerns. A woman told a friend of mine that she hoped to see the streets stream with the blood of Papists. But nothing shows more evidently what base arts have been practised to rouse the fears of the people, and excite them to madness, than a hand-bill which was distributed about the streets on the morning of Tuesday. I will transcribe it *verbatim*, for it now lies before me. "England in blood! On Thursday morning, the 8th instant, will be published *The Thunderer*, addressed to Lord George Gordon and the glorious Protestant Association, showing the necessity of their persevering and being united as one man against the infernal designs of the Ministry to overturn the religious and civil liberties of this country, in order to introduce Popery and slavery. In this paper will be given a full account of the bloody tyrannies, persecutions, plots, and inhuman butcheries exercised on the professors of the Protestant religion in England by the See of Rome, together with the names of the martyrs and their sufferings, highly necessary to be read at this important moment by every Englishman who loves his God and his country. To which will be added, some reasons why the few misguided people now in confinement for destroying the Romish chapels should not suffer, and the dreadful consequences of an attempt to bring them to punishment." The author of this paper has been since taken into custody.

Lord George Gordon underwent an examination last Friday before the Privy Council during three hours. Nothing more, it is reported, appeared against him than an inflammatory letter which he had sent to be inserted in one of the newspapers, wherein he applauded the rioters for what they had done, and encouraged them to further excesses; and some private letters to confidential friends in Scotland, relating the events that had passed in London, and speaking of them in terms of high approbation; but there was no evidence of his having planned any revolution. The Privy Council committed Lord George a prisoner to the Tower. From what I knew of Lord George Gordon before the present disturbances, (which, by the way, was only by having heard him often speak in the House of Commons,) I never thought him a man from whom his country had much to dread. He spoke, indeed, upon all occasions; but his speeches were incoherent and ridiculous. One day, I remember, he read a newspaper as part of his speech; at another time, he kept the whole House waiting two hours while he read them an Irish pamphlet. He seemed the less dangerous as he had not the support of either party; one day he attacked the Ministry, the next the Opposition, and sometimes both the one and the other. It has happened to him to divide the House, when he alone voted for a question, to which every other member gave his negative. Yet what dreadful effects may not a mistaken zeal produce even in such hands as these! though it must be confessed that Lord George Gordon is not destitute of qualities which, in an age when religion had greater influence upon the minds of men than it has at present, might have raised him to be the scourge of his country. He is endowed with a spirit of enthusiasm, and with the most determined resolution; add to this, that his manner of speaking not being in the least declamatory, but in the style of conversation, is most capable of working an effect upon an ignorant audience.

I believe I did not mention in my former letter that these civil broils have converted me into a soldier. Gray's Inn was one of the places which these determined enemies to all law threatened to lay in ashes. All the law societies (for Lincoln's Inn and the Temple were likewise threatened with destruction) resolved to stand upon their defence. Accordingly, we all armed ourselves, and kept watch at our different gates for several nights. The Temple, however, was the only Inn of Court that was attacked; and there the rioters retreated very precipitately when they found what resistance was made to them. This example is followed all over the town: the inhabitants of almost every parish are forming themselves into associations to protect their houses and property; so that, hereafter, should any disturbance of this kind happen, it will be very shortly quelled, without the assistance of the soldiery. And we shall esteem it no small happiness to be able to do without them; for, though we are greatly indebted to the military power for saving our effects from being plundered, and our houses from being burned, it is no very comfortable sight to Englishmen to see encampments at their very doors, and soldiers patroling all their streets. I should not omit to mention that the government have conducted themselves very prudently in not using any unconstitutional remedies against these outrages: they have taken prisoners all the rioters they could find, and mean to let them have a fair trial by jury. We have just received news, that at Bath they have been disturbed with the same riots as broke out here: several Romish chapels and houses have been burned; but when this intelligence was sent from thence, peace was pretty well restored. This information is certainly authentic; but the reports we have of the same fury raging at York, at Bury, and in other parts of the country, are, I hope, entirely groundless; indeed, we have had so many false reports, that one knows not what to believe. At one time it was said that the rioters had broken into the Bank, at another that they had attempted the Tower; again, that Lord Peters's house in the country was levelled with the ground, and that he himself was murdered; in short, every tale of horror to which the fears and the credulity of the people could give birth and strength, was circulated with astonishing rapidity throughout every part of the town.

It has been no small comfort to me, amidst all these tumults, to reflect that you and my dear sister were far removed from them. I could not turn my thoughts to you, without agreeably contrasting in my mind the quiet you enjoy at Lausanne, amidst all the riches of nature, a fertile country, and a benignant climate, to the rage and uproar that revelled among us, and set before us, in the most shocking points of view, the enormous vices of some of our fellow-creatures, and the miseries and afflictions of others. Not but that I was aware how far the baneful influence of these disorders must have spread, and that they must have occasioned some uneasy moments, even at Lausanne. Nature did not form you to say with the inhuman Lucretius, —

> " Suave mari magno, turbantibus æquora ventis,
> E terrâ magnum alterius spectare laborem ; "

especially when those you saw struggling with the tempest were united to you by the tenderest bonds of love and friendship. But how happy am I that I can tell you (so fully is peace restored to us) that the tranquillity of my beloved hermits need not hereafter be disturbed by any melancholy reflections on the situation of affairs with us. Enjoy then, my dear Roget, that repose so congenial to your disposition, and may it soon restore you to perfect health.

Your affectionate brother,

SAML. ROMILLY.

LETTER IV.

Dear Roget, Gray's Inn, Oct. 27. 1780.

Your inquiries after my health, as well as those of my dear Kitty, are so frequent and so pressing, that they seem to require of me a short history of my indisposition ; it shall be but short. I dignify it with the name of history, because, as I am now very nearly, if not quite recovered, nothing will be wanting to make it complete. It begins, then, with the late riots. For several days before they commenced, I had attended constantly at the House of Lords to hear the debates, where one is obliged to stand the whole time. This slight fatigue was increased by being pressed in the crowds of the petitioners, and still more by my sitting up three successive nights when the confusion was greatest, and by running about all day instead of taking rest or even giving my usual application to study; for I cannot boast the same command over myself with Archimedes, to wrap myself up in meditation when my city is given up to be plundered. After this, you will easily imagine I was not in a condition very proper for entering upon military discipline; yet, without refusing to join an association which I wished ardently to see formed, and which I had warmly promoted, I could not avoid it. Accordingly I began to learn my exercise. The ardour of our association determined them to indulge in no relaxation, but to exercise every day, for two hours each day, without intermission; and this, too, in very warm weather. The consequence was, that after persevering for some time, I was obliged to withdraw. Nor was I the only person who found the fatigue too much. The cold bath, from frequent use, was no longer a remedy. I was advised to try the sea. I did so, but unfortunately had a slight fever at the time; bathing increased it, and so much that I arrived in town very ill. The care of my good friend, Dr. Watson, soon delivered me from my fever; my strength returned by degrees, and I am now so well recovered that I should resume my regimentals, were it not that, most of our association being out of town, our summer campaign is at an end. My physician tells me that I shall have better health as I advance farther in life: so that, unlike most men, I may regard the revolution of time, and the approaches of old age, as desirable. The worst effect of my illness has been to make me lose some time. My doctor forbade me to look into any books but such as are merely amusing. I followed this prescription at first; but I had soon the courage to disregard it, and found myself grow much better by my disobedience.

There is great reason to presume that the character of our new Parliament will not differ materially from that of its predecessor; for there are but 150 new members. The greater number of the old members who have been thrown out at this election are of the court party; but, as the ministry always commanded such great majorities, one cannot thence conclude that the opposition have gathered any strength. The most famous of those rejected members of the last Parliament is Burke. Though he was thrown out at Bristol, he certainly might have been elected for some borough; but it seems he is resolved to retire altogether from public affairs. To withdraw his assistance from the public counsels at so difficult and dangerous a crisis does not, in my opinion, admit of any excuse; even though one should make every allowance for what a man of nice honour must feel under the disgrace of being rejected by his former constituents, and under the torrent of abuse which the newspapers have long vomited forth against him. Surely, the nicest sensibility to injury can never so disorder a man's judgment, as to make him mistake the sordid traders of Bristol, and venal gazetteers, for an ungrateful public. But it is not in the dregs of modern patriotism that we must look for a Phocion exhorting his son, as he drinks off the poison to which he has been sentenced by an ungrateful country, never to forget that even veneration of his father's memory is a duty subordinate to love towards his country.

I have lately read a pamphlet published by the Protestant Association about a year ago, and entitled, *An Appeal to the People of Great Britain*. Had I read it before, and known how much it had been circulated among the common people, I should not have been at a loss to account for the violence of the petitioners' religious zeal. It is extremely ill written ; the reasoning such as refutes itself; but the author addresses himself to the passions of his readers in a strain of furious declamation, well calculated to work up enthusiasts to very madness. He professes to favour toleration ; but his book is such an exhortation to revenge and persecution, as the days of Charles the Ninth never, perhaps, produced. But judge yourself whether I exaggerate. "Let us call to remembrance," these are the very words of the appeal — "Let us call to remembrance the massacre at Paris ; there Popery appeared in its true colours, drunken with the *blood of the saints and with the blood of the martyrs of Jesus*. Whilst Popery has existence upon earth, let it be remembered, though, to the disgrace of humanity, let it be remembered with horror, that on Saint Bartholomew's day thousands and tens of thousands of Protestants were murdered in France in cold blood. Smithfield, Oxford, Cambridge, and many other places have a voice crying aloud, 'Beware of Popery.' O Britons! let not the blood of the martyrs be forgotten, or their sufferings effaced from our memories, or from those of our children to the latest posterity. Are there none living in these days whose ancestors suffered by the unparalleled massacre of Ireland?" Is not this dictated by the vindictive spirit which animates the war-song of the American savages? Do you remember that inserted in Dr. Robertson's *History of America?* — "The bones of our countrymen lie uncovered; their bloody bed has not been washed clean; their spirits cry against us. Let us go and devour the people by whom they were slain. Lift the hatchet; console the dead; tell them that they shall be avenged." They certainly will bear comparison; and so far it is to the advantage of the savage, that he honestly owns himself to be actuated by a principle of revenge, while the pious Protestant affects to have at heart the good of mankind and the glory of God. He has not omitted the argument of all persecutors, that they seek the happiness of those they persecute. "To tolerate Popery," he says, "is to be instrumental to the perdition of immortal souls now existing, and of millions of spirits that at present have no existence but in the prescience of God, and is the direct way to provoke the vengeance of an holy and jealous God, to bring down destruction on our fleets and armies." So that, according to the arguments of this wretch, persecution is a religious duty!

Adieu, believe me to be, &c.,

SAML. ROMILLY.

Letter V.

Gray's Inn, Dec. 12. 1780.

You ask me, my dear sister, if the circle of my friends is as small as ever. Yes, to the full; less, I should rather say. All the few friends I had here two years ago are now scattered in different parts of the earth. Yourselves banished to the distance of above six hundred miles; Greenway, always in camp, or in winter quarters, does not pass a month in town in the whole year; Joseph Garnault, in China; and even Appia (with whom you know I had contracted some intimacy), at Petersburgh. My brother and our dear Jane are all I have left to console me for being separated from you: with them I dine almost every day, and frequently pass my evenings. New acquaintance I have none; how, indeed, should I make them, since I am still as backward to introduce myself into company as ever? One acquaintance, it is true, I have made since you were in England; a friend I ought to say, if to take the greatest interest in my concerns, and to load me with unaffected civilities, can give a claim to that title. I mean Mr. Spranger, a name, I believe, perfectly new to you. He is a counsellor, under whom I have studied almost ever since you quitted England. Mrs. Spranger is one of the most amiable women I know; not very young, indeed, for she has four children, but still handsome, and possessing the most engaging manners. At their house, where I frequently dine or sup (though less often than I am pressed to do), I meet a good deal of company, which, consisting mostly of men of sense and education, is very agreeable. But the most engaging society, that, my dear Catherine, of your amiable sex, I seldom enjoy, for I am hardly ever of their card parties; besides that, it is not at a whist table that your sex appears in its native charms. With so small an acquaintance, you will easily conceive that I seek for amusement in my studies, and there I am never disappointed. My rooms are exceedingly lively, and capable of themselves to secure me from indulging in melancholy, so that you may discard those apprehensions which I persuade myself I discover under your inquiries. In the depth of winter, the moment the sun peeps out, I am in the country. A cold country indeed it is; for, having only one row of houses between me and Highgate and Hampstead, a north-west wind (sharp as your piercing *bise*) blows full against my chambers: fortunately I am sheltered from the north-east. What renders my chambers very comfortable is a tolerable collection of books, which, I confess, somewhat extravagantly, I have lately purchased. Thus far to my dear sister; and now, without taking leave of her, to her husband.

Alas! my dear Roget, you quite despair, then, of returning to England. For myself, I cannot yet resign that hope. So much, indeed, is my happiness attached to it, I must be cruel to myself were I forward to give it up. As to your little boy, if you should be resolved to have him over in the spring, be assured that, thinking every other concern of less importance than your happiness, I shall not hesitate, whatever may be my emyloyments, to quit them all, and to be the bearer of joy and comfort to my dear friends. But, at the same time, I am forced to add that, should you (as I hope you will) alter your intention of having him sent to you, or should there be any other means of sending him with safety, you must not think of seeing me. It can hardly be necessary to dwell upon my reasons for denying myself the happiness such a journey would afford me. Having so much to do before I can be qualified for the employment I have chosen, and so short a time in which to do it, all my moments are precious; they are now, indeed, become still more so, by reason of the time which I was obliged to lose during my illness in the summer. Were I actuated by the bad ambition of gaining honours or of winning applause, this would be but a poor apology for being remiss in the duties of friendship; but with you I need not enforce the necessity of fulfilling the prior duties one owes to one's country, and unless I much mistake the intention of my heart, my greatest ambition is "*patriæ impendere vitam.*"

What do you think of Arnold's conduct? You may well suppose he does not want advocates here. I cannot join with them. If he thought the Americans not justified in continuing the war, after the offer of such favourable terms as the commissioners held out to them, why did he keep his command for two years afterwards? In my opinion, they must be very extraordinary circumstances indeed which can warrant a man's bearing arms in a civil war on opposite sides. Arnold will certainly, from his knowledge of the people and the country, prove a very useful man. He has published a proclamation, inviting the Americans to enlist under his standard, for Clinton has empowered him to raise a regiment for the service of the King. It abounds with invectives against France and the Congress, and, what seems to me to come less from the heart, with high professions of zeal to serve his country and assert its liberties. One word in this proclamation I think very remarkable. He says that the Americans might have been spared the calamities which they have suffered for these two last years if, as prudently as the Irish, they had accepted of the *liberality* of Great Britain. Either the Americans were, at first, contending for their rights, or they were not; if they were, it was not liberality, it was but strict justice in us to acknowledge those rights,—a piece of justice not very meritorious in us, since we were forced into it. If, on the other hand, what they contended for was not their *undoubted* right, but an usurpation they sought to make upon the parent country, the war on the side of the colonies was, from the first, rebellion, and Arnold a traitor. My brother says the word may have been inserted inadvertently. What! a word on which so much depends: and in a solemn proclamation! But Arnold, they say, may in truth have discovered his error; he may now think that the Americans were wrong from the beginning. But, admitting this, surely the discovery of an error so fatal, and which has been attended with such an effusion of blood, should have left an honest man no inclination to form new schemes of ambition, and to embark with as much alacrity as ever in new enterprises, where I see no reason why he may not be as much mistaken as before.

The Congress, to justify their generals in the severity exercised over Major André, who, as he was returning from concerting measures with Arnold, was taken and hanged, have published a very long account of that affair, with all the letters that passed between the generals upon the occasion. Major André's case was laid before a board consisting of fourteen field-officers, and it was their unanimous opinion that he ought to suffer death; but they gave no other reasons for their sentence than that it was conformable to the rules of war. The arguments used by Clinton and Arnold in their letters to Washington, to prove that André could not be considered as a spy, are, first, that he had with him, when he was taken, a protection of Arnold's, who was at that time acting under a commission of the Congress, and, therefore, competent to give protections. Certainly he was, to all strangers to his negotiation with Clinton, but not to André, who knew him to be at that time a traitor to the Congress; nay more, whose protection was granted for no other purpose but to promote and give effect to his treachery. In the second place, they say that, at the time he was taken, he was upon neutral ground; but then they do not deny that he had been within the American lines in disguise. The letters written by André himself show a firm, cool intrepidity, worthy a more glorious end. Writing to General Clinton, he requests that his mother and sister may have the sale of his commission; as for himself, he says, he is "perfectly tranquil in mind, and prepared for any fate to which an honest zeal for the King's service may have devoted" him. There is another short note which he wrote to Washington the day before his execution; it concludes with these words: "Let me hope, Sir, if aught in my character impresses you with esteem towards me, if aught in my misfortunes marks me as the victim of policy and not of resentment, I shall experience the operation of these feelings in your breast by being informed that I am not to die *on a gibbet*." "But," say the Congress, "the practice and usage of war were against his request, and made the indulgence he solicited inadmissible." The fate of this unfortunate young man, and the manly style of his letters, have raised more compassion here than the loss of thousands in battle, and have excited a warmer indignation against the Americans than any former act of the Congress. When the passions of men are so deeply affected, you will not expect to find them keep within the bounds of reason. Panegyrics on the gallant André are unbounded; they call him the English Mutius, and talk of erecting monuments to his memory. Certainly no man in his situation could have behaved with more determined courage; but his situation was by no means such as to admit of these exaggerated praises. Arnold, in his letter to the Americans, charges the Congress with having rejected the offers of the English commissioners by their own authority, and without ever consulting the different Provinces. This, if true, was a very bold step indeed; but it may be said, that if the Provinces have re-elected the same members to represent them in Congress, they have tacitly confirmed all their former measures; but whether the fact is so I cannot tell.

Burke has lately published the speech he made to the people of Bristol, in which he had the courage not only to vindicate the act for the toleration of the Roman Catholics, but to give it the highest encomiums. He concludes a very noble panegyric on Sir George Saville, by saying, that one of the actions which in his whole life does him the greatest honour, is his having been the man who brought so just and wise a bill into Parliament.

Your friend and affectionate brother,

SAML. ROMILLY.

LETTER VI.

Dear Roget, Gray's Inn, Jan. 1. 1781.

Use has not at all lightened your loss to me. After an absence of eighteen months, I still regret as much as ever that I am debarred the happiness of your conversation. In my studies I miss you yet more: I long to consult you upon what I read, and to read over to you and take your opinion on what I write. I have lately learned Italian: do not censure me for such a waste of time. I began to apply myself to it when I was ill, and was forbidden any severer studies;

and so easy a language is it, that I soon began to read its prose writers with pleasure. I have just read Machiavel's famous book, *Del Principe*. Had Cæsar Borgia, his hero, been as successful as he was cruel and profligate, he would have been exactly the unjust man, stained and polluted with every vice, whom Plato, in his *Republic*, proves to be miserable in the midst of his prosperity, and to whom he opposes his just man, despised and persecuted. Though, in the end, his crimes availed not this monster, Machiavel does not scruple to propose him as a model for the imitation of princes; and seems to lament that his great talents could not give him the disposal of events. The picture this Italian politician gives of human nature is the blackest that ever was painted; but it seems probable that he never travelled out of his native country; and though his acute penetration may have given him a full insight into the character of his countrymen, he was assuredly but ill acquainted with human nature in general. When he says that men are by nature hypocrites and cowards, ungrateful and rapacious, this may possibly be as exact a copy of the manners of Italy, in an age just emerging from barbarism, as his gloomy imagination could trace; but for a representation of the human species, how false and preposterous is it! "Princes," he says, "are not to be bound by promises and oaths, for all men are perfidious; and were monarchs alone observant of their faith, they would find themselves the dupes of their own ridiculous scruples."[1] He is the first

[1] Principe, chap. 18.

writer, perhaps, who, regarding mankind with the eyes of a sullen misanthrope, has expressed no indignation at what he saw, and seemed well contented that things should remain as they were. Seeing men in the odious light in which he represents them, Machiavel could not but have conceived a deadly hatred against them; and, if so, his book seems to me no longer a prodigy: for in this institute of a tyrant, he has, consistently with that hatred, set himself to arm with force, and with every destructive art, the most cruel scourge of mankind. The author of the *Anti-Machiavel*, published by Voltaire, seems to have formed his opinion of the human heart from the manners of France, as much as Machiavel did from those of Italy. Machiavel says, that no oppression of a prince will so soon draw on him the hatred of his subjects, as to rob them of their property or wives; for these are wrongs which raise a more implacable resentment than the murder of a father. The Anti-Machiavelian, falling into the opposite extreme, says, that such gallantry, using that fashionable phrase of the language he writes in, never renders a prince odious. The story of Lucretia, indeed, stands a little in his way; but he dexterously removes that obstacle by supposing the whole story a romance, — a convenient mode this of getting rid of the great examples of ancient virtue, where they obstruct a modern system or remain a reproach to modern depravity.

Without doubt, you have had some account of the dreadful hurricane and earthquake in the West Indies; but not, I imagine, such particular relations as we have had here. They exceed in horror any thing I ever read of. Wherever the storm directed its course, it was attended with desolation and death. The letters from the inhabitants of Bridgetown, in Barbadoes, contain descriptions of the night they passed, when the storm was at its worst, which are horrible beyond conception. To the howling of the tempest was added the noise of the houses falling on every side, and of the shrieks and groans of the inhabitants who were crushed by their ruins,— this, too, in a night impenetrably dark, interrupted only by sudden gleams of lightning, which discovered imperfectly the havoc suffered in every quarter. The return of light, which had been so long and so fervently prayed for, brought no abatement of the storm; and only served to display the most dreary prospect that the imagination can devise: what was, the preceding evening, a well-built populous town, was now a vast heap of ruins, interspersed with the bodies of the dying and the dead. Those who have escaped this calamity find themselves only reserved for greater misfortunes: reduced from affluence to beggary, without any shelter to protect them from the inclemency of the weather, and with all the horrors of a famine staring them in the face; for the devastation has been so universal, that they say it will scarce be possible to avert that dreadful evil. It is hardly credible, but the same letters declare it to be a fact, that, in the midst of this shocking scene, numbers of the negroes were employed in pillaging the houses. Great allowances are certainly to be made for a race of men so oppressed and trampled on, in any vengeance they take upon their oppressors; but one would think no human being had a heart so hardened, either by natural stupidity or by the longest course of oppression, as not to be melted or appalled at so awful a spectacle.

Jan. 5. — I intended, you see, to send this letter by the last post, but I was unluckily prevented from finishing it in time. I have since received yours of 16th December. You profess yourself unequal to the task of criticising Rousseau; what presumption would it then be in me to undertake it? I have lately read a great part of his works. It astonishes me that I should not formerly have been more struck with the merit of the *Emile.* "Mon cœur a béni cent fois pendant cette lecture l'homme vertueux et ferme qui ose ainsi instruire les humains." I sincerely lament with you that he abandoned the plan he had formed for its continuation. I am much surprised that any one should ever have questioned his speaking his real sentiments, in his Discourse upon the Arts. Surely never had any piece of oratory the marks of coming warm from the heart, if that has not. Some parts of the *Lettres écrites de la Montagne,* and that addressed to the Archbishop of Paris, to me appear superior, for forcible reasoning and a strain of irresistible eloquence, to any modern production I ever read. Had I the arrogance to judge of originals, some of which I know but from translations, I should possibly give to some passages of Rousseau the preference over the great masterpieces of antiquity. At least, after reading Rousseau, I am inclined to confess that, after all, my favourite Cicero "n'était qu'un avocat." Among other of his writings, one I had never heard of, a Letter addressed to Voltaire, on the subject of his Poem on the Earthquake at Lisbon[1], has given me great pleasure. Do you recollect it? It is in that he makes the very just distinction, that we should not say, "tout est bien," but "le tout est bien."

Yours, &c.

SAML. ROMILLY.

LETTER VII.

Dear Roget, Gray's Inn, Feb. 9. 1781.

It was not till last Monday that I received your letter of the 13th of last month, in which you paint in such strong colours the very alarming occurrences which have lately happened at Geneva. It will be needless to trouble you with any reflections on that subject; though you must think they could hardly fail of presenting themselves to me in abundance upon reading your letter. Let me particularly beg of you not to fail to inform me of every event of any importance, which may happen in consequence of what I am already acquainted with.

The Dutch have not yet published their counter-manifesto: we wait with impatience to hear how they will justify their conduct: they have some very able defenders here. Having lately heard a debate in the House of Lords upon the Dutch War, which lasted seven hours, you must needs think I am pretty well master of the arguments on

[1] The date of this letter is Aug. 18. 1756.

both sides of the question. The substance, or rather the heads of them, I will state to you as concisely as I can. The Ministry represented the conduct of the Dutch, ever since the breaking out of the war with America and France, to have been, in the last degree, injurious and faithless to England. Mention was made of their supplying the enemy with stores, contrary to the treaty subsisting between them and us; of their giving refuge to American privateers, not only at St. Eustatius, but even in the Texel, and refusing to surrender them up to our ambassador; of their denying us the succours they were by treaty bound to furnish; and, lastly, of their having actually signed a treaty with our subjects in open rebellion against us, nay, of their having assented to American Independence almost as early as France, for the treaty bears date September, 1778. On the other hand, the conduct of Great Britain towards the Dutch was represented to have been in every respect friendly, moderate, and even indulgent: we did not persist in our demands of having Paul Jones delivered up to us; we suffered them for a long time to carry on an illicit commerce with our enemies; and, when we were at last obliged to stop their ships, we scrupulously paid them for all their cargoes, and indemnified them from loss. We did not so much as demand the stipulated succours, to which we had an undeniable right, till our coast was threatened with an invasion; and even now, when fortune has thrown into our hands their secret treaty with America, we have still left them room to repair their fault, by only demanding that the pensionary Van

Berkel, who had signed it, may be punished. So much for the justice of the war.

As to its expediency, they say it is now clear that the Dutch are secretly our enemies. It is, then, prudent in us to strip them of their disguise, and force them to meet us face to face; as open enemies, they cannot do us more prejudice than they have already done as false friends. St. Eustatius has been the continual source which has supplied vigour to the Americans. Had some violent convulsion in nature sunk that island in the sea, before the breaking out of the war, America must long since have submitted to our arms. The Dutch were, once, powerful as a maritime state, it is true; but ships are now constructed in so different a manner, and lie so much deeper in the water than they did formerly, that their harbours are totally incapable of containing any formidable fleet. They are a people naturally averse to war, and fond of that peace and security by which alone commerce, their great idol, can thrive. This innate disposition has been nourished by the torpor of a century, passed in ease and quiet. As they are thus indisposed, so are they wholly unprepared for war; their possessions are every where open and exposed to an enemy: St. Eustatius, the Cape of Good Hope, the Isle of Ceylon, the Spice Islands, in short, all their distant possessions, are in a state to invite invaders. One vigorous blow will strike an alarm through all the States; will open the eyes of the better part of the nation, and rouse them to shake off the yoke of that French faction, which has gained so entire an ascendant over them as to make them forgetful of their faith, and blind to their true interests.

The Opposition, on the other hand, contend: First, That the war is unjust. The Dutch, they say, are, by the now subsisting treaty, allowed to furnish our enemies with stores. They are, as every body knows, so rapacious of gain, that they have supplied even their own enemies with stores, particularly in a very memorable instance, the siege of Bergen-op-Zoom; and how can we then expect they will do for us what they will not do for themselves? The pretended treaty which has been found is, in fact, no treaty; it is only a rough draft; it purports to be no more, for its initial words are, "We agree upon this as the proper plan for a treaty," &c. Our demand of punishment on Van Berkel is insolent, ridiculous, and illegal. How is he punishable? by what law? Suppose an Englishman, some years ago, had, in his cabinet, drawn up a treaty with Corsica, or that he had actually agreed upon terms with some Corsican chief, and the French had demanded punishment on him; should we have inflicted it? or rather could we? Our demand to the States is not unlike that of the Czar Peter, who, when an ambassador of his was arrested in London for debt, demanded the heads of the persons concerned in the arrest!

Secondly, As the war is unjust, so is it inexpedient and rash. War is at all times an evil; what then must it be to a nation already engaged in hostilities with three of the greatest powers in the world, sinking under the enormous weight of its debt, with all its resources exhausted;—a war against our natural ally, whose interests are inseparable from ours? What though they have been long lulled in peace; their indefatigable industry will shortly put them in a state, not merely of defence, but of annoyance. The severest blows our naval power ever sustained were from the Hollanders. The names of Van Tromp and De Ruyter are still dreadful. Who knows how soon the rashness of our councils may raise up other commanders as formidable? We talk of the weakness of the Dutch settlements, but we forget the condition of our own; that our oppressions in the East Indies have made for us there as many enemies as there are natives; that we are already engaged in war with the fierce Marattoes; that discord and enmity rage among the servants of the Company, particularly at Bengal, where all is anarchy. A war with Holland must be a war with all the powers of Europe; for, as the Dutch have acceded to the armed neutrality, there can be no doubt that all the neutral powers will make theirs a common cause.

I leave you, my dear Roget, to determine on which side the arguments preponderate. However weighty the arguments of Opposition, it must be confessed they come with a bad grace from men who have so often blamed the timidity of the Ministry. Our circumstances, you will say, have greatly changed, and it would be madness in us to hold the same language now, which, a few years since, would have been moderate and reasonable; but it was only last summer, at a moment the most alarming we have ever known, when great part of London lay in ashes, and rebellion and civil war seemed at our very doors, that the Duke of Richmond reproached the Ministry in the severest terms for not proceeding rigorously to punish a Russian, who was said to have been concerned in burning the chapels. The Duke was then for despising the Russians, and the armed neutrality. No matter what the consequences. "Fiat justitia et ruat cœlum."

I must how conclude by informing you of the death of Mrs. Facquier.[1] You know too well the great obligations we have to her, and were yourself too well acquainted with her excellent disposition, not to conceive how much we all should feel her loss, were it not lightened by the consideration that her death is a deliverance from a painful existence. Considering what she has gone through for many years past, one cannot call it a cessation of life, but the conclusion of a lingering death; "non erepta vita sed donata mors est." She expired, free from all pain, in a state of composure and tranquillity which could hardly be expected after what she so long had suffered. Though she had never any apprehension of quitting this life, (for it had proved to her a state of too severe probation for her to be attached to it, nor could a life of such piety and charity leave her any dread of futurity,) yet having so often experienced such sharp pain from disease, she always expressed some fear of what she might suffer at the moment of dissolution; but her death was like sleep. So true is it that half the terrors of death are of our own creation. Adieu. Yours most affectionately,

SAML. ROMILLY.

[1] See *antè*, p. 9.

Letter VIII.

Gray's Inn, March 27. 1781.

When I have told you, my dear Roget, that your little boy and all your friends here are in perfect health, I have concluded all the most interesting intelligence I have to send you, and must have recourse to public news to fill my letter. I might, indeed, indulge myself with planning schemes of future felicity: the probability of our seeing each other next summer in Switzerland already affords me the dream of a transient happiness; but of happiness it becomes us to be economists.

Little business of consequence has come on lately in our Parliament; the Lords have scarcely any debates; the Duke of Richmond, Lord Shelburne, and Lord Camden never attend. In the Commons, some unsuccessful attempts have been made to curb that system of corruption which is the bane of our constitution. One was a Bill against contractors sitting in Parliament; the same Bill which last year passed the Commons, and was thrown out by the Lords. The debate was short; for the majority were so confident of victory, and so vociferous for the question, that few deigned to speak on one side of the House, or were permitted on the other. One argument used against the Bill was, that it was unjust and cruel to suppose that members of Parliament would be induced to vote against their conscience by the hope of being favoured with lucrative contracts; as if men of honour and fortune would prefer their own interests to those of their country. Another objection was, that the Bill would, in its effects, prove an exclusion of merchants from Parliament. You observe how these arguments destroy one another. If these contractors are so disinterested as to prefer the public to their own private good, they will sooner resign the advantage to be made by contracts than quit the service of their country in Parliament; consequently, the Act will not operate as an exclusion. If, on the contrary, preferring an increase of their private fortunes to the honour and satisfaction of promoting the public good, they keep their contracts and resign their seats, it necessarily follows that they are not men who have the welfare of their country at heart, not men who can safely be entrusted with the rights of their fellow-citizens and the interests of their country. Another Bill, which has been thrown out by the House of Commons, was for disqualifying officers, employed in the collection of the Excise and Customs, to vote at elections of members of Parliament. The opposers of this Bill dared to profane the name of Liberty by saying that the Bill was destructive of it, and that it would rob a very large class of men of their dearest privilege; though they well know that this dear privilege is a hateful burden to all but those who are dishonest enough to make a profit of it: that the rest, threatened with the loss of their places if they vote against the court, find themselves, at every election, reduced to the dilemma of choosing between a sacrifice of fortune or of conscience.

The conduct of the English judges in India is

become a matter of public inquiry by a committee of the House of Commons, in consequence of petitions which have been presented to the King and the Parliament from the British inhabitants, and from the Gentoos and Mahommedans in India, complaining of great injustice and oppression in the administration of justice. But, before I proceed, it may be proper to remind you that this English court of justice was established in the year 1773, and that the Act, under which it was erected, confines its jurisdiction to British inhabitants and natives in the service of the Company. Our countrymen complain that they are refused the trial by jury in civil causes; that the judges have, in many particular cases, acted partially and illegally; that they have denied Magna Charta to have force in India, &c. &c. But the wrongs of the natives are much more insupportable. The judges, in order to extend their authority, have given to the Act of Parliament the most literal, rigid, unfair construction; for example, all persons who rent farms of the Company are, they say, servants of the Company, and therefore, by the letter of the Act, subject to the English court of justice. By such means, multitudes of Indians are brought under the English law; that is, a complicated system of law, so voluminous that years of study are requisite to enable even Englishmen to acquire a knowledge of it, is at once transplanted into a country whose inhabitants are strangers even to the language in which it is written. The arbitrary institutions of a commercial republic, in which all men are equal, are made the laws of a despotic empire, where distinctions between every different class of men are religiously observed, and where such distinctions are even become necessary to subordination and government. In a word, a law is given them which clashes with their own law and their own religion, and shocks their manners and prejudices in a thousand instances. But, independently of the laws themselves, they detest the practice of our courts, our pleadings and mode of trial, as founded in absurdity and injustice. Why, they ask, must we employ an attorney to prosecute our suits? How is it to be conceived that another man, a stranger, whose acquaintance we must seek for the purpose, will defend our cause as zealously as we should ourselves? Money can be the only inducement for his becoming our friend; so that our adversary has but to offer a higher bribe, for this mercenary friend to sell his friendship again and to betray our cause. The monstrous expense, the perpetual delays, and enormous length of your proceedings ruin us before our cause is heard; and, after all, when it comes to a hearing, ignorant of your language, we remain strangers to what passes in court, to the rules of your decisions, to every thing, in short, but the sentence we are to undergo and the fees we are to pay.

Though it was scarcely possible to reconcile the Indians to the novelty of our laws and the practice of our courts, however cautiosuly and gradually it might have been attempted, yet by prudent conduct the yoke might have been made to feel less galling at first; but our judges seem to have sought to aggravate its weight. They were attended to India by a swarm of desperate adventurers, debtors, and bankrupts, who went to repair their ruined fortunes by the plunder which was to be made under sanction of the law. These wretches, upon their arrival at Calcutta, assumed the character of attorneys, officers of the court, servants of the judges, &c. &c.; and are described to have spread themselves over the fertile provinces of Bengal, Bahar, and Orissa, like the locusts over Egypt, carrying with them ruin and desolation; breathing a spirit of discord and litigation wherever they went; opening public shops to supply a redress for every imagined wrong, or rather to gratify the malevolence and resentment of every restless and revengeful spirit; instigating slaves to bring actions of assault against their masters, and culprits to recover on the judges of the country for false imprisonment, and reviving causes which had long been terminated; for, what seems incredible, the judges gave the law a retrospective force, and property was disposed of, and crimes adjudged and punished by positive laws, which were not in being, in that country, at the time of the transactions. The confusion that followed from all this is hardly to be conceived. On the principle that all men are equal, writs were issued out indiscriminately against persons of every description, no matter what their sex, rank, or consideration in the country. Gentoos, who think themselves polluted by the touch of any but those of their own particular sect, were personally arrested, thrown into a common dungeon with malefactors of every description, and there left with the alternative either of perishing with hunger, or offending against their religion by eating of food prepared by profane hands. The harams, the apartments of the females, which are held sacred in that country, and which it is profane in any male to approach, were violently forced open by bailiffs, and the bodies of the women arrested; an indignity which they complain of as more cruel than death itself. Judges were seized in the administration of justice, and torn, with circumstances of contempt, from their tribunals in the sight of the prisoners they were trying. The administration of justice was at a stand; murders were committed with impunity; and the country judges refused to punish the murderers, lest they should draw down on themselves the severity of our Supreme Court by some error in their proceedings, or by interfering with the English jurisdiction. The petition of the Gentoos concludes in these words, "If (which God forbid!) it should so happen that this our petition should not be accepted, those amongst us who have power and ability, discarding all affections to our families, will fly to any quarter we can: whilst the remainder who have no means or ability, giving themselves up with pious resignation to their evil fate, will sit down in expectation of their death. After this, let the soil of the country remain, and the court of justice! Let the court of justice remain upon the earth, or the earth cover it!" Though I have read a great many of the papers and publications upon this subject, yet, as I have not seen any thing written in defence of the judges, I ought to suspend my judgment upon their conduct, but with very great allowances for exaggeration and misrepresentation, they still seem very guilty.

I must now take my leave of you.

Your affectionate brother,

SAML. ROMILLY.

LETTER IX.

Gray's Inn, April 4. 1781.

It gave me great pain, my dear Roget, to find you in your last letter speak in so disconsolate a manner of life, as if you had lost all relish for any of its enjoyments. I own I did not expect it; for, though I am sure no one has felt your afflictions more sensibly than I, yet I have often pleased myself with thinking that your life was not destitute of enjoyment; for, knowing that ambition and the tumultuous pleasures of the world never had charms for you, I confess I thought I still saw room for many happy hours in a life of quiet and obscurity, with the company of a few friends and our dear Catherine for the partner of your exile; above all, in the prospect of educating your son. I know that the purest intellectual pleasures are poisoned by bodily pain; but you have flattered us, or you are free from that evil. You speak of your life as precarious; but who is certain of existence till to-morrow? and what thinking being would have the idea of death less present to his mind than you say it is to yours? You know, my dear Roget, how we always exaggerate to ourselves our past happiness and our present misery: so much, that were we to live over again some of the most envied moments of our past life, we should be surprised to find that that happiness which, seen through the delusive medium of time, appeared with so many charms, was, in reality, possessed of so few; and yet it is by comparisons with this distant magnified happiness that we add to the bitterness of all our present sorrows.

You ask me how I spend my time: in a manner so uniformly the same, that a journal of one day is a journal of all. At six o'clock, or sooner, I rise; go into the cold bath; walk to Islington to drink a chalybeate water (from which I have found great benefit), return and write or read till ten; then dress and go to Mr. Spranger's, where I study till three; dine in Frith Street, and afterwards return to Mr. Spranger's, where I remain till nine, or else stay in Frith Street, and read with my brother and Jane. This is the history of every day, with little other variation than that of my frequently attending the courts of justice in the morning, instead of going to Mr. Spranger's, and of my often passing my afternoons at one of the Houses of Parliament; for I have lately been so fortunate as to find the means of gaining admittance to both Houses whenever I choose. Indeed I am grown as great a politician as Appia was, though it is not mine, as it was his, favourite topic of conversation. "Peace is my dear delight," and peace and our politics are incompatible. My father is still as warm an advocate as ever for the Ministry[1], and I as deeply affected as ever with the miseries and disgrace

[1] The administration of Lord North.

they have brought upon my country. The moment the conversation turns upon public affairs, I impose it upon myself as a law not to take part; and yet I am often weak enough to let the subject carry me away by degrees, in which case our conversation never ends without my sincerely repenting, and reproaching myself with want of firmness in not keeping my resolution. Mr. Spranger is as warm a friend of the opposition as my father of the court; too warm a friend for me to concur with him; for, though I believe many of the minority to be as disinterested and truly patriotic as any men in the kingdom, yet some of the leaders of the party are such, that one must be prejudiced to blindness, not to see that their only view is to raise themselves upon the ruins of the party they oppose. At Mr. Spranger's I pass for a ministerialist, and at home for a patriot — an epithet not very honourable in the sense in which it is used.

As for political news, we have none, except that the minority are very angry with Lord North for the terms upon which he has made the loan of this year, and for his distribution of it among the subscribers. I should not be very intelligible, I fear, if I were to endeavour to explain what those terms were; suffice it to say, that they were so advantageous to the subscribers, and, consequently, so disadvantageous to the public, that the next day after they were declared, they bore a premium of 10 per cent., and have remained ever since at a premium of between 10 and 7 per cent. The distribution is complained of as having been made to none but the friends of the ministry, and a very great part of it to Members of Parliament, who are thus bribed with the public money to betray the public, and whose interest it thus becomes to ratify the most improvident bargain a minister can make, when they themselves share the spoil. They are not the guardians of the people, but the usurers who profit by their prodigality.

Adieu; believe me to remain, my dear Roget, your warm friend and affectionate brother,

SAML. ROMILLY.

LETTER X.

Dear Roget, May 22. 1781.

The conduct of Rodney and Vaughan in confiscating all the property at St. Eustatius, has lately been brought before the House of Commons by Burke. As his motion, though it was only for papers necessary for an inquiry into that transaction, led to a censure upon the Ministry, if the orders of confiscation were sent from hence, and if not, to a censure upon Rodney and Vaughan, you will not be surprised that it was rejected, though it was supported by very strong arguments, at least in my opinion; but you shall judge for yourself. It was admitted, that to confiscate all the property of a place taken in war is contrary to the law of nations observed by all civilized states, and particularly as that law is laid down by Vattel, the last writer of authority upon the subject. But then, it is said, a distinction is to be made between a people openly at war with you, and one who, like the Dutch, have perfidiously violated their treaties, and secretly supplied your enemy with succours. The answer to this is: their perfidy was the cause of our declaring war, but, war being once begun, we must conform to the rules of warfare established in Europe; and it is a principle laid down by every writer on the law of nations, that each state at war must be presumed to have justice on her side. Besides, it is impossible to punish the perfidy of a nation by severity in carrying on war against it; for the only effect of such severity would be to draw retaliations from the enemy, and finally to establish a more cruel law of nations than what now prevails. But then, it is said, St. Eustatius is not a settlement; it ought not to be compared to Grenada, or any other conquered island; it is nothing but a depôt or magazine. But how does this alter the case? The only question is, whether, in a place which has surrendered at discretion and without resistance, the private property of individuals is liable to confiscation. Lord George Germaine[1] said, that the orders sent from home were, that the property of the inhabitants established in the island should not be touched. But this is a reason for going into an inquiry; for, if it be true, Rodney is highly criminal in having departed from his orders, and that to commit an act of the most wanton injustice. With respect to the Jews, it was said that the orders that were given for transporting them, were given unknown to the Com-

[1] Secretary of State for the Colonies.

mander-in-Chief, and that they were countermanded the moment they came to his knowledge. An inquiry, then, is still more necessary, in order to discover who it was that dared to give orders so disgraceful to the nation. With respect to the property of English merchants, it is said the trade was improper, and supplied the enemy with strength: the cargoes that were consigned to St. Eustatius might, with much more safety, have been sent more to the north. To this it is answered, that the trade was perfectly legal; that it was protected and encouraged by acts of parliament, made since the commencement of the American war; that more to the northward the cargoes might, it is true, have been safe from capture, but they would not have been sold, they would have found no market. But that this dread of supplying the enemy is only a mask to cover the most flagrant injustice is evident, for the Commanders-in-Chief sold all the effects they seized, — sold them much cheaper indeed, but exactly in the same manner as the merchants would have sold them; so that to supply the enemy by a fair trade is with them a crime, but not, to supply them by dint of violence and plunder. After all, it is said, what injury has been done? Whoever think themselves aggrieved, may have recourse to law. Without doubt they may; but it is only because they have been injured that they must recur to law. Are we to thank Rodney and Vaughan if our courts of justice are open, and our judges impartial? Was it a merit in Verres that the Sicilians found a Tully to plead their cause, and a tribunal to hear their complaints? When one considers who they are whom those men advise to go to law, one must see that it is adding insult to injury. It is telling the wretches whom they have reduced to beggary, that they may follow them home if they will, engage in an expensive lawsuit, and try whether the goodness of their cause alone will enable them to overcome men crowned with laurels, elevated with popular favour, and loaded with riches. And what redress will the law give them? at most only the restoration of their property. But who will compensate them for a long separation from their families, and for the injury their commerce must have sustained by a tedious attendance on our courts of justice? But the strongest ground on which the motion was opposed was, that it would be unjust to condemn Rodney and Vaughan unheard and absent; and yet this argument comes with an ill grace from those who are so confident of their innocence; for being innocent, they cannot fear a condemnation. These confident friends of Rodney, to be consistent with themselves, should be the most earnest for the proposed inquiry, which will clear his character from the foulest stain which, whether justly or not, it has certainly contracted. Let us be just to our officers, but let us not be unjust to these miserable sufferers who are reduced to want bread; let us not be unjust to ourselves, nor suffer the honour of the nation to be blasted by a flagrant violation of the laws of nations.

Did I ever inform you that, among the variety of disputing societies which were established here in such abundance last winter, there were several for debating topics of religion? Having never been present at any of them, I cannot speak of them from my own knowledge; but, according to the representation I have had given me of the company which usually frequent them, the auditors are mostly weak, well-meaning people, who are inclined to Methodism; the speakers partly fanatics, who persuade themselves that a jargon of scriptural words, as unintelligible to themselves as to their hearers, is inspired eloquence; some designing villains, who are anxious to poison the minds of the people, and by means of their religious prejudices to work their own bad ends; and a few coxcombs, with more wit than understanding, and who go there for the purpose of ridiculing religion, or rather of displaying their own talents to advantage, by placing them in contrast with the imbecility of their opponents. That such meetings, where the cause of religion is probably no less injured by its defenders than by its assailants, are at all times pernicious, can, I think, admit of no dispute; but at present they are particularly dangerous, as they tend to keep alive that rage of persecution against the Catholics which has of late so unhappily infected the minds of the people. Nothing, one would imagine, could raise up panegyrists of these societies but what has lately happened, an attempt to suppress them. The Solicitor-General[1] has lately brought a bill into Parliament for this purpose. The bill is drawn artfully enough; for, as these societies are held on Sundays, and people pay

[1] Mr. James Mansfield.

for admittance, he has joined them with a famous tea-drinking house, involving them both in the same fate, and entitling his bill, A Bill to regulate certain Abuses and Profanations of the Lord's Day. This bill has met with no opposition in Parliament but from two or three members; but among the common people, I am told, it is exceedingly odious. It is called a persecution, an inquisition, and many other names equally reproachful and inapplicable. Could one, indeed, expect that those turbulent spirits who have sought to blow up the wildest fanaticism among the people, would patiently suffer so powerful an instrument to be wrested out of their hands?

Have you ever heard of a book published here some time since by a Mr. Howard, upon the State of the Prisons in England, and in several other countries of Europe? You may conjecture from the subject that it is not a book of great literary merit; but it has a merit infinitely superior. It is one of those works which have been rare in all ages of the world; it is written with a view only to the good of mankind. The author was some time ago sheriff in the country; in the execution of that office a number of instances of abuses practised in the prisons came under his observation. Shocked with what he saw, he began to inquire whether the prisons in the adjacent counties were on a better footing. Finding every where the same injustice prevail, he resolved, — a private individual, — to attempt to reform abuses which he found were as general as they were shocking to humanity. Accordingly, he made a visit to every prison and house of correction in England, with invincible perseverance and courage; for some of the prisons were so infected with diseases and putrid air, that he was obliged to hold a cloth steeped in vinegar to his nostrils during the whole time he remained in them, and to change his clothes the moment he returned. After having devoted so much time to this painful employment, he set out on a tour through great part of Holland, Germany, and Switzerland, to visit their prisons. What a singular journey!—not to admire the wonders of art and nature, not to visit courts and ape their manners; but to dive into dungeons, to compare the misery of men in different climates, to study the arts of mitigating the torments of mankind! What a contrast might be drawn between the painful labour of this man, and the ostentatious sensibility which turns aside from scenes of misery, and, with the mockery of a few barren tears, leaves it to seek comfort in its own distresses! The result of all his inquiries Mr. Howard has laid before the Parliament, and some steps have, I believe, been taken towards putting our prisons on a better regulation; but I am sorry I cannot particularly inform you what they are.

Adieu, yours most affectionately,

S. R.

Letter XI.

[TO ——.]

La Grande Chartreuse, near Grenoble, Sept. 8. 1781.[1]

This is but the third day, my dear ——, that I find myself in this monastery, and I seem already to have inhabited it for years. The sight of the same objects, and of the same faces, and the precise order which reigns here, soon destroy the novelty of the life of a recluse; and I can hardly persuade myself, since I have been in this place, that I am ever to quit it. It was dusk when we arrived, and we were so much fatigued with our journey that we paid little attention to any thing but the hospitality of our religious hosts, and the excellent supper they set before us. As for myself, when I was shown into my chamber, I was so overwhelmed with drowsiness that I took notice of nothing in it but a bed, into which I threw myself with the impatience of a weary traveller. The next morning, after a slumber of nine hours without interruption, — except once, indeed, that I was waked by the melancholy bell which summons the fathers to the midnight service, — I found myself lying on a small wooden bed, in a little cell paved with tiles, and furnished only with two wooden chairs, and a desk for prayer, over which hung a very indifferent print of the passion of our Savour. My window looked over the spacious court-yard

[1] Mr. Romilly made a journey to France and Switzerland in the summer of this year. See "Narrative of his early Life," p. 60.

before the house, which was vast, but solitary; the grass grew between the stones, and in the midst stood two fountains, the melancholy splashing of whose waters alone interrupted the deep silence. The aspect of the country was well suited to the building, and presented to the view a dreary mountain rising above, one end wholly covered with woods of gloomy pine. I quitted my little cell to walk about the house of this solitary community. Every object struck me with awe and respect. As I walked through the long cloisters, nothing broke the profound silence of the convent but the sound of my steps on the pavement, faintly echoed by the vaulted roof. The cloister led me by a small burial ground in the midst of the building, where a number of tombstones in the form of crosses were placed in a kind of irregular order, — some high, some low; some new, others mouldering away and broken or fallen down, and with inscriptions scarce legible. This is the burial-place of the Generals; and they are never permitted to be far distant from it after their elevation to the supremacy of their order; for the General must not step beyond the precincts of the monastery. I began to read the inscriptions; and while I was remarking the very advanced age to which a life abstemious even to excess had been prolonged by these venerable fathers, and was observing the slight distinctions which some of them derived from the addition of a few years to their uniform lives, or by having died, some in the present century, and some three hundred years ago, I heard the distant steps of some person in the cloister. I quitted the cemetery to see who it might be; a white figure at a considerable distance was advancing towards me; it was one of the fathers. I walked to meet him, and should have spoken to him; but he had arrived at the door of his cell, which opened into the cloister: he entered and shut-to his door. I reproached myself for having forgotten that the fathers are not permitted to speak, and for having exposed him to the temptation of opening his lips; for he seemed in that instant to regret that the laws of his order imposed silence on him. The falling-to of the heavy door rang through the building, and left an awful impression on my mind. In imagination I followed this venerable monk into his cell. I fancied myself, like him, imprisoned from the world, and separated from the grave by nothing but the unvaried round of fasts and prayers; and that I should never quit my cell, except to rehearse the vigils in the chapel, to eat one weekly meal in silence with my brethren, or to walk about the lonely mountain, till I was carried into my tomb.

S. R.

Letter XII.

Ostend, Nov. 10. 1781.

Once more better than my word, I write to you, my dear Roget, from this place, though I did not give you reason to expect to hear from me till I should have arrived at London; but I deserve no thanks for this letter, for it is the fruits of the most irksome leisure which an unfavourable wind inflicts on me, by confining me to this place. I cannot look back on the manner in which I have spent the last five months, without owning myself much indebted to you for having induced me to take a journey, part of which has afforded me much pleasure, and all, if I do not flatter myself, much instruction; at the same time that I have gained by it this great advantage, that I now find myself possessed of a tolerable stock of health and strength, both of which I was poor in when I landed here in June last.

Pray inform me in your next letter whether the last part of Rousseau's works has yet been published, and whether you hear any thing of the edition of Berne. I have talked a great deal about that our favourite author with Mr. Romilly * of Paris, who was one of the very few persons who remained connected with him till his death; though, what is singular, he did not sacrifice to that connexion his friendship with Diderot. The manner in which these two authors used to speak of one another well exemplifies their different dispositions. Rousseau, though fully persuaded that Diderot had used him exceedingly ill, used to tell Mr. Romilly that he did well to continue his acquaintance with him, for that there was much to be learned in his conversation. Diderot, on the contrary, could not forgive Mr. Romilly for seeing Rousseau, whom he loaded with the most opprobrious names, though he never would particularise the injuries he pretended to have received from him. The acrimony of Diderot against Rousseau, instead of abating,

[1] The Mr. Romilly here mentioned was no relation of the writer. See p. 64.

seems to have increased with the death of that unfortunate man.[1] His remains were hardly cold before Diderot, in his *Life of Seneca*, treated him in vague and general terms, as a monster of hypocrisy and impurity. In one of the visits I made Diderot, I purposely turned the conversation on Rousseau. The reason which Diderot gave for not attacking him till after his death was, that several private persons were involved in the transactions in which Rousseau had used him so ill, and that, if he had mentioned those affairs before, Rousseau, "qui n'avait point de pudeur," would not have scrupled, in defending himself, to have blasted the characters of those other persons. This reason seems a very strange one; and the rather so, as Diderot's accusation, entirely vague and uncertain, particularises neither things nor persons. However, he is going to publish a second edition of the *Life of Seneca*, increased by a whole volume, in which he is to defend his accusation of Rousseau in the former edition against the editors of the *Journal de Paris*, among whom are Mr. Romilly and Mr. Corancez, who severely criticised it. I talked with Diderot a good deal about this work, of which he said he would send me a copy. I find that, among other very extravagant means which he has hit on to defend and exalt the character of his hero, one is to destroy the veneration with which the world has hitherto regarded Thraseas; though, in truth, the extravagant design of abusing Thraseas is but a consequence of a former extravagance, that of exalting Seneca. When I see

[1] Rousseau died in 1778.

these two men compared together, I cannot help thinking of the two architects[1] of antiquity: in Seneca I see the eloquent speaker who talks of the greatest virtues; in Thraseas, the godlike stoic, who shows those virtues in action. The chimeras of Seneca were realized in Thraseas.

In the little I have seen of the French, I have found them to be much less gay than they are commonly said to be. They are merry and serious by starts; but they are strangers to cheerfulness, and still more to serenity of temper. When Mr. De Luc was at Paris, he often observed to a gentleman whom I am acquainted with, as he walked out with him on Sunday evenings, that he never saw in England that mirth and gaiety which appeared on the countenances of the French. The observation has often been made before, but by men of less sense than Mr. De Luc; and thence one is to conclude, that the French are a happier nation than the English, and consequently that a despotic government is preferable to a free one! I greatly doubt the happiness of the French; but, if they are happy, they are more to be pitied than if they were discontented, because, in their situation, it is not possible they can be happy till their souls are debased to a level with their condition. Slaves must be insensible indeed to the misery and ignominy of their state, when they can hug the chains that dishonour them, and lick the feet by which

[1] Competitors for the erection of a public building at Athens; the one of whom fascinated the people by his eloquence, whilst the other, who had more knowledge of his art than of oratory, said only, "Men of Athens, all that he has spoken will I perform." — *Vide Plutarch. Reip. Ger. Præc.*

they are trampled on. Such men can never taste of real happiness; to them all its genuine sources are dried up. It is ever the policy of a tyrant to enervate the minds of his subjects, and to give them a fondness for false grandeur and empty pleasures. When he has once wrought this change in their disposition, he may at an easy price glut them with all that they are greedy after: they will never feel the want of pleasures which they no longer have souls to enjoy. So it was that, in the worst days of the Roman empire, its tyrants fed a populace, whom they had rendered stupid and sensual, with offals and gaudy shows. It is not more surprising that a people ignorant of liberty are contented with servitude, than that a man blind from his birth laments not the want of the most delightful of the senses. I have never seen a troop of children who appeared more cheerful and contented than the deaf and dumb scholars of the Abbé de l'Epée; but ought I from thence to conclude, that they are as happy, or perhaps happier than we, and that Providence, in giving us our senses complete, bestowed on us a superfluous, if not a pernicious gift?

At Versailles I assisted at the mass. The service was very short, though it was on a Sunday; for kings are so highly respected in that country that even Religion appoints for them less tedious ceremonies than it imposes on the people. The moment his Majesty appeared, the drums beat and shook the temple, as if it had been intended to announce the approach of a conqueror. During the whole time of saying mass, the choristers sang, sometimes single parts, sometimes in chorus. In the front seats of the galleries were ranged the ladies of the court, glowing with rouge, and gorgeously apparelled, to enjoy and form a part of the showy spectacle. The King laughed and spied at the ladies; every eye was fixed on the personages of the court, every ear was attentive to the notes of the singers, while the priest, who in the mean time went on in the exercise of his office, was unheeded by all present. Even when the Host was lifted up, none observed it; and if the people knelt, it was because they were admonished by the ringing of the bell; and even in that attitude, all were endeavouring to get a glimpse of the King. How can a king of France ever be brought to regard his subjects as his equals, when, even before the throne of heaven, he maintains so high a superiority over all around him? What an idea must he not conceive of his own importance, when he thus sees his God less honoured than himself?

S. R.

Letter XIII.

Gray's Inn, Nov. 16. 1781.

At last, my dear Roget, you find I am safe arrived at my dear home. It was very fortunate that I took advantage of the first favourable moment which presented itself for crossing the sea, as the wind has been contrary ever since, and there are, at present, no less than four mails due.

I have not yet had time to do any thing in the

commission you gave me; but I shall now set about it immediately, and give you an account of it in my next.

I forget what it was I wrote to you from Ostend; I know I mentioned something of Diderot, but did I tell you how zealously he preaches his system of materialism? In the first visit I paid him, after we had talked a little on political topics, he turned the conversation to his favourite philosophy; he praised the English for having led the way to true philosophy, but the adventurous genius of the French, he said, had pushed them on before their guides. "Vous autres," these were his words, "vous mêlez la théologie avec la philosophie; c'est gâter tout, c'est mêler le mensonge avec la vérité; il faut *sabrer* la théologie." He spoke of his acquaintance with Hume. "Je vous dirai un trait de lui, mais il vous sera un peu scandaleux peut-être, car vous Anglais vous croyez *un peu* en Dieu; pour nous autres nous n'y croyons guères. Hume dina avec une grande compagnie chez le Baron D'Holbach. Il était assis à côté du Baron; on parla de la religion naturelle: 'Pour les Athées,' disait Hume, 'je ne crois pas qu'il en existe; je n'en ai jamais vu.' 'Vous avez été un peu malheureux,' répondit l'autre, 'vous voici à table avec dix-sept pour la première fois.'"

He said that Chancellor Bacon was one of the greatest men our country had ever produced, and that Bacon says, "Causa finalis est virgo, Deo sacrata, quæ nihil parit;" that Plato, too, the author of all the good theology that ever existed on the earth, says, that there is a vast curtain drawn over the heavens, and that men must content themselves with what passes beneath that curtain, without ever attempting to raise it; and in order to complete my conversion from my unhappy errors, he read me all through a little work of his own, — a Dialogue between himself and a lady of quality much attached to religion, whom he attempts to convince of her folly.[1]

You know that the Queen of France was brought to bed at the time that I was at Paris; but I never had time to give you any account of the rejoicings on that occasion. What seemed to me most extraordinary was, that they were commanded. The day the Dauphin was born, an order was posted up in all the streets, enjoining the citizens to illuminate their houses for three successive nights, and to shut up their shops, and commanding the officers of the police to look to the execution of this order. Who would have thought that a people so famous for their fond attachment to their kings could have needed such an order! an order which, even when rendered necessary by the disloyalty of a nation, can never answer any purpose, unless it be to lull a feeble government into a childish joy by an outward show of happiness, by making an oppressed and discontented nation for a moment act the part of a happy and a grateful people!

At night I walked about Paris to see the illuminations; the streets were crowded with people, and

[1] This is published in his works, under the title of *Entretien d'un Philosophe aveç la Maréchale de* ——.

the public edifices were well lighted up; but in many of the private houses there appeared only one glimmering lamp at each window, hung up, not in token of joy, but of reluctant obedience to the Sovereign's will; and some of the citizens were daring enough not to illuminate their houses at all. In many of the squares were little orchestras with bands of music playing to the populace, some of whom danced about in wild irregular figures. But it was at the Place de Grève that the greatest crowd was assembled. The Town-house there was richly illuminated, a fire-work was played off, and afterwards the people were invited to dance to the music of four bands in different orchestras. The company, which consisted of the very lowest and dirtiest rabble of Paris, soon began to dance in a ring; but they were noisy rather than merry, and none seemed happy, unless happiness can be found in a tumultuous oblivion. My opinion of the Parisians, with respect to gaiety, is so different from that of all travellers, that I hardly dare trust to it; but I must describe things as I see them, and not borrow from others my opinions and observations. However, as the idea one forms of a people commonly depends, in a great measure, on the disposition of mind one happens to be in one-self, I ought not to conceal from you, that the ragged and miserable appearance of the people, the sight of the guards drawn up on every side, the frequent appearance of the horse-guet, who came upon one every now and then unexpectedly, and the reflection that the pavement on which I stood had been so often wet with the blood of the wretches whom the barbarous justice of the country dooms to expire in excruciating and lengthened agonies, spread over my mind such a cloud of melancholy as nothing could dissipate.

Forgive me for not making this long letter still longer; but as yet I have hardly found a moment's leisure since my return. Pray write to me soon, and often think of your sincere friend and most affectionate brother,

SAML. ROMILLY.

LETTER XIV.

Dear Roget, Gray's Inn, Dec. 4. 1781.

I have just received your letter of the 14th of last month, wherein you mention a former letter addressed to me at London, which unfortunately has not yet come to hand. I fear it was on board that packet which has been lost, and which sailed the last before the one in which I came over. As there is no prospect of my ever recovering it, I shall be much obliged to you to repeat, in your next, the most interesting of its contents which you recollect. The hopes you give us of your returning to England have given me the greatest joy. When we have you here again, we intend it should be for life. I hope, therefore, you will be careful to lay in a good stock of health before you undertake the journey.

And now, to speak of public news, which is of much too serious a nature to be passed over in silence. When I arrived home, I found every body in great anxiety for the army under Lord Cornwallis. His situation was very critical; an army, vastly superior in numbers to his own, surrounded him on every side; and no person seemed to doubt that, unless Clinton arrived in time to relieve him before his provisions were consumed, he would be obliged to surrender up himself and his army prisoners, and the disgrace at Saratoga would be renewed in the Chesapeak. It was thought, however, that Clinton might reach the Chesapeak before it was too late; and much was then expected from the valour of two such British armies against forces so unnaturally allied together, and so unaccustomed to act in conjunction as those of America and France. At any rate, it was supposed that the event must be quite decisive of the war; and the public was eager and burning with impatience to hear whether America was to return to her dependence, or be dissevered from us for ever. In this uncertainty, the day on which the Parliament was to meet drew near. The King's speech was prepared, had been read at the Council, and was to have been delivered to Parliament the very next day, when news arrived that Cornwallis and all his soldiers were prisoners. This report, which came with such authority as not to admit of any doubt, filled many persons with the deepest consternation: they saw blasted all our hopes of ever attaining what, in the course of so many years, we had pursued at the cost of so much blood and treasure. Others, instead of turning their views back, looked forward to the evils we had escaped, and thought we had more reason to rejoice at an event which had delivered us from a war so destructive to the nation; an event which, by happening thus early (for they considered it as inevitable at some time or other), had spared us many millions of debt, and the loss of many gallant armies, which the ministers would certainly have sacrificed in the pursuit of a favourite, but unattainable object. But none (at least none that I have heard of) saw this calamity with the terrors with which it has since been heightened; for none imagined that, after another so awful lesson, there would be any talk of continuing our inauspicious war in America.

The debates, which were to be had on the following day, promised to be very interesting; and so much had they roused the attention of men, that the lobby of the House was full long before the Speaker arrived; nor was it without difficulty that he could make his way into the House. The moment he had entered, the people crowded after him; it was impossible to shut the doors, and the gallery was in a moment filled with a promiscuous crowd. I, among the rest, had the good fortune to get a seat. As you have, without doubt, already seen the King's speech, you have as certainly observed that, after boasting of successes in the East Indies, which nobody had heard of before, announcing the disaster in Virginia, and declaring his resolution to prosecute the war with vigour, he goes on to involve the future conduct of the war in darkness and uncertainty. Let me recall his words to you, for they are very material. "I should not answer the trust committed to me as the Sovereign of a free people, &c., if I consented to sacrifice, either to my own desire of peace, or to their temporary ease and relief, those essential rights and permanent interests, upon the maintenance and preservation of which the future strength and security of this country must ever principally depend;" and afterwards, "the late misfortune calls loudly for your firm concurrence and assistance, to frustrate the designs of our enemies, equally prejudicial to the interests of America, and to those of Great Britain." In both Houses, all the speakers, on the side of Opposition, understood these words to intimate that the war in America was still to be carried on; and the address, which echoed them back to the throne, they understood as pledging the House to give their sanction to that measure: but the Ministerial speakers denied that to be the sense either of the speech or of the address, and many of them declared that, if they had understood it so, they certainly would have voted against the address; not that they were clear that the war in America ought to be abandoned, but because it was a question of too great moment to be thus hastily decided.

But let me confine myself to the debate in the Commons which I was myself witness to. The gentlemen who moved for an address, echoing, as usual, every sentence of the speech (men so little known that I shall not trouble you with their names), prefaced their motion with harangues of a very singular kind; giving the most dismal picture of the nation, yet saying we ought not to despond; boasting that our empire had numberless resources, yet omitting to point out any one of those resources; confessing that we were overcome in America, yet insisting that we ought still to maintain the style and deportment of conquerors; reminding the House that it became a renowned and high-spirited nation not to sink under its misfortunes, but, like ancient Rome, to take courage and a more determined resolution from its defeats: that, though every man must be deeply affected with the late calamity, it was not for Britons to indulge an unmanly sorrow; and that it better suited the character of the nation to appear before their King on this occasion as the bold Barons, our ancestors, are recorded to have done in former times, upon a like disaster, when for mourning they put on suits of armour. To these declamations they added an abundance of angry invectives against the ambition of the Bourbons, threw out many vague accusations against the Opposition as the real authors of all these measures, whose mischievous conduct they contrasted with the wise schemes and prudent measures of administration, which the seditious harangues of their opponents had frustrated.

When the last of these gentlemen had ended, Fox rose to move as an amendment to the proposed address, the omission of all the words which I have above transcribed, and the insertion of others which said nothing of continuing the war, but recommended a change of measures. This motion he introduced by a very long and passionate speech, in which he said that he had to set before the House a picture of the nation, melancholy indeed, but much less melancholy than had been drawn by the gentlemen who preceded him. He would use to the House the same reasoning with which Demosthenes addressed the people of Athens: "If your country had been reduced to its present miserable state under a wise and virtuous administration, as these men pretend, your situation would be desperate indeed; but if, as I insist, your affairs have been foolishly, imprudently, and perhaps treacherously administered, you have still hopes of retrieving them under other men, and by some other system." He said, that for the party of administration to stand forth the accusers of the minority on a day of such shame and humiliation to themselves was insolence not to be endured; that their accusations were the severest condemnation of themselves, for what could be thought of those men whose best digested plans and profoundest schemes were all disconcerted and scattered into air by the breath of one seditious orator! that the authors of the ruinous measures which had been pursued sought to shift the responsibility for what they had been guilty of from their own shoulders, to those of the men who had from the first seen the folly of these measures, had foretold their failure, and had endeavoured in vain to open the eyes of the nation before it was too late. He then entered on the subject of the address: he said he must call back the attention of the House to the events of the war; events which, though the movers of the address had passed them over in silence, should and must be often mentioned that night; events which would long be remembered with horror in the history of this country, and the effects of which he hoped would soon be felt upon its scaffolds. At this, the Solicitor-General smiled. Fox perceived it, and hastily asked him if he was not yet contented. "What," continued he, "are we still to suffer before the Ministry are called to account? Is not all they have done sufficient,—not the loss of thirteen provinces,—the effusion of so much blood,—the waste of so much public money,—the annihilation of so many branches of our commerce? What crimes can be imagined black enough to provoke the severity of justice, if deeds so atrocious, if such accumulated treasons to their country, do not bring their authors to the scaffold?" He then went through the history of the war, pointing out everywhere the misconduct of Ministers, and concluded with saying that, though he would not assert that they were pensioned by the King of France, he would be bold to say that France had not, among all the statesmen whose memory she reveres the most, one who had done her half such essential services as the present English Ministry. They railed, indeed, at the French King with empty words, as the Miso-philippoi, of whom Demosthenes speaks, railed against the King of Macedon; but, like them, they were bent on securing to him the most substantial benefits. They disdained to pursue, like Louis XIV., vain and ostentatious schemes of superficial greatness—they had industriously gained for the country they favoured the greatest and most solid advantages—an extension of her commerce, and the annihilation of the only rival which could check her power. Nor was this great design more meritorious than the admirable mode of its execution; the Ministry having so contrived it that America should separate from England, not by treaty, but by the decision of war, in order that sentiments of resentment and hostility might remain for ever impressed on either party. Nor was this all; they had so managed matters as to render the union between France and America indissoluble; they had made the concluding blow proceed from their joint efforts, and had taken care, by letting the French be their deliverers, that a sense of gratitude to that people should be with them eternal, like the memory of their deliverance. He ended with showing the folly and cruelty of still continuing the war in America, and said the Ministers had dared to suggest to his Majesty the speech of a hard-hearted unfeeling prince, who was not to be moved by the affliction of his much injured and exhausted people, but was determined madly to prosecute the same measures as had already driven them to the brink of ruin. Burke made another very violent speech, in which he promised soon to move for an impeachment against the Ministers: but the amendment to the address was lost in the Commons, by 218 to 129; and in the Lords, by 75 to 31.

Adieu, yours most affectionately,

Saml. Romilly.

Letter XV.

Gray's Inn, Jan. 11. 1782.

That I have suffered so many posts to pass without writing to you, my dear Roget, you will have ascribed, I hope, to its true causes, — a great deal of business, and no news to send you.

In a letter which I received at Paris you desired me to procure for you the papers which the Congress published at their first meeting, their petition to the King, and their addresses to the people of Great Britain and to the Canadians; but I suppose you have since discovered that they are all printed at length in the *Annual Register* for 1774.

You desire me to send you characters of Lord Dartmouth, Lord George Germaine [1], &c. Their private characters I am quite unacquainted with; and it is not easy to distinguish their characters as statesmen, for no one minister has appeared to be the author of any particular measure. All that has been done, has had the apparent approbation of the whole administration; and there are persons who go so far as to assert, that the real authors of all the proceedings against America are still behind the curtain. Of the whole administration, however, taken together, the principal characteristics are, want of system and irresolution; and the latter, indeed, is but a consequence of the former. Having little, confined views, they seem never, from the first, to have formed any comprehensive plan; and this original defect has increased with

[1] Members of Lord North's administration.

ill success. Perplexed and confounded with the mazes and dangers into which they have run, like children they rather turn away from what affrights them than endeavour to prevent it. They ward off the present evil that presses on them, but leave the morrow to provide for itself; they may truly be said, according to the Latin phrase, *in diem vivere*. Their plan of operations (for system they have none) changes with every new occurrence; with every various accident, every various passion takes its turn to rule them; regarding only the immediate object before them, they magnify its importance; they are now confident of success, now plunged into despair. The idol they erected yesterday is cast down to-day, and perhaps will be enshrined again to-morrow. In prosperity they are proud, contemptuous, and overbearing; in adversity supple, mean, and abject. At the commencement of the disputes with America, they treated the refractory colonists as a despicable gang of ruffians; but the moment a league was formed with France, they prostrated themselves at the feet of those rebels they had spurned, and offered them much more than ever had been demanded. This panic was soon dissipated by a gleam of success; the ministers resumed confidence, and one of them was imprudent enough to hint, even in the House of Commons, that unconditional submission was alone to be listened to;

> "Quidlibet impotens
> Sperare, fortunâque dulci
> Ebrius."[1]

[1] Horat. Car. lib. i. 37.

Nay, only last winter, flushed with the successes of Lord Cornwallis, they were already, in imagination, masters of all the Southern provinces; and masters so absolute, that they thought it time to send out again Lord Dunmore to chastise, not to govern Virginia.

The petitions and remonstrances I mentioned in my last go on very languidly; the nation seems fallen into a deep sleep. There are calamities, I fear, enough in store to awaken them; God forbid that it be then too late! The first business the Parliament is to be engaged on, when it meets again, is an inquiry into Lord Sandwich's conduct.[1] The cause, however, is already prejudged; for Lord North has declared that this inquiry will prove his colleague to be honest, able, and vigilant. William Pitt, the late Lord Chatham's son, of whom I believe I talked with you, has made a great figure this session in Parliament; he has spoken only twice, but both his speeches have gained him uncommon approbation. Applause was echoed from one side of the House to the other; and Fox, in an exaggerated strain of panegyric, said he could no longer lament the loss of Lord Chatham, for he was again living in his son, with all his virtues and all his talents. He studies for the bar; and, to whatever he applies himself, whether to law or politics, he is likely soon to take precedence of all our orators. He possesses those talents which are said to have been peculiar to his father — warmth of utterance, command of language, strength and closeness of reasoning, and, above all, an energy and irresistible vigour of eloquence.

[1] First Lord of the Admiralty.

As I could not have published an article about Geneva in *The Annual Register* before next year, I sent the account I had written to the printer of *The Morning Chronicle;* and it has been inserted in two very long articles in that paper of last Tuesday and of this day. The account is exactly the same as when you saw it, except as to corrections of the style, which, after all, I have not had time to make other than indifferent, and except a continuation from the time when that account broke off to the present moment. I will send you both papers with your parcel of books.

I must now leave you, for I have a great deal to say to our dear Catherine.

My dear Sister,

If my ascending the Dent d'Oche had answered no other purpose, I should not regret my excursion, since it serves sometimes to recall me to your memory, and to that of your dear little boy. Pray, when he knows his Uncle by no other description than that of the man who went up the high mountain, do not fail to assure him that I am not very much taller than Roget, lest the gigantic ideas his little imagination may form of me should be sadly disappointed when we are happy enough to meet. I hope he always talks English to you, though all his soliloquies are French.

I was very sorry to hear that you were somewhat uneasy about your future plans, whether to return to London or Geneva: you seem to think that whichever part of the alternative you embrace, it will be decisive where you will spend the remainder of your days. If I thought so too, I should not hesitate to entreat you to return without delay to England. But why not pass one year more at Geneva or at Lausanne (for as affairs are at Geneva, I every day rejoice that you are out of it), and then with Roget's increased stock of health, come and make us all happy here? Nay, suppose you should be obliged to remain two or three years longer abroad, they will seem as nothing when we meet. Life, it must be confessed, is short enough, but at our age two or three years is no very considerable portion of it. Should it happen, which God forbid, that Roget's health should render it unsafe for him to return to England, I hope we shall both learn to endure separation with patience. I will not preach to you that the satisfaction of acting properly in every station of life into which we are thrown, and of bearing with composure every misfortune, is a pleasure to compensate every want, and to remove all the uneasiness of absence. I feel too painfully, by the concern I experience at being so far from a sister I so dearly love, that that doctrine is too sublime for me, and therefore not to be preached by me to others. But yet, my dear Kitty, when we are guided only by the emotions of our hearts, we are very often misled. Great as is the pleasure of being amidst our friends (and how great it is I believe no one knows better than myself), I fear we often magnify it much beyond the truth. Separation gives to what is absent a thousand charms which vanish on a nearer approach. Yes, I really believe that even the charms of my dear father's society, and the pleasure of remarking continually, by a close observance, the uncommon excellence of his heart, may be exaggerated by an imagination always flying back to the paternal house, and hovering over it with habitual fondness. Let us, my dear sister, be cheerful as long as Heaven permits.

You must needs think me a very insipid traveller, for as yet I have not given you an account of any thing that I saw since I left you; but if such accounts will afford you any amusement, you have but to write me word, and we will make together a great many excursions to Paris; but we will not take Roget with us, lest, while we are gazing at its magnificent buildings, its spacious squares and extensive gardens, at the costly grandeur of Versailles, its superb gallery, and its almost animated pictures and statues, he draw us away, and exclaim in the words of our favourite Rousseau, "Prétendues grandeurs! frivoles dédommagemens de la servitude, qui ne vaudront jamais l'auguste liberté!" I know your *penchant* for the fine arts; but to describe all the beautiful masterpieces of the best masters, which I have seen in the collections of the Duke of Orleans and the French King, would be almost an endless, and I fear, after all, a tedious task. The living artists at Paris, in every branch except sculpture and architecture, are, I think, much below mediocrity. These two arts, indeed, are not yet on the decline; architecture, on the contrary, seems better cultivated now than it has ever been. Have you ever heard of Houdon, a famous sculptor at Paris?

he it was who carved the bust of Rousseau, which is now so common at Geneva: he is a man of great merit, I think I may say of great genius. I was particularly struck with two of his designs for sepulchral monuments. In one, Virtue with a serene and cheerful countenance, and Friendship weeping with dishevelled hair and in an agony of grief, are laying the dying man in his tomb: on one side appear Envy and Calumny, hovering aloof, and not daring to approach the grave; and on the other, the Dignities, the Pomps, and Follies of the world dissolving into air. The other is a monument for a Princess of Saxe Gotha: she is represented walking in a kind of chapel; at the end is a recess, with a curtain half lifted up by the image of Death, who has seized upon the princess, and is dragging her with an irresistible arm into his dark abode: the princess seems resigned to her fate, and is turning a farewell look upon her subjects. In both these monuments the thought is noble, but they both leave in the mind a sentiment of despair; and such is the effect of what, at Paris, is called Philosophy: they boast that it has made men wiser; I am sure that it has not made them happier than they were before. I must confess I regret those times when Religion gave awful lessons from the graves of the dead; when she appeared, as on the tomb of Richelieu, mitigating the pangs of death; when the dead were seen rising from their sepulchres, as in one of the master-pieces of Roubillac, and the proud monuments of human grandeur mouldering away at the sound of the last trumpet. But I must take my leave of you;

it is with that regret which I always feel on quitting you.

S. R.

Letter XVI.

Grays Inn, Jan. 24. 1782.

At last, my dear Roget, I have sent your books; Pache set out last Monday.

Has Mr. Berenger heard any thing of De Lolme? his bookseller here has had no news from him since he left Ostend, from which, and I believe some other circumstances, it is supposed that he is in the Bastille; and it is likewise supposed that the crime he is accused of is being the author of the invectives against M. de Vergennes[1], which appeared in the *Courrier de Londres*. It is true he is not the author, but no matter for that. It is the policy of an arbitrary court to make sure of all those whom they suspect; if he is guilty he deserves his fate, if innocent there is no harm done. They will be convinced of their error in some four or five years, and then, with true *politesse, on lui demandera mille excuses*, and set him at liberty. I was very much surprised to hear that such a zealot of liberty had set out on an errand so humiliating and so hopeless, as to sue a minister of France for permission to sell his papers in that kingdom. If it be true that he is in the Bastille, I fear he is there for a long time; for to write against a minister is, in the religion of government, the sin against the Holy Ghost.

[1] Minister of Louis XVI.

You ask what I think of Diderot. I did not suppose you would have thought that question necessary, when you had read the account of my visit. With respect to the atheists of Paris, among honest men there can hardly be two opinions. A man must be grossly stupid who can entertain such pernicious notions on subjects of the highest importance without strictly examining them; and much is he to be pitied if, after examination, he still retains them: but if, without examination of them, and uncertain of their truth, though certain of their fatal consequences, he industriously propagates them among mankind, one loses all compassion for him in abhorrence of his guilt. He is like a man infected with some deadly contagious disease, for whom one's heart bleeds while he submits in secrecy to his fate; but when one sees him running in the midst of a multitude, with the infernal design of communicating the pestilence to his fellow-creatures, indignation and horror take the place of pity. I am not vain enough to pronounce what is the extent of Diderot's and D'Alembert's learning and capacity; but, without an over-fond opinion of myself, I may judge of the subordinate atheists, the mob of the Republic of Letters, the Plebecula who have no opinions but what those their arbitrary tribunes dictate to them; and in these I have generally found the grossest ignorance. The cause of modern atheism, I believe, like that of the atheism of antiquity as Plato represents it, is the most dreadful ignorance, disguised under the name of the sublimest wisdom. You do well to say that Plato does not favour their opinions. I fear these self-erected idols of modern philosophy, had they been born among the philosophical magnates, would have been but outcasts and exiles; for, if you have read Plato lately, you will remember that, among his laws, some were to be enacted for maintaining an uniformity of language in matters of religion in all times and places, in all writings and conversations; others for obliging all men to worship the gods with the same ceremonies, and to prohibit all private sacrifices; others, again, for inflicting the severest punishments on any who should dare maintain that the wicked can be happy, or that the useful can be distinguished from the just. So totally does the authority of the ancients, on which the advocates for unbounded toleration build so much, upon occasion fail them.

You have long since read the account of the taking of St. Eustatius. What infamy! The Governor is too prudent, undoubtedly, ever to return to England; he must either drag on the load of his life in France, in the receipt (for he cannot know the enjoyment) of the wages of his treachery, or be more actively infamous, and take up arms against his country. I am wrong, perhaps, to speak as if his treason were proved, but can it possibly be doubted? How unfortunate we are in our commanders; some cowards, some traitors, others brave, indeed, but the slaves of party, or the more abject slaves of avarice! The Ministers have often availed themselves of some circumstances which seemed for the moment fortunate, to boast that we had Providence on our side.

What will they say now? Never did the hand of Providence appear more conspicuously than at present. We took St. Eustatius like pirates, violating in the persons and property of the prisoners the law of nations; but we did not profit by our guilt. The effects seized were retaken in their passage home, and the island itself is lost in the most disgraceful manner. We encouraged treachery in the rebel Arnold, but all we gained by it was empty promises; the same treachery is retaliated on us, and what we lose by it is the only pledge we had, by which we might have purchased back the friendship of the Dutch.[1] And, indeed, when one looks upon all the dreadful events of the war, and upon all the calamities which this administration has brought upon us, one is tempted to exclaim, "Nunquam atrocioribus cladibus, magisve justis indiciis approbatum est, non esse curæ Deis securitatem nostram, esse ultionem!"[2] Lord Cornwallis and Arnold are both arrived at Plymouth; the latter is said to have brought with him a very great fortune. The Parliament met last Monday, but they have not yet entered on any business of importance.

Admire my self-sufficiency; for I am going to censure a fault in the language of your last letter. You say "depuis *lors*," a phrase which is used only in the territory of Geneva, and which, as you are now in the Canton of Berne, you are not entitled to. The *literati* of Paris are all agreed to

[1] St. Eustatius was taken from the Dutch, February 3d, 1781; and was taken by the French, under the command of Marquis Bouillé, on November 26th, 1781.

[2] Tac. Hist. 1—3.

say "depuis *ce temps*." And how came I to be so learned? By the favour of D'Alembert, who told me that "depuis lors" was one of the Genevanisms which blemished the style of Rousseau. This piece of knowledge is not to be despised, for it is almost all I learned in two visits I made to the reserved D'Alembert. Whatever subject I talked of, he found means to turn the discourse upon what was to be seen at Paris; as if I visited him for the purpose of gaining imperfectly that intelligence which was to be had completely in the *Curiosités de Paris*.

Your most affectionate

Saml. Romilly.

Letter XVII.

My dear Kitty, Gray's Inn, March 1. 1782.

When, after having read your first letter, where you are all joy with the thoughts of soon living with us again, I came to the second, where that scheme is quite abandoned, where you talk of taking a final leave of me, and of teaching your boy the history of our family and of his country, as if we were to be only a tale in his memory, and he to be for ever an alien to his native land, I sincerely lamented the mischief I had undesignedly done; and reproached myself a thousand times with coming like a cruel invader and carrying off the little sum of happiness you had been so long scraping together: but how is it possible, my dear sister, you could find any thing in my letter tend-ing to fix you in so cruel a resolution! My intention, when I wrote, was only to persuade you not to come to a determination at present either way. Not but what I knew how painful it is to remain in suspense; but I strongly suspected, what your last letter has convinced me of, that your seeming resolution had left you in a very undecided and uneasy state, and that your thinking so continually on what was far distant only served to weary and harass you by anticipating again and again the fatigues, and by multiplying tenfold the dangers of the journey. Let me preach to you a philosophy which I have myself often found successful; it is to command one's imagination, and not to suffer it to carry one astray into the midst of tragedies *which are but possible;* for though it is, I think, our duty in all cases to be prepared for the worst, it cannot be necessary that we should afflict ourselves by entering into all the detail of misery, and by dwelling on objects which we see but darkly, and through a medium that always magnifies and distorts them. It becomes us to look forward to futurity, but not to pry into it with too curious an anxiety. Another consolation which my little share of misfortunes in life has taught me, is to trust that every evil will bring with it some cause or means of comfort. The greatest of our joys and afflictions are but in imagination. Learn then, my dear sister, with me to treat those waking visions, which you so forcibly describe to have thrown you into alternate ecstasies of joy and starts of fear, and to have made you pass many uneasy days and sleepless nights, as the vain representation of what never was and never will be. I flatter myself I am not teaching you any ideal philosophy, but what I have myself practised with success.

Thank you, my dear Roget, for giving me so constantly accounts of what passes at Geneva: my paper is too short for me to waste it in compliments; I shall therefore thank you by a like service, and tell you the news we have here.

In my last I think I mentioned a motion which Fox made in the House of Commons, censuring Lord Sandwich. He has since repeated it to the fullest House that has been known for several years, there being 453 Members present. The division was, for the motion 217, against it 236. Lord Sandwich is, nevertheless, still continued in his office. A motion has since been made by General Conway, whose name, I suppose, you are by this time well acquainted with, as he was principally concerned in the repeal of the Stamp Act. His motion was for an address to the King, praying that the impracticable plan of subduing America by force might be abandoned, and that proper means might be taken to effect a reconciliation with the American Colonies. I omit, as unnecessary, the arguments by which it was supported: it will naturally occur to you, that the principal topics of argument were, the distress of this country, the impossibility of succeeding in the conquest of America, the much worse situation we are in now than at the very commencement of the war, &c.

The Ministers opposed the motion with all their strength: they said that to vote such an address would be to apprize the enemy how we intended to act, and to teach them how to counteract our designs; it would be to encourage the Americans by showing our despondency, and instead of forwarding peace would set it at greater distance. The expression of the proposed address was, they said, much too loose and extensive; it was impossible to know how to comply with it. Was it intended to withdraw all the troops from America? The motion might be so understood; and yet nobody had pretended that this would be expedient.

The Ministers disclosed to the House, but in a very unsatisfactory manner, their design for carrying on the war. They said they meant to keep the posts; and when it was asked what they meant by a war of posts, the Secretary at War said they meant to keep the posts they had already, and to take more if they saw occasion. This explanation produced a roar of "Hear, hear!" from the Opposition. Fox said it was evident, from this and many similar expressions dropped inadvertently, that the plan of the war was changed only for the moment, and that the faintest glimmering of success would awaken all the vain projects of the Ministers; that they would indulge new dreams of conquest, that new armies would be marched through the country, and unconditional submission be again the only terms to be listened to. The new Secretary of State for the American department, Welbore Ellis, spoke in the debate, little to the purpose, though in a great many words. One objection he made to the object of the motion was, that it would be to abandon our friends in

America. The state of those friends, Colonel Barré declared, and, as he said, from very good information, to be this: those who were called our friends in the Northern Provinces hardly troubled themselves to know whether we were in existence, and those in the South remembered us only to pour execrations on our heads. The Ministers were asked why, if the war was to be merely defensive in America, had Sir Guy Carleton been appointed to the command in chief? They answered that, unless the troops were recalled, an officer must be sent to take the command, as, otherwise, the chief in command, when Sir Henry Clinton leaves America, would be a foreigner. But the argument which the Court party seemed to rely on most, and which, I presume, was meant to operate by way of threat (though, if the event had been foreseen, it would surely never have been used) was this: the Opposition, they said, to act in a fair and manly manner, ought not to have made such a motion as that before the House, but to have moved at once for a change of ministers; for that was the effect which the motion must indirectly have if it were carried, since no ministers could possibly remain in office, if the Parliament could not trust them with the executive power, but took upon itself to direct it. The House was exceedingly full when I left it, which was about one o'clock in the morning; but several Members went away before the division. The motion was lost by a majority of only a single vote; the numbers being 193 to 194. The House did not rise till three in the morning.

The Minority resolved to try their strength again upon the same question: accordingly, the day before yesterday, General Conway moved the following resolution: "That, after the long and fruitless continuance of the offensive war in America, for the purpose of subduing the revolted Colonies by force, it is evident that that object is impracticable, inasmuch as it takes from our exertions some part of that strength which ought to be employed against our European enemies, and is contrary to his Majesty's inclination, expressed in his speech to both Houses, in which he declared it to be his royal wish to restore peace and tranquillity." I was not in the House, but the arguments used in the debate were much the same as had been employed before. The House did not divide till half past one o'clock, when the motion was carried against the Ministry by a majority of 19; 234 for the motion to 215 against it. This happy event occasioned, the next day, a rise of the stocks of one and a half per cent.

Letter XVIII.

Dear Roget, Gray's Inn, March 8. 1782.

In my last letter I mentioned General Conway's motion: as soon as it had passed the House, a motion was made for putting it into the form of an address, and carrying it up to the Crown. An address was accordingly carried up, to which the King answered, "that the House might be assured that, in pursuance to their desire, he would take such measures as should appear *to him* to be most conducive to the restoration of harmony between Great Britain and the revolted Colonies." The day after the motion passed, there were rejoicings in several places; the bells were rung, and a great many houses were illuminated; and papers were cried about the streets, "Good news for England, Lord North in the dumps, and peace with America." The Ministers affected to take the alarm, and sent advice to the Lord Mayor, that they had notice of intended riots; but every thing was very peaceable, as, I believe, every body expected. The joy of this victory over the Ministers was much damped by their still continuing in office. Lord North, a few days after, when pressed with his own declaration, did not scruple to say he would stay in his place till the House voted that he should be removed; which may be fairly interpreted thus, that as his administration had lasted in calamity to his country, so it should end in utter disgrace to himself. Since the success of his last motion, General Conway moved the House to come to a resolution, "That whoever should be hereafter concerned in advising, or by any means attempting, the further prosecution of offensive war on the Continent of North America, for the purpose of reducing the revolted Colonies to obedience by force, were declared and should be considered as enemies to their King and country." The Ministry said the motion was useless; that when the House voted the address, that implied a censure upon those who should dare to disobey it: but the Ministry, probably feeling their weakness, would not divide the House upon the motion, and it passed. We have since received news of the loss of Minorca and of St. Christopher's in the West Indies. Some very important motion is to come on to-day in the House of Commons; it is said to be for a total change of Ministers: in my next I will tell you the fate of it.

I forgot to mention before, that the Attorney-General has brought in a Bill preparatory to a peace with America. Charles Fox said, a few days ago, in the House, that he knew peace with America might be had immediately; that there were persons in Europe empowered by the Congress to treat for peace; and that he himself, as much as he detested the Ministry, would, if they would give him authority, negotiate with those men. Lord North answered, that services so offered he disdained.

I am much surprised you thought any thing in my letter worth communicating to M. de Végobre. On the subject of the *Cross Elections* he seems to think that political energy is not essentially necessary in your commonwealth [Geneva], except in such a crisis as the present; and that such a crisis is not likely soon to recur. He may be assured it never will recur if the citizens are once unmanned and enervated. Perhaps I am mistaken; but it is my opinion that political indifference must at all times be mortal to a small republic. If the *cross elections* do not produce the effect which I think most natural, that of stifling all zeal for the people, they will be still more dangerous to the peace of the community. A demagogue in office is infinitely less dangerous than when excluded and persecuted into importance. In office, the demagogue is fettered by the known extent of his power, his views are restrained and his proposals overruled by his colleagues; but when excluded and kept in a private condition, he stands alone; his power being illegal knows no limits, and, as he cannot take a single step without an infringement of the constitution, as, to be active at all, he must come under the animadversion of the law, he little heeds how desperate may be his measures. Suppose him to be actuated by the ambition of acquiring honours; which is wisest, to cut off the possibility of his gratifying that ambition without the subversion of the state, or to lure his attention from more dangerous objects by leaving certain places in view, which, when he attains them, disarm him of half his power? When Wilkes was forced into popularity by expulsions and exclusions from Parliament, his power over the populace was little less absolute than that of eastern despots; they yoked themselves like slaves to his coach; they rescued him out of the hands of the ministers of justice; and, when afterwards he voluntarily surrendered himself up, they besieged his prison, and shed their blood in his cause: but the moment he was admitted into the House of Commons, his power fell to be that of a single vote in a small minority; for none of the talents which make a demagogue important with the multitude have much influence in a senate. What avails it ten members of a council that each is a Demosthenes in eloquence, in zeal, and in patriotism, if they have to oppose the silent votes of eleven *pedestrian*[1] senators?

Adieu. Yours most affectionately,

S. R.

Letter XIX.

Dear Roget, Gray's Inn, March 24. 1782.

Though I have received your and my dear Kitty's letter of the 2d of this month, I must postpone answering it, till I have given you some account of the fortunate event which has taken place here since the date of my last letter.

You may remember I then talked of a motion that was to be made that day in the House of Commons, and from which much was expected. The motion was for a removal of the whole administration: it was lost by 226 votes against 216. The Friday following, another motion was made, different in form, but the same in substance; that, too, was lost by 236 against 227. How the Ministers began already to tremble for their places you may judge by the topics on which they were defended in the debate; the principal of which were, that the Ministers were not the authors of the American war, which, it was admitted, was the source of all our calamities: that that war was the unavoidable consequence of measures, adopted before any of the present Ministers came into office, particularly the Stamp Duty and the Declaratory Act: that to enforce our right of taxation over the Americans

[1] Roman senators who voted but did not speak were called *Pedarii*, from their expressing no opinion but with their feet.

was not a project of the Ministers, but of the whole nation, expressed by their representative, the House of Commons: that if the present ministry were now to be removed, they must be succeeded by men who entertained the most dangerous and unconstitutional principles of government, and who had pledged themselves to the nation to reduce those principles into practice (for Charles Fox had protested a few days before, that, if ever he came into office, he would act upon the same principles which he had always professed in opposition, and that he should hold any man who did otherwise in the most sovereign contempt and abhorrence): that we should soon see half the boroughs in the kingdom stripped of their rights of election, Parliaments made triennial or even annual, and the populace assembled to give their advice in matters of legislation and government: that unanimity was now more than ever requisite: that it was unanimity to which we owed all our success in the last war: that a change of ministers ought to be effected, not by turning out one party and bringing in another, which was to aggravate, not to heal our divisions; but by a coalition of all parties, who, uniting cordially in the common cause, might destroy the very name of opposition.

To all this it was answered, that the question was not now who were the authors of the war, but whether, after that series of disasters and disgraces which had overwhelmed us under the present administration, it was proper to intrust them any longer with the conduct of our affairs: that the sanction of Parliament, under which the Ministers sought to shield themselves, had been obtained by deceit and misrepresentation of our having innumerable friends in America, of all the powers of Europe being resolved to remain at peace, of the certainty of our being always able to command a fleet equal to that of the House of Bourbon: that, whatever the political principles of a new ministry, no innovation could be established till after it had received, in the constitutional form, the assent of the King and both Houses of Parliament: that unanimity was desirable, but not an unanimity obstinately to pursue impracticable schemes of ambition, and complete that ruin which was so far advanced: that the unanimity of the last war was produced by no coalition, but by discarding an obnoxious administration and forming a new one agreeably to the wishes of the people: that a coalition with the men now in office was impossible, for what the nation required was, not a change of men, but of system; and that the government should no longer be founded on corruption, but on the affections and confidence of the people.

Upon this motion being lost, notice was given that another motion to the same effect would be made upon the Wednesday following. On that day, accordingly, the House met; but, just as the motion was about to be made, Lord North rose and informed the House that the business they were going to proceed upon was quite unnecessary, as the King had come to a resolution to change all his ministers. He, therefore, moved that the House might be adjourned to Monday (to-morrow), in order that the new ministry might be properly arranged. We are all very impatient to know who will compose this new administration: I will send you a list of them if it be settled before I close this letter, for it is greatly apprehended that the House will be obliged to adjourn again to-morrow.

I am not surprised that you so much admire Burke's speech; but, though it is somewhat cruel to tell you so, it is far inferior to some of his later compositions, particularly to a speech made at Bristol at the last election, in justification of his own conduct, which is perhaps the first piece of oratory in our language. The passages which you pointed out are those which I the most admire, particularly that of General Conway's quitting the House of Commons after the repeal of the Stamp Act. Certainly, never had any writer a more luxuriant imagination than Burke; he is more a poet than an orator; but do not you think that he indulges that poetical imagination to a fault? When he has once hold of a beautiful image, he forgets that its only use is to illustrate; the ornament becomes with him the subject, and he employs many phrases to decorate and enrich the figure, while the matter of his speech is quite neglected. I think I could point out several instances of this in the speech I sent you[1] if I had it before me. One I recollect in the character of Lord Chatham's second administration, which he calls a motley composition, a piece of joining work, a tesselated pavement, making several other allusions of the same kind; and, in the very first words of his speech, where an orator ought surely to be very

[1] Burke's Speech on American Taxation, April 19. 1774.

temperate in the use of figures, having, in describing the uniformity of the arguments upon the American question, called it a circle, he pursues the metaphor, and says, "we have been lashed round it till our heads are giddy and our stomachs nauseate." The imagination of Burke properly restrained, and united to the force and irresistible reasoning of Fox, would form a perfect orator as to composition; for in delivery they are both defective. The account of the European settlements was written when Burke was a very young man; though it certainly bears no marks of being a juvenile performance. However, I should suppose he is much less to be relied on than Robertson, who everywhere cites his authorities. You certainly could not read, without being much struck with, *A Description of the Feast of the Dead* [1], extracted from Lafitau. When I read it, it recalled to my mind a passage of one of Saurin's sermons, where, upon occasion of the title of a book, *Rome Souterraine*, he carries his hearers into the subterranean world, the regions of the dead as they lie scattered there in all the various stages of corruption. Do you know Lafitau's book? I should be curious to see it from Burke's commendation of it.

You ask whether I do not think there may be circumstances, in which an Englishman should begin his political career by a solemn engagement never to accept of any place. I think there hardly can be any circumstances in which such an engagement would not, in a man of great abilities, be culpable. In one of an inferior capacity it is

[1] Burke's *Account of the European Settlements in America*, vol. i. p. 225.

indifferent whether he make such a declaration or not; for, though his integrity admit not of the remotest suspicion, his opinions will have very little weight. We have an instance of this in Sawbridge, who has done exactly what you mention, solemnly professed that he will never come into office; but who seldom speaks in the House, and never commands attention. When a man is endowed with very distinguished talents, there can be no question that he owes the utmost exertion of them to his country; and you certainly know too much of our politics to think that he can render his country the hundredth part of that service in opposition that he can in administration. In politics, above all things, I think it the highest imprudence to bind one's self down to any determinate rule of action, except that supreme rule of conforming one's self in all things to the dictates of virtue and to the public good. Imagine a Chatham having, in the days of his country's prosperity, bound himself by such a vow as you allude to. Suppose, after the lapse of some years, his country brought to the verge of ruin; the ministers driven from the helm by public indignation; and every honest man deterred, by the dangers to be encountered, from venturing to take their place. What is he to do, who by the suicide of his incomparable talents has made himself useless to his country? A second Jephthah, he would have to choose between perjury and parricide. I very much doubt such an engagement having the good effects you seem to expect from it. To men of honest minds, who cannot easily bring themselves to think that others have no nobler motives for their public actions than their private interest, it would be superfluous; and the envious and suspicious would not be debarred every means of misconstruction, even by such an engagement. It would still remain for them to doubt its sincerity, however solemn it was; or to allege, as you have heard it alleged at Geneva, that, the ambition of riches and titles removed, there still remained the more captivating ambition of fame and popularity.

26th March.—Yesterday morning nothing was known of the new ministry. The Parliament, however, met, and it is said that an announcement was there made of all the members of the new administration; but no business was done, for I was there at four o'clock, and both Houses were adjourned.[1]

I am, dear Roget, &c. &c.

SAML. ROMILLY.

LETTER XX.

Gray's Inn, April 12. 1782.

The news of the change of ministry will, I hope, my dear Roget, have revived your spirits, and disposed you not to think any longer that we can expect a peace but from the generosity of our enemies. Not that I am yet very confident in my

1 On the 25th of March, 1782, Lord North's administration was replaced by that of Lord Rockingham, in which Lord Shelburne and Charles Fox were the secretaries. On the 1st of July Lord Rockingham died, and a few days after Fox resigned his office. Lord Shelburne then became prime minister, Lord Grantham and T. Townshend secretaries, and William Pitt chancellor of the exchequer. This ministry was succeeded early in 1783 by the coalition ministry, in which Lord North and Charles Fox were the two secretaries.

expectations; one may almost doubt whether things have not gone too far to be retrieved, even by such superior talents as are found united in the new administration.

Lord North has had two places, which he held only during pleasure, settled on him for life; so that you may judge he is not very much chagrined at being displaced. He attends regularly in the House of Commons as a private member of Parliament. In private company the other day he said, that the Opposition, who had always complained of his publishing lying Gazettes, were no sooner in office than they set off with a Gazette more full of lies than any of his had been, for it contained a string of paragraphs, each beginning, "His Majesty has been pleased to appoint," &c., when it is certain that the King was not pleased at any one of those appointments. It would amuse you to see how most of the pensioned newspapers have changed their style; they now pay assiduous court, with compliments and panegyrics, to the men whom, a few weeks ago, they constantly persecuted with libels and lampoons. We hear of nothing but the public savings they are to make, of the peace we are to have with America, and of the peace with Holland.

It is generally imagined that the new ministry will meet with no opposition of any kind in Parliament. Out of it, indeed, there is an impotent attempt to oppose them. Lord George Gordon is endeavouring again to poison the minds of the public by dispersing handbills, in which he has not unsuccessfully imitated the style of the Puritans of the last century. He inveighs against the new ministers; says that they are no better than their predecessors; that they are despised by the public; that Fox is a Papist; that the present disturbances in Ireland are to be imputed to the toleration of Catholics; and laments that no person moved to amend the resolution proposed to the House, "that the Ministers had lost the confidence of the people," by adding, "and the Opposition have not found it."

Are you not very curious to know what will be the first measures of the new administration? Is it not too much to expect they should perform literally all they promised when in opposition? Will Fox, agreeably to his promise, impeach Lord Sandwich, even though he may now find affairs of more pressing importance on his hands; or is not this another instance of the imprudence of not leaving one's future political conduct free? The Ministers seem likely, at the very commencement of their administration, to have great difficulties to encounter in the affairs of Ireland. You know the Irish have long talked of throwing off the supremacy of Great Britain. A motion for that purpose has been made this Session in the Irish Parliament, but lost by a very great majority, since which the different associations in Ireland have come to resolutions to assert their independence. This has been followed by tumults at Dublin; Lord Carlisle, the Lord Lieutenant, has not dared to stir out of his castle, and Eden, his Secretary, was near receiving personal violence from the populace as he was setting off for England. The object of his journey was to bring Lord Carlisle's resignation of his vice-royalty, and to represent to the Ministers the state of affairs in Ireland; but, on his arrival here, he found the ministry changed, Lord Carlisle deprived of the honorary office of Lord Lieutenant of the East Riding of the county of York (which was now restored to the Marquis of Carmarthen, from whom it had been taken two years ago, because that nobleman presumed to vote with the Opposition), and deprived of the vice-royalty of Ireland, which was now conferred on the Duke of Portland. Piqued at this affront, as he considered it, to Lord Carlisle, he refused to give the Secretaries of State any information, but told them he should, on the first day of the Commons meeting (for they were then adjourned), make a motion relative to the affairs of Ireland. Accordingly, last Monday, he moved to repeal a clause in an Act of George I., which declares the supremacy of the British over the Irish legislature. The Ministers, particularly Fox, complained loudly of the very uncandid manner in which Eden had behaved. They said that, for themselves, having no information of the state of affairs in Ireland, or of that people's demands, they could not judge how far the measure proposed was proper, but that it seemed, like all the measures of the late ministers, designed to palliate, not eradicate the evil; that the present ministers intended to make such a settlement of the affairs of Ireland as should be agreeable to both countries, and remove all fears and jealousies for the future. Eden was desired by a number of members to withdraw his motion;

for a long time he refused; General Conway talked of moving a vote of censure on him; at last he complied with the wishes of the House. Fox, in the course of his speech, said that, if the motion were persisted in, he should be obliged to move for the order of the day, though he should be sorry to do it, for then the House must adjourn immediately; and he wished that, on the very first day of their meeting under the new administration, something might be done towards that reformation which they had promised. Accordingly, after this business was over, a motion was made for leave to bring in a Bill to exclude all persons concerned in collecting the customs or excise from giving their votes at elections. In another part of his speech Fox said, that since he and his colleagues had come into office, they had found many more instances of the shameful neglect and mismanagement of the late ministers even than they had suspected; such instances of mismanagement as would render public inquiries on the subject necessary. So much for politics.

Yours affectionately,

S. R.

Letter XXI.

Gray's Inn, May 20. 1782.

I always write to you, my dear Roget, on the supposition that you take as much interest as ever in English politics; and certainly, if you were at all changed in that respect, these letters must be very dry and unentertaining; but I cannot suppose you are; and the present situation of our affairs should rather increase than abate your curiosity.

I mentioned to you in my last letter the object and the fate of Mr. William Pitt's motion[1]; it remains to give you some account of his speech, and of the arguments used in opposition to the measure. The account you have had in the *Courrier de l'Europe* has, I suppose, been very indifferent; as the Parliamentary intelligence of that paper is borrowed from the English newspapers, and in them there have been but very imperfect accounts of that debate, for the fame of Mr. Pitt's eloquence had drawn such a crowd down to the House that many of the news-writers could not get in. I was more fortunate.

Mr. Pitt began by establishing as propositions which could not be controverted, first, that every free state, to maintain its liberty and the vigour of its constitution, must be frequently brought back to its original principles; and next, that the English constitution has departed widely from the principles on which it was originally founded, inasmuch as the House of Commons, which ought to be the representative of the people of Great Britain, was become a partial representation, having no connexion with the people at large, and from which the sense of the nation could not be collected. He then went on to this effect: — "That this is so cannot be disputed; we all know it by reason, we all know it much more feelingly by fatal experience; we have all been the melancholy witnesses of a war carried on obstinately and ruin-

[1] In favour of parliamentary reform.

ously against the sense of the nation, but with the approbation and support of Parliament. We have seen ministers, obnoxious and hateful to the nation, retained in their places by Parliament, in the nation's despite; and plans of economy, brought forward in consequence of the people's demands, and supported by their earnest petitions, rejected with scorn by Parliament. We all know that many of the constituents who send members to this House are not men zealous for the honour and happiness of their country, but venal electors, who carry their votes — the noblest privilege of Englishmen — to market, like some vile and contemptible commodity; not populous and commercial towns, but miserable boroughs, the drains of all that ill-got wealth which from the East pours in upon us like a deluge. After having seen all this, all these fatal symptoms of the approaching ruin of a state, can it be doubted that the original principles of this constitution are lost? Nay, it is past all doubt; our shame and our misfortunes cannot be dissembled. This House is not the representative of the people of Great Britain; it is the representative of nominal boroughs, of ruined and exterminated towns, of noble families, of wealthy individuals, of foreign potentates; and this is surely the most to be-dreaded of all the misfortunes that can befall a nation, for there can be no stronger symptom of the approaching dissolution of a state than that foreigners have gained an interest and an ascendant in the national council. Our laws have, with a jealous care, provided that no foreigner shall give a single vote for a representative in Parliament; and yet we now see foreign princes, not giving votes, but purchasing seats in this House, and sending thier agents to sit with us as representatives of the nation. No man can doubt what I allude to. We have sitting among us the members of the Rajah of Tanjore, and the Nabob of Arcot, the representatives of petty Eastern despots; and this is a thing notorious, publicly talked of, and heard with indifference; our shame stalks abroad in the open face of day, it is become too common even to excite surprise. We treat it as a matter of small importance that some of the electors of Great Britain have added treason to their corruption, and have traitorously sold their votes to foreign powers; that some of the members of our senate are at the command of a distant tyrant; that our senators are no longer the representatives of British virtue, but of the vices and pollutions of the East." He then strongly recommended a reform of the representation, as the only effectual means to restrain the influence of the Crown, which had lately manifested itself with such dreadful symptoms, and which had brought the nation to the verge of ruin.

The speakers against the motion insisted on the danger of innovation in a constitution, which had ever been the boast of this country, and the admiration and envy of all others. They urged that, in matters of government, visionary projects could not be put to trial innocently; for a failure of success might involve a whole nation in anarchy and confusion: that to vote for the motion was, in effect, to open a wide field for innovation of every kind; it was no less than, by destroying the old constitution, to dissolve all the bands of government, to reduce men to the primeval state of nature, and to prompt every individual to propose such a form of government as the wildness of a luxuriant imagination, or the frenzy of ignorant enthusiasm, might suggest: that though the motion did not directly propose a general representation of the people, yet it must necessarily hold out that idea to the public; it would raise among them mighty expectations, which must end in disappointment and apparent deceit, because a general representation is a thing absolutely impracticable: that nothing could be more dangerous than to infuse into the people's minds vast expectations of franchises and privileges, which, by frequent and habitual reflection, they would come to consider as their undoubted rights, and as such would think themselves justified to assert and contend for: that this inconvenience would arise from the mode in which the measure was proposed,—the motion did not offer any specific plan, which might be canvassed and duly considered, and passed or rejected according to its merits or defects; but generally it pledged the House to do something upon the subject without ascertaining what, thus leaving it to the people to imagine, as they should please, what it was the House was bound to do, and then to accuse it of deceit if the new-modelled representation did not come up to the wild expectations of every hardy reformer: that no time could be more improper for such a motion than the present, at a moment the most perilous this country had ever known; when we were surrounded by enemies, when the greatest exertions were necessary, and when as (Mr. Fox had lately declared) ten times the abilities of the Ministers would not be more than was requisite for the salvation of the country. At such a time, instead of fixing all our attention on our own defence, and on the annoyance of the enemy, the bands of government are to be dissolved, a new constitution is to be formed, visionary schemes of perfection are to be debated. Will the measure proposed help, in any degree, to extricate us from our difficulties? Will it strengthen the hands of the Ministers? Will it weaken our enemies? Will it give us allies? Will it supply our navy with one ship, or our army with a single man? If not, let us save the country from the dangers which threaten it on every side, and then aim at its political perfection. But it is said that a more equal representation is the only effectual remedy that can be found against the influence of the Crown, and that it is to that influence over Parliament that we owe all our present calamities. If this be so, why did that influence never appear with such dreadful effects before? Is the representation different? Is it more unequal than it was? Nay, it never has been altered from the time of Charles II. It was what it is now, during all the illustrious reign of King William, at the time of our immortal victories under Queen Anne, during our unrivalled greatness in the last war. Where has this baneful influence lurked during all this long period? Either an unequal representation is not the cause of influence in the Crown, or that influence cannot be very fatal to the strength, the happiness, or the glory of a nation, which, under its shadow, can flourish at home, gain victories abroad, and rise to be an object of universal terror and envy.—As I suppose the answers to all these arguments will present themselves directly to your mind, I shall not dwell any longer on the subject than to say that Charles Fox supported the motion with all his force.

I turn abruptly from one subject to another; but you do not, I hope, expect method in my letters.

The more I reflect on the reasoning of the atheists of France, the more I wonder at their absurdity. I cannot forgive them that, not content with starting doubts, they are for utterly destroying every thing that falls not under the notice of the senses, which they preposterously regard as unerring nay, as the only guides to truth. Wholly absorbed themselves in matter, they will allow nothing else to have existence. Do you not think that the absurdity of their reasonings on this subject might be put in a very strong light by the fable of some imaginary island, not unlike those one meets with in the *Travels of Gulliver?* An island, suppose, inhabited by none but blind men, who should have a traditionary religion which taught them to believe, that, if they observed all their natural duties to God, themselves, and their fellow-creatures, they should be rewarded, at some future time, with the gift of a fifth sense; a sense which would open to them enjoyments which, in their present imperfect state, they had not capacities to conceive; a sense by which they would, as it were, feel things at a prodigious distance, which would enable the soul to expatiate, as it were, apart from the body, to soar into vast regions of space above their heads, and to contemplate thousands of celestial luminaries which were placed there; in a word, which would make them infinitely happier than they then were, though it was impossible to give them any clear notion of that happiness. With this tradition, and this prospect before them of unknown joys, they may be supposed to have long lived happy and virtuous, till there arose among them a sect of philosophers, who captiously scrutinized these religious doctrines, and ridiculed the believers of them, who demanded proof that these pretended future blessings were not imaginary. Prove, said they, that the soul, which is clearly inseparable from the body, and reaches no farther than the extension of the body, can otherwise than by the hearing know what is passing at a distance from it. How shake off this material frame, and wander into superior regions? If not, how feel at a distance? Are men to be equipped with organs of feeling that shall reach miles? Must not they obstruct one another? &c. &c. One might thus, to prove the impossibility of there being a fifth sense, employ similar arguments to those which our dogmatizing philosophers use to prove the impossibility of the soul's existing apart from the body, or rather to prove the non-existence of spirit, because it falls not under the notice of the senses. But you laugh, perhaps, at this ridiculous conceit of mine.

Letter XXII.

Gray's Inn, June 11. 1782.

Your last letter, my dear Roget, put me a little out of humour with you, not because it followed so quickly upon its predecessor, but because it began with an apology for such diligence, as if I did not always, when I had read one of your letters, begin to be impatient for another, and count the days until it should arrive.

You have heard, before this time, all the particulars of Rodney's victory over De Grasse, and you perceive undoubtedly the very great advantages resulting from it; that, besides depriving the enemy of eight line-of-battle ships, it has frustrated all their designs upon Jamaica, and will probably enable us to recover many of our islands. The thanks of both Houses of Parliament have been voted to Rodney; they have likewise been voted to the other admirals and captains who were in the engagement, and to every common seaman on board the fleet. A monument, too, is to be erected in Westminster Abbey to Lord Robert Manners, and two other officers who were killed in the action. Rodney has, besides, been made an English Peer, and Admiral Hood, who commanded under him, a Peer of Ireland. Rodney, however, was recalled, and Admiral Piggot sent to supersede him before the news of the late victory arrived here; and the Ministers have not since sent to countermand Rodney's recall. In all this they have, in my opinion, done exceedingly right; they did well to recall him; and to have afterwards countermanded his recall must have made them appear ridiculous and contemptible, as if they were wholly uncertain and undecided in their measures. However, this step of recalling Rodney has displeased many people, and raised something like an opposition to the Ministry. You have seen an account of the debates upon this subject, I suppose, in the newspapers. A motion of censure was offered to the House, but not made, and the speakers against the Ministry were very few. Governor Johnstone was the most violent. You recollect him, I suppose; he went out as one of the Commissioners to America. In the character of a warm friend of Rodney, he has delivered two Philippics against the Ministry, in which he styles the recall of Rodney a disgrace, and the moving of thanks to him by Fox an insult; and, because Fox and Burke had said that, though they thought Rodney deserved great thanks and rewards from his grateful country, yet they could not change their opinion of what had happened at St. Eustatius from anything he had done since; that they thought, however, that the nation ought entirely to forget the transaction at St. Eustatius, and drop all inquiries into it; all the errors of Rodney were hidden under the trophies he had won from France. But this, Governor Johnstone said, he would never agree to; he defied the Ministers to prosecute the inquiry which was afoot; he would agree to no compromise; his gallant friend would never consent to be dressed up with honours and titles, while the world was made to believe that he was a plunderer and a corsair. Don't you think it would have been a more friendly part to have left it to Rodney to determine about this matter for himself; especially as the Admiral seems to be so little anxious to have the inquiry prosecuted, that, this very session, he voted in person against its being gone into by the House? Lord North made a kind of speech which is very usual with him; uncertain, undecided; wishing, but not daring to join in opposition; saying that he should vote against the motion, but exhausting his invention to find arguments in its support; and saying he was sure such a motion would have been made against him, had such a measure as the recall of Rodney been adopted in his administration. Fox answered with a degree of warmth and indignation which a cooler politician than myself would blame; he bade Lord North speak his sentiments boldly, and not, with an affectation of candour and delicacy, vote against a motion which he sought obliquely to recommend to the House. Fox seemed to despise the man, and to scorn his assistance, and indeed,

> " Non tali auxilio, nec defensoribus istis
> Tempus eget." [1]

But if it is impolitic to provoke enemies by such warm language, it is surely much more so to irritate them by the severity of sarcasm. When Governor Johnstone complained that Fox was an improper person to move the thanks of the House to Rodney, Fox said that he was actuated only by zeal for the public, and promised to move the thanks of the House even to Governor Johnstone,

[1] Virgil. Æn. ii. 521, 522.

if ever he should render any service to his country. And again, when Johnstone, giving an account of his being himself employed by the late ministry, said that he was applied to to command an expedition to South America to foment a rebellion that was said to have broken out there, but that at first he refused it, as not thinking himself equal to such an expedition, Fox observed that he was much too modest when he supposed himself not qualified to excite seditions and rebellions in the dominions of any prince upon the earth. Are not these the "facetiæ asperæ, quæ acrem sui memoriam relinquunt?"[1]

By Rodney's being created a Peer, his seat in Parliament is become vacant. Hood has been proposed to succeed him; but the Westminster committee have named another candidate. This opposition to Hood is said to be ungenerous and ungrateful; but why, is more than I can tell, unless a seat in Parliament is to be considered merely as a reward, a titular dignity; or unless it be proved that the same qualities are requisite to make a good senator as to constitute a brave admiral. What man, who was engaged in a lawsuit, would, out of gratitude to Hood, take him for his advocate? and yet that would be as reasonable as making him a member of Parliament, only because he fights well; besides that it is impossible he should do his duty as a member of Parliament, without giving up that station in which he is so much better calculated to serve his country.

No material change has yet been made in our

[1] Tac. Ann. xv. 68.

constitution. Sawbridge has made his motion for shortening the duration of Parliament, but it was lost by a great majority. If the Ministry are sincere in their desire to bring about the great changes that have been talked of, they must dissolve the Parliament; and a dissolution is what I fully expect, although it does not seem to be generally thought of. So much for politics, with which I fear I have very much tired you.

What I mentioned that I had written about Geneva has been printed: I will send it to you by the first opportunity, though I should be sorry it were seen at Geneva, for this among other reasons, that it might in some measure (what above all things I wish to avoid) influence the conduct of the citizens; for the opinions of the obscurest individual, when they appear in public, are often mistaken by foreigners for the opinions of a nation.

Pray continue to be very particular about the affairs of Geneva, whose patriots I regard more as my countrymen than all the *literati* in the world. But I must answer my dear sister, so adieu with more than fraternal affection.

S. R.

Letter XXIII.

Gray's Inn, July 16. 1782.

Your letter of the 29th of June left me, my dear Roget, in very anxious suspense about the fate of Geneva. The news I have since heard of the city's opening its gates has relieved my mind from many of the horrors which I began to paint to myself; but I still wait with impatience for the circumstantial account of this event, which I hope you have sent me, before I determine with myself whether to rejoice even at the restoration of peace, and the sparing of many precious lives.

The news I have to send you from hence is not of a nature to afford you any consolation for the misfortunes of Geneva. The fair prospect which the change of the ministry opened to us is at present very much overcast. No doubt, you have heard of the death of the Marquis of Rockingham, and of the unhappy division among our Ministers which followed that event. Fox, Burke, Lord John Cavendish, and Lee the Solicitor-General, have all resigned; and Keppel, it is expected, will very shortly follow their example. On the first day of the Parliament's meeting after this political schism, the expectation that Fox would explain the motives of the step he had taken drew an uncommon crowd to the House of Commons. I was fortunate enough to be carried along with those who forced their way into the House, so that you may depend on the account I send you.

The business began by Mr. Coke, a very independent county member, moving a vote of censure against the Ministry for having granted a pension of 3200*l.* a-year to Colonel Barré, which is to take place whenever he shall be out of office; a pension which has been hurried through the House with unusual expedition, that it might be beforehand with the Bill for the Reform of the Civil List Expenditure, because that Bill provides that no pension shall be granted for more than 300*l.* a-year, and that all the pensions in any one year shall not amount to more than 600*l.* per annum. This very culpable measure (for as such I must consider it) was but weakly defended by an exaggerated representation of the great services which Colonel Barré has rendered his country, and by an enumeration of the honourable and lucrative employments of which the persecution of the late ministry deprived him; and it was very soon quite forgotten in the more important discussion which the debate produced. For, when a member of the late administration drew a comparison between them and their successors, each being, as he pretended, alike eager to enrich their friends, and alike disunited in opinion, Fox rose and denied that it was true that he and his friends, when in opposition, had ever blamed any of the late ministers for differing in opinion from their colleagues, but said that they had blamed those who, though divided in opinion and disapproving the political system they saw adopted, were still mean enough to continue in place, and, through the criminal dread of losing the emoluments of office, lent their name and authority to measures which they knew threatened inevitable destruction to their country; that, for himself, he disdained such conduct, and no sooner had he seen the political system of the last ministry likely to be revived by the present, than he had resigned. This called up General Conway to declare that he saw no symptoms of any renewal by the present administration of the ancient system; he said that he understood the principles upon which the present administration had come into place to be these:—1. That the independence of America should be made the basis of a peace. 2. That economy should be observed in every department of the State. 3. That the influence of the Crown should be diminished. 4. That Ireland's dependence on the British Parliament should be preserved inviolate, as it had lately been established. These, he said, he believed to be the political principles of the whole administration; he was sure they were his own; he never would forsake them; and the moment he saw them abandoned by his present colleagues he would stand forth, he pledged himself, as one of the warmest members of opposition. What were Mr. Fox's motives for resigning, General Conway said, he did not know. The opinion he entertained about the necessity of making America independent differed so little from the sentiments of other members of the Council, that to himself it appeared to be only a subtle distinction, merely a shade of difference in opinion.

This declaration led Fox into a general explanation of his conduct in a speech an hour and a half long, delivered with more than his usual eloquence. The sum of what he said is shortly this: that his opinions have been overruled at the Council on several subjects, particularly respecting the independence of America. What the difference exactly consisted in he did not explain, because, he said, that if he were to speak without reserve, it would be said that he had transported to America suspicions to which the Americans had before been strangers, and made them more exacting in their demands than they would otherwise have been. He declared that he should not be surprised to see the war revived in America on its original plan. As to what Conway had laid down as the principles of the administration, they were principles which he had never heard of before, and which, if really adopted by the Ministry, had been adopted since he had retired, and justified his resignation; for they showed that he had much more weight at the Council out of administration than in it. He then mentioned the backwardness of the Ministry to correct and punish the abuses and peculations that have been committed in the East Indies; and said that, finding his opinion always overruled at the Council table, he had formally signified to his colleagues, before the death of Lord Rockingham, that he should resign; a step which he would have taken immediately, had he not feared it might affect the declining health of that nobleman. But when Lord Rockingham died, and Lord Shelburne was made First Lord of the Treasury, he was then confirmed in his resolution, and immediately resigned. Since that promotion, he said, the administration was no longer that which the Parliament and the nation had brought in; that, for himself, he had not the least confidence in the present administration; and that he had, as was his duty, resigned: that he had made a very great sacrifice: that he did not affect such a stoic indifference for what all the rest of the world earnestly aspired to as to pretend that he had, without regret, resigned high distinctions of fortune, power, honour, and glory; but he did not hesitate a moment to give up all these advantages, and, what he prized above them all, near political connection with those he was most united to by blood and affection (meaning the Duke of Richmond, who stays in), rather than submit to the treachery and infamy of continuing in office, and patronizing by his name an administration and its measures which in his conscience he disapproved, and believed dangerous and fatal to the country. He then prophesied that all the real friends of the constitution and of the people would soon be in opposition again, and that Lord Shelburne would be in administration with all the old ministers.

Burke spoke against the appointment of the First Lord of the Treasury. He exclaimed with uncommon warmth (uncommon rage I should rather say), that he had no confidence in the administration, constituted as it now was; that he saw in them, indeed, "*satis eloquentiæ sed sapientiæ parum;*" that in his soul he believed the Government was more safely intrusted to the hands of the late ministry; that the country was sold, betrayed, and ruined; that his own conduct in resigning could not appear interested, for it was certainly most prejudicial to his fortune, most adverse and repugnant to his nature; that his disposition was an attachment to business, a desire to exert his little talents to the utmost for his country, to promote the public good, and assist in the public business; that, by a strange fatality, he had been doomed to pass his days in opposition, and now, after three months spent in a manner congenial to his nature, he found himself condemned to pursue, during the remainder of his life, the same unprofitable course that he had formerly taken.

William Pitt answered Burke and Fox in severe terms; said that their great talents ought to be considered at this time as public property, and that to withhold their assistance from the public at a time when it stood so much in need of them was a species of treachery. To him, he said, the dispute between the Ministers appeared to be only a contest for power.

The new promotions are as follows:—Lord Shelburne, First Lord of the Treasury; William Pitt, Chancellor of the Exchequer; Thomas Townshend, and Lord Grantham, who was lately ambassador at Madrid, Secretaries of State; Sir George Young, Secretary at War.

The Americans have refused to enter into any separate negotiation, so that peace seems much more distant than we hoped. To this bad news must be added the loss of the Bahama Islands. But let us quit this ungrateful subject. Adieu. Love to our dear Kitty.

S. R.

Letter XXIV.

Gray's Inn, July 26. 1782.

I am not to expect, then, my dear Roget, any more letters from you on the melancholy subject of Geneva. The few words which my dear sister inclosed for me in her last letter, too fully confirm all the fatal intelligence we had before received. The warm interest which you know I took in the cause of your fellow-citizens will have enabled you to conceive the concern I feel at the issue of their affairs. I lament it, too, from a more general consideration; for I do not doubt that the conduct of the pretended patriots of Geneva will be remembered hereafter by the advocates for arbitrary power; who, when they find the arguments by which the people's cause is defended unanswerable, betake themselves to an attack upon its defenders, and triumph in showing the insincerity and selfishness of seditious demagogues. Thus are the people alike the victims of the treachery of their pretended friends and of the tyranny of their open enemies. I am less astonished at the want of public virtue and patriotism, which has appeared in the chiefs of the *Representants*, than at their folly and inattention to their private interests. For, admitting that they were careless about the honour and freedom of their country, surely prudential and interested considerations alone might have induced them to risk their lives in defence of their own fortunes, their character and consideration in their country, rather than to preserve, at any rate, a miserable existence, embittered by the reproaches of their own consciences, and the contempt of mankind, —

> "Et propter vitam vivendi perdere causas." [1]

My dear sister gives me room to hope that she will write me a detailed account of this melancholy catastrophe. I am the more desirous of this, as I think of continuing my account of the

[1] Juvenal. Sat viii. 84

affairs of Geneva, not (undoubtedly) with a view to its appearing in any publication, but merely as an exercise and a matter of instruction and improvement to myself.

What do you think of the Abbé St. Pierre's project of perpetual peace, and Rousseau's observations on it?[1] A much stronger objection might, I think, be made to the proposal than either of those writers have foreseen and answered, which is, that the ultimate consequence of instituting, as supreme arbitrator of all the affairs of Europe, a Diet, of which the majority would be the representatives of arbitrary princes, must be the total extirpation of liberty. For the internal political disputes of every country must be submitted to the decision of the Diet, there being no other alternative but an appeal to war; and the project supposes war never to be made but by the whole confederacy. To explain my meaning better — Suppose the project to be adopted, and a general European confederacy to be formed; a dispute arises in England between the Crown and the Commons about the extent of the royal prerogative; and the King and the people are both alike inflexible in their pretensions. The confederates, who are the guarantees of each national constitution, must be recurred to, to decide the contest; and no doubt the weight of royal influence, the necessary ignorance of the judges with respect to our constitution, and the despotic principles of government prevalent in their own states, will render their decision favour-

[1] Entitled, *Jugement sur la Paix perpétuelle,* and published with Rousseau's political works.

able to the King. Nor is it any answer to this objection to say, that the confederates are guarantees of every distinct constitution of government, such as it exists at the time the confederacy was formed; because, in disputes between different members of a government, the question always is, what is the constitution? and every ambitious prince has prudence enough to cover his encroachments, and the stretches of his power, with the name of the exercise of his constitutional prerogative. Besides it may often happen, from a change in the character and manners of a nation, that to maintain its present constitution is to destroy its liberties; witness England at this moment; or granting that the confederacy should violate the first principle on which it was formed, who shall take advantage of the violation and refuse obedience to its decrees? Shall a populace, unused to arms, and ignorant of discipline, array themselves for war against a league of all the powers of Europe? There would be nothing then to restrain the general diet from deciding every contest for the prince, and against his subjects. One victory of this kind would encourage the prince to excite fresh troubles, which must be brought before the same partial tribunal, and the example would soon become general. It is absurd, as Rousseau says, to imagine that, if the project took place, many of the confederate princes would unite their forces for the purpose of making conquests; but it is not absurd to suppose that they would unite their counsels in order to extend their authority over their subjects: and it would be to be dreaded that not only princes, but even aristocratical governments, would join in this cruel policy, by turns assisting each other to become the tyrants of their country. The evil would be without the possibility of a remedy; for what would it avail a country that she had many Brutuses among her sons, if their virtue was overawed and rendered useless by a mighty league of all Europe, firmly resolved "ut e conspectu libertas tolleretur."[1] Whether Europe would not be compensated for the loss of liberty in the very few states that still retain any shadow of it, by having war banished from all its quarters, is a question which I should not hesitate to decide by saying, "Mihi potior visa est periculosa libertas quieto servitio."[2] But it is time to put an end to this long dissertation.

Adieu! believe me, &c.,

SAML. ROMILLY.

LETTER XXV.

Gray's Inn, Oct. 25. 1782.

I was obliged to send my last letter to you, my dear Roget, in so great a hurry, that I had not time to read over what I had written. I hope, however, you were able to make it out. From that time till the present moment I have never had leisure to write to you, and the hour which I now devote to you is stolen from occupations which, compared to any thing that I had less at heart than

[1] Tac. Agric. 24. [2] Sallust. Hist. Fragm. lib. i.

writing to yourself, I should think necessary. All this is not so much to apologize (for apologies to you would be ill placed) as to account for my silence, and to prevent your being uneasy whenever I am thus forced to interrupt our correspondence. Do not imagine, by my seeming to be thus immersed in business, that I am yet called to the bar. I cannot be called before six months; and a just diffidence, or rather knowledge, of myself will make me postpone it for six months longer. Indeed, the nearer I approach the term, which I have formerly so often wished for, the more I dread it. I sometimes lose all courage, and wonder what fond opinion of my talents could ever have induced me to venture on so bold an undertaking; but it too often happens (and I fear that has been my case), that men mistake the desire for the ability of acting some very distinguished part. Of those who may truly say

> "aliquid jam dudum invadere magnum
> Mens agitat mihi; nec placidâ contenta quiete est,"[1]

very many were never designed by nature for heroes. But not to lose all the little time I have upon no better a subject than myself, let me inform you of news in which I presume you must take the deepest interest.

It has been determined, in the Privy Council of Ireland, to recommend the King to offer to the Genevese a permission to establish themselves in Ireland, and to grant them a sum of money for the purpose. The King has agreed to

[1] Virgil. Æn. ix. 186.

give 50,000*l.* It is proposed that the colony shall consist of 1000 persons, who understand the watch manufacture; and they are to have a charter of incorporation, by which they will be enabled to elect their own magistrates, and to regulate entirely their own internal police. The Duke of Leinster, by letter, invites the colony to settle upon his estate in the county of Wexford, in the province of Leinster. He offers to give them, by a pure and perpetual donation, a very large tract of ground which he now lets (though much below its value) for 600*l.* a-year; he engages to procure them places of abode, and particularly offers his own house, Leinster Lodge, a mansion capable of lodging one hundred persons, till they can build houses for themselves. The spot of ground where he proposes that they should build their little city is, he says, in one of the most fertile and temperate parts of Ireland, at the confluence of two rivers, at a convenient vicinity to the sea, and distant about thirty miles from Dublin. All this news you may depend on, for I have seen the order of the Irish Council, and the letters of Lord Temple and the Duke of Leinster. Other noblemen have invited the colony to settle upon their estates, but none offer terms so advantageous and so noble as the Duke of Leinster. You will wonder how I gained all this intelligence, but your astonishment will cease when I inform you that I have had some visits from D'Ivernois. He hinted to me that, besides the watch manufactory, there was some thoughts of instituting a French College at the New Geneva (for so the city is to be called).

It is to resemble the old Geneva in every thing, except in having an upper and a lower town,

> "et parvam Trojam, simulataque magnis
> Pergama, et arentem Xanthi cognomine rivum
> Agnosco, Scææque amplector limina portæ."[1]

You were perfectly right in supposing that no such opinion is to be found in Hume, as M * * * ascribes to the *philosophe Anglais*. That writer does say, it is true, that England has not produced any orator who may be compared with those of antiquity; but far from prophesying that it never will, he writes purposely to exhort his countrymen to the imitation of those great models; and instead of imputing the want of success in oratory of the English to their great sense, he entirely refutes that opinion.

The Essay of Hume, which I suppose is alluded to, is, in my opinion, a very indifferent performance. In examining all the causes of our inferiority in eloquence, the writer passes over in silence that which seems to me to be the most material — I mean the different application which the ancients gave to that science from that which we give it. Our great men are every thing; geometricians, historians, poets, orators, and I know not what. Demosthenes was an orator alone. Till we have seen men of genius shut themselves up for whole months, to study only the force and beauty of their language, transcribing with their own hands eight several times the works of an eloquent writer, and struggling with unremitting efforts to overcome every imperfection in their nature, we cannot

[1] Virgil. Æn. iii. 349.

wonder that we have not a modern Demosthenes. Hume is the more surprised that we have had no orators (though he must or might have heard Lord Chatham, Mr. Pulteney, Lord Hardwicke, Lord Mansfield, and Lord Camden), when we have had such a writer as Lord Bolingbroke. You know Lord Bolingbroke's history: during the greater part of his life he was debarred a seat in Parliament, or, in his own words, he was "stripped of the rights of a British subject, of all except the meanest of them, that of inheriting;" but, if his delivery was equal to his style (and according to Lord Chesterfield it was so), he was, at least, capable of rivalling Cicero. You are unacquainted, I believe, with his writings; let me, therefore, give you a specimen of some of his figures. I have a multitude of them present to my memory. Speaking of the criminal indifference and gaiety of some of his contemporaries, he says, that "*they were men ready to drown the dying groans of their country in peals of unseasonable mirth and laughter;*" of Catherine of Medicis, that "*she first blew up the flames of religious faction, and then endeavoured in vain to extinguish them in a deluge of blood;*" of Philip IV. of Spain, that "*he languished rather than lived from the cradle to the grave.*" To Sir Robert Walpole he speaks of the many crimes which might now be proved against him, of the many more which were ready to *start into light* the moment the power by which he concealed them should determine.

Pray, thank my dear Kitty for her letter; I mean to answer her soon, and am rejoiced to find she continues to draw the beautiful prospects that surround you. To gaze on those sublime views, to be conversing with you and my dear sister, and walking with you and your little boy over your grounds, are the frequent, but, alas! the imaginary occupations of your affectionate brother,

SAML. ROMILLY.

LETTER XXVI.

Gray's Inn, Dec. 10. 1782.

Before I take any notice, my dear Roget, of the contents of your letters of the 13th and 23d of last month, I must hasten to communicate to you the agreeable news I have to tell you. It is much less agreeable, however, than we were flattered with hopes of, a fortnight ago. We have had the greatest expectations of peace: the Parliament, which was to have met the 26th of last month, was adjourned to the 5th of the present: a letter was sent from the Secretary of State to the Governor of the Bank, informing him that a negotiation had been begun, and was very far advanced, and that, before the meeting of Parliament, either peace would be concluded, or all negotiations would be at an end. The dealers in stocks were immediately in an uproar and tumult, which has lasted almost ever since. The stocks rose and fell, one, two, and sometimes three per cent. every day; from 57, the price at which they were when this news arrived, they one day rose to 65. The opening of Parliament, however, has disappointed much of our expectations: how much of them has been fulfilled, I cannot state to you more accurately than by transcribing a part of the King's speech. It shall be only a part; for, whatever other merits it may possess, it has so little of that "imperatoria brevitas" which Tacitus commends, that it fills very nearly two columns in the newspapers.

"Since the close of the last Session, I have employed my whole time in the care and attention which the important and critical conjuncture of public affairs required of me. I have pointed all my views and measures, as well in Europe as in North America, to an entire and cordial reconciliation with the colonies. Finding it indispensable to the attainment of this object, I did not hesitate to go the full length of the powers vested in me, and *offered* to declare them free and independent States, by an article to be inserted in the treaty of peace. *Provisional articles are agreed upon, to take effect whenever terms of peace shall be finally settled with the court of France.* In thus admitting their separation from the crown of these kingdoms, I have sacrificed every consideration of my *own* to the wishes and opinion *of my people.* I make it my humble and earnest prayer to Almighty God, that Great Britain may not feel the evils which might result from so great a dimemberment of the empire, and that America may be free from those calamities which have formerly proved, in the mother country, how *essential monarchy is to the enjoyment of constitutional liberty.* Religion, language, interest, affections may, and I hope will, yet prove a bond of permanent union between the two countries. To this end, neither attention nor disposition shall be wanting on my part. While I have carefully abstained from all offensive operations against America, I have directed my whole force, by land and sea, against the other powers at war, with as much vigour as the situation of that force, at the commencement of the campaign, would permit. I trust that you feel the advantages resulting from the safety of the great branches of our trade. You must have seen, with pride and satisfaction, the gallant defence of the governor and the garrison of Gibraltar; and my fleet, after having effected the object of their destination, offering battle to the combined fleets of France and Spain on their own coasts; those of my kingdom have remained, at the same time, perfectly secure, and your domestic tranquillity uninterrupted. This respectable state, under the blessing of God, I attribute to the *entire confidence which subsists between me and my people*, and to the readiness which has been shown by my subjects to stand forth in the general defence. Having manifested to the whole world, by the most lasting examples, the signal spirit and bravery of my people, I conceived it a moment not unbecoming my dignity, and thought it a regard due to the lives and fortunes of such brave and gallant subjects, to show myself ready, on my part, to embrace fair and honourable terms of accommodation with all the powers at war. *I have the satisfaction to acquaint you that negotiations to this effect are considerably advanced.* * * * *I have every reason to hope and believe that I shall have it in my power, in a very* *short time, to acquaint you that they have ended in terms of pacification,* which I trust you will see just cause to approve. I rely, however, with perfect confidence, on the wisdom of my Parliament, and the spirit of my people, that, if any unforeseen change in the belligerent powers should frustrate my confident expectations, they will approve of the preparations I have thought it advisable to make, and be ready to second my most vigorous efforts in the further prosecution of war. * * * I must recommend to you an immediate attention, above all things, to the state of the public debt. Notwithstanding the great increase of it during the war, it is to be hoped that such regulations may still be established, such savings made, and future loans so conducted, as to *promote* the means of its *gradual* redemption, by a fixed course of payment."

These are the most important passages in the speech ; but it wanders over a multitude of subjects, calling the attention of the Parliament to the affairs of India, the scarcity of corn, a revision of our commercial system, the late increase of robberies, the Mint, the King's revenue, particularly the royal forests, the money voted for American sufferers, &c. The King assures the Parliament, too, that he has carried into strict execution the Act passed in the last session for making reductions in the civil list expenses.

There was not, in either house, any opposition to the address. In the House of Lords, Lord Shelburne explained the offer of declaring America independent, not to be a present and irrevocable recognition of her independence, but a mere offer, which, if peace did not follow, was to be entirely at an end. Fox, in the other house, understood it to be a full acknowledgment of the independence of America; supposed the word "offer" to be a mere inaccuracy of expression; and, upon this ground only, approved the measure. But his speech is worth giving you a fuller account of.

It appeared, from some parts of the speeches of the mover and seconder of the address, that great sacrifices must be made to purchase peace. The cession of Gibraltar was hinted at; that fort was represented to be an empty honour of little advantage to the country; and it was said that, by giving up to the Spaniards what they had so set their minds upon, and what seemed to have been the sole object of their ambition in the last wars, England would secure the permanency of peace. Fox commended the speech; praised a part of the present administration, but said that he saw great danger in some members of it;—declared that he never would make any opposition to them, while they acted so wisely as they did at present. He enlarged upon the wisdom of signing a separate treaty of peace with America, by which our acknowledgment of her independence was made certain and irrevocable. It was a measure which he had always himself recommended when in administration, but which was then disapproved. He did not doubt, however, that, less powerful in the ministry than out of it, he had much contributed to the adoption of that measure; and that, speaking in the House of Commons on the opposite side from that of the administration, his sentiments had had that weight with his ancient colleagues which they never obtained in the council. He said that the acknowledgment of the independence of America was an act so wise and so expedient, that he was only sorry to find in the same speech which announced it words expressive of reluctance and regret, of distrust and apprehensions of its consequences: that those apprehensions, he would venture to affirm, were groundless; the consequences must be happy to this country; the Ministers need not fear, they had acted well and wisely; he would defend them against themselves; he would maintain against any eloquent lord, that when America was independent, the sun of Britain's glory was not set (such had been once the expression of Lord Shelburne): on the contrary, that sun would now shine out brighter than it had done for years before. He would pledge himself to the world that no learned lord (alluding to a former speech of Dunning, now Lord Ashburton) should move for an impeachment against the first minister; that minister might be secure; his life was in no danger; the independence of America should not be granted with such gloomy auspices as impeachments and public executions; it should not be sealed with Lord Shelburne's blood. He owned that peace was most desirable; yet he thought too high a price might be paid for it. He would not say that it could not be expedient, in any possible situation of this country, to give up Gibraltar; but he would say that, Great Britain and Ireland excepted, it was the last of his Majesty's dominions that ought to be ceded; that it was the most effectual instrument of war in our hands; and that, had it been properly employed by stationing a fleet there, early in the present war, to have prevented D'Estaing from sailing to the West Indies, we should probably have had peace at this moment. To part with Gibraltar was to resign the Mediterranean altogether into the hands of the house of Bourbon, to be theirs as completely and as absolutely as any lake or pool in their own dominions. Gibraltar was an important possession as a means to gain us allies; but when foreign powers saw that we could afford them no assistance in the Mediterranean, they would be little solicitous of our alliance. To suppose that the cession of Gibraltar would secure a longer duration of peace was as unphilosophical as it was impolitic; for one must be strangely ignorant of human passions to suppose that ambition could be extinguished by enjoyment; on the contrary, it was a passion whose appetite was sharpened by being gratified; a passion with which every success was the parent of a thousand new projects, and which the farther it advanced the more unbounded were the prospects that opened before it. It had been said that the failure of the Spaniards now would be a lesson to them hereafter; and that the more important the advantages which we had reaped from Gibraltar during this war, the more certainly would it be a useless possession in future, when our enemies would have learned to neglect it, and to point their arms against some vulnerable part. But this reasoning proceeds upon a notion (the vainest that ever was conceived), that states are exempt from human follies, prejudices, and passions; but that states, and those who are entrusted with their government, are, in fact, subject to all the weaknesses incident to humanity, is a truth, of which we need not go far to find a striking example. It was not a first, a second, or a third campaign in which we had exhausted our strength, lavished our treasures, and poured out our blood upon the plains of America, quite as ineffectually as the Spaniards have wasted their efforts against the impregnable rock of Gibraltar, that taught us to desist from our design. The ministers of that day gained new obstinacy from every repulse; and, though their object was every day more distant, they would still have pursued it with as much eagerness and rage as ever, if this House had not timely interposed, wrested the sword from their hands, and saved the country. Let us trust for the duration of peace, not to so frail a hope as that the ambition of the Bourbons will be satiated, but to the terror of our own arms.

Lord North, too, spoke much upon the importance of Gibraltar. It had one advantage, he said, above what anything we could receive in return for it could possess; it was impregnable. He recommended that, notwithstanding all our domestic divisions, we should be united against France and Spain as one man. Peace was desirable to us, but it was also desirable to our enemies. America was exhausted; an attempt had been made by the Congress to raise taxes, but without success: Holland was divided in herself, and as likely to consume her strength in intestine wars as to annoy her neighbours: Spain was impatient till she could turn her arms against her own revolted subjects in South America; and even France was in no condition to supply her allies with money. He claimed merit to himself and his ancient colleagues for our late successes, and for the happy change in the aspect of public affairs. It was they who had made the mighty preparations for the last campaign, and had laid in such abundant naval stores. He said he would tell our naval Alexanders that, if they had conquered, they had conquered with the troops of Philip.

The day after the address had been voted, Fox said in the House that he had quite mistaken the purport of the King's speech; that, as the *offer* of independence to America had been explained by Lord Shelburne in the House of Peers, he by no means approved of it, but retracted all he had said the preceding day in its praise. Burke made a similar declaration, and talked of moving an amendment to the address, which Fox affirmed he would second. After so long a detail all reflections of my own may well be spared.

To pass, then, to another subject. I am much obliged to you for giving me so particular an account of the difficulties which are supposed to stand in the way of an emigration from Geneva. You seem to think, as I do, that they are too weak to merit a moment's consideration. One would think the Genevese imagined their manufacture to be the sole means by which they could support themselves, or be useful to society; and that, ceasing to be watchmakers, they would cease to be men. I confess I augured very ill of the project when my dear sister was asked whether coals were burned in Ireland, whether wine was drunk there, and was importuned with other such minute and frivolous inquiries. How different was the manly conduct of the Hollanders, when, to preserve their liberty, they resolved to transport their common wealth to Batavia, the most pestilential climate upon the whole face of the globe. Were I of Geneva, I should be tempted to apply to my countrymen the words of Brutus, "Nimium timemus mortem et exilium et paupertatem. Hæc videntur Genevensibus ultima esse in malis. Servitutem luxuriosam modo et honorificam non aspernantur: si quïdquam in extremâ ac miserrimâ contumeliâ potest honorificum esse."[1] To many I hope they will be inapplicable; but all those who can bear to live under the present government of Geneva deserve all its severities, and all the contempt which attends the condition of slaves. But perhaps there is more of resentment than of reason in what I have said, for I confess I am impatient with the prospect of this second disappointment.

I have never read Locke's book on education which you speak of, but I have always heard it esteemed as one of his best works. From the idea Rousseau himself gives me of him, I should have supposed that our admired author had borrowed all the physical part of his education from Locke, but none of the moral part. Locke's plan seems to have been to exercise the reason early, instead of burdening the memory, according to the usual

[1] Cic. Epist. ad Brutum. 17.

method; but you know it is not Rousseau's design to make children reasoners. Madame Genlis is very ungrateful if what Roustan tells me is true (and he is an admirer of hers), that the best part of her book is borrowed from the *Emile*. Rousseau's reason for refusing to educate a prince, namely, that his scholar would afterwards refuse the title, flows necessarily from the best maxim of practical philosophy, *that we should avoid temptations*; a maxim which is so little of a paradox, that no person of the plainest understanding can refuse his assent to it, and that it is recognised by every Christian in his daily prayers. Rousseau might, with more propriety than any other writer, have used the exclamation which I have somewhere read was frequently in the mouth of a Spanish polemic, "Ye powers that preside over controversy, give me, I ask no more, give me an adversary that understands me."

S. R.

Letter XXVII.

London, Jan. 7. 1783.

It would seem, my dear Roget, by your last letter, that you thought I had affected doubt of succeeding in the way of life on which I am to enter, only to draw from you such praises as might encourage me in my pursuit. That object, had it been mine, must have been fully gratified by your silence, which, introduced as it is, is a greater encouragement to me, and is more offensive to modesty even than a panegyric upon talents which your indulgence might have supposed me to possess. However, I assure you I had no such wish, and that what I wrote to you was but a faithful transcript of what I felt. Could I but realize the partial hopes and expectations of my friends, there could be no doubt of my success, almost beyond my wishes; but in myself I have a much less indulgent censor, and, in this perhaps alone, I cannot suffer their judgment to have equal weight with my own. I have taught myself, however, a very useful lesson of practical philosophy, in order to make myself easy in my situation, which is, not to suffer my happiness to depend upon my success. Should my wishes be gratified, I promise myself to employ all the talents and all the authority I may acquire for the public good. Should I fail in my pursuit, I console myself with thinking that the humblest situation of life has its duties, which one must feel a satisfaction in discharging; that, at least, my conscience will bear me the pleasing testimony of having intended well; and that, after all, true happiness is much less likely to be found in the high walks of ambition than in the "secretum iter et fallentis semita vitæ." Were it not for these consolations, and did I consider my success at the bar as decisive of my future happiness, my apprehensions would be such that I might truly say, "Cum illius diei mihi venit in mentem, quo mihi dicendum sit, non solum commoveor animo, sed etiam toto corpore perhorresco."[1]

My account of the new edict of Geneva did not come from the republican Beauchateau, but from

[1] Cic. In Q. Cæcil. Div. 13.

one who feels no less indignation at it than yourself. I hear of articles in it more insulting and tyrannical than any you mention; such as the abolition of the liberty of the press; a prohibition under a severe penalty to bear arms, or even to have any weapon in one's house; a law to make all clubs unlawful, even those for amusement; to make it unlawful to speak of politics in a coffee-house, or even in a private family; to punish every transgression with great severity, and to compel the master and servants of the coffee-house, or the master of the family where the words are spoken, under a heavy penalty, to inform against their guests. But you must tell me that you have read all this in the edict before I can give credit to it. Not that I suppose men who can resolve to destroy the liberties of their country, are likely to be guided by any sense of decency in the choice of the means most proper to effect their object; but a tyranny so complete and so atrocious as this, seems quite repugnant to the manners of the age we live in. It is only under the detested tyrants of Rome that one can find its parallel; and it is the wonderful pencil of Tacitus that alone can paint all its horrors. "Non aliàs magis anxia et pavens civitas, egens adversùm proximos; congressus, colloquia, notæ ignotæque aures vitari; etiam muta atque inanima, tectum et parietes circumspectabantur."[1] I rejoice, however, that the Government has not deigned to assume any mask: one has at least the satisfaction to reflect that none will suffer its severities but willing slaves.

1 Annal. lib. iv. 69.

Besides, the instructive lesson, which Geneva affords the world, acquires tenfold weight from the horrors of such a tyranny. How much is it to be lamented that such a subject should not find an historian worthy of it. Why is not there some Genevan who, now that he has lost his own country, will enlarge his patriotism into a divine philanthropy, and, considering the world as his country, turn the miseries of his native city to the advantage of mankind? I would fain see the history of Geneva written, not by a member of the commission, whose talents must be prostituted to palliate the faults, and it may be to excuse the treasons, of himself and his colleagues; but by one who has no interest in the subject but the interest of virtue: "Uni æquus virtuti atque ejus amicis."[1] If you know a citizen of this character (as you assuredly do), an enthusiast of virtue, one who to a Roman's patriotism adds the utmost sensibility of heart, conjure him to undertake the subject; entreat him not to doubt his talents; let him be assured that the energy of his mind and the tenderness of his heart cannot fail to render him eloquent. Exhort him to write with no view to interest, with no view even to reputation, but only for the benefit of mankind, and most of posterity. Find such an historian, and let me have the honour to be his translator; for that is the only literary character in which I can venture for many years, if ever, to appear before the public. I have attempted, indeed, the very subject which I am now exhorting you not to suffer to remain without

[1] Hor. II. S. i. 70.

an historian; but my attempt, which (for I had scarce any materials) was only an exercise, and consisted but of detached parts, such as seemed to afford the greatest scope for imagination, has corroborated my opinion that it is not for me yet to think of being an author. Most of what I wrote I had the grace to destroy immediately after. Some passages, however, I preserved; and, though it may seem inconsistent with the rest of what I have said upon my composition, I shall, if I do not find wherewith to fill this letter, send you, for your opinion, some of the characters which I had drawn*; not for your opinion as to

* "Duroveray was at this time Attorney-General of the Republic; an honour which he owed less to acquired talents than to his zeal for liberty, and to the bold and decided manner in which he had engaged in the party of the citizens. His natural eloquence was little improved by study or by art; but the violence of his temper supplied him with bold and imposing images, and the warmth and quickness of his passions with a rapid and impetuous elocution. These natural endowments soon rendered him one of the most conspicuous characters in the commonwealth, and the citizens the more willingly gave him their confidence, as he was an entire stranger to artifice; the ingenuous openness of his character displayed qualities less proper to conciliate the affections, than to command the applause of his fellow citizens. He was violent, resolute, uncomplying, warm and overbearing in dispute, exacting rather than courting approbation, and impatient of contradiction as well from friends as from enemies.

"Clavière, who might be considered, next to D., as chief of the *representant* party, was of a character very unlike that of the Attorney-General. Not born in the city, nor the son of a citizen, his zeal in the popular cause wanted the animating warmth of national prejudices; for which sentiments of philanthropy and general principles of politics are but a feeble substitute. His reason might convince him of the people's rights, and the government's injustice; but his heart had not inherited the enthusiasm of liberty, or the stern hatred of tyranny. Nor were his passions strong and energetic to conceal or supply his want of patriotism. His genius was penetrating and subtle, not bold and enterprising. Though artful and cautious, he was incapable of that firm and deliberate calmness which is the most requisite quality in a popular leader. His timid ambition, intoxicated by the prospect of success which a delusive imagination painted to him, yet startled and was checked by the least suspicion of a reverse of fortune: even his art forsook him when it was most required, and he knew not, in any critical

style or composition, for in that respect they are beneath your notice, but as to truth of design; in a word, to know whether you think I have caught any of the features of their characters, and have made any progress in that which Pope calls the proper study of mankind.

There are those, then, it seems, who think the plenipotentiaries justified, because they acted under their royal master's commands. I, on the contrary, have always been taught that no commands, no fear, not even of death, can ever excuse the author of the instrument of a flagrant injustice. There once, too, were men of honour in France who thought so; witness the gallant soldier who re-

---

moment, how to dissemble his fears, or to conceal his intemperate hopes.

"Vernes had all those qualities which can adorn and render amiable a tranquil and studious life, but nothing of the republican's force and energy. Tender, mild, affectionate, learned, eloquent, and polite; the friend of Rousseau, but, at the same time, the friend of Voltaire; his love of virtue was blemished by an intemperate love of letters, of glory, and of applause. Nature designed him for an ornament to a Trajan's court, in whose pure serenity every lesser virtue flourishes and is embellished with all the innocent elegancies of life; and not to embark amidst the tempests of a divided republic, where occasion may call for those higher virtues at which vulgar natures shudder. She had denied him the masculine vigour of mind which shrinks not at the sight of blood when liberty can be purchased at no less a price.

"Lamotte was a true republican, born in a low condition of life, and destined to a mechanic trade. His rude bluntness, the boldness of his language, and his ostentatious contempt of the accidental distinctions of fortune, challenged attention to his singular character, and he delighted in that singularity. He affected alike to despise the foppery of artificial manners, the refinements of systematic politics, and the resources of study and of learning. Yet he possessed a rough and nervous eloquence, whose vigorous sallies produced the greater effect as they were the less expected; but his arguments were mingled with coarse and unseasonable jests; his language was uncouth, his pronunciation vulgar, his tone of voice loud and clamorous. Such manners could not fail of being highly offensive to the wealthy families, who looked down with scornful pity on a man, who, glorying in the meanness of his condition, had yet the presumption to be ambitious."

turned for answer to the mandate of the most bloody tyrant of France, "Je supplie votre Majesté d'employer mes bras et ma vie à choses faisables."

Our ministers seem, in the House of Commons, to be very weak in orators, however strong they may be in numbers. If Mr. Pitt had more experience, and were more accustomed to business, in short, if he were some years older than he is, he might almost alone support the administration; but talents as wonderful even as those he possesses can hardly qualify a man, at the age of twenty-three or twenty-four, for the arduous part he has to sustain. With a great command of language and quickness of parts, it is no difficult task to support any side in a debate; but to propose taxes in such a manner as may be palatable to the Parliament, when almost every resource of finance is exhausted, and to be ready to answer the multitude of objections which are started from every quarter of the House, is an undertaking to which one would suppose nothing but long habit and the most perfect knowledge of the subject could render any man equal. Mr. Pitt is soon to propose some plan for a reform of the parliamentary representation; but who is so sanguine as to hope that it will be adopted by the present Parliament;—a Parliament elected under the predominant influence of the late ministry, and many of whose members cannot be ignorant that a new-modelled representation will, in effect, be an exclusion of themselves from Parliament? The present Parliament was tried last session upon both questions, of a new representative system, and of shortening the duration of Parliaments, and rejected both by a majority of almost two to one; since when, I cannot see that any thing has happened to convince them of the necessity of these reforms.

Your most affectionate brother,

SAML. ROMILLY.

LETTER XXVIII.

Dear Roget, Gray's Inn, March 21. 1783.

I am very sorry my silence should have occasioned you any uneasiness; my letter of the 10th of last month ought to have arrived at Lausanne before the date of your last; I make no doubt you have received it since. You do me but justice when you suppose that I am prevented from writing to you by business, and that you are never forgotten by me. I lost no time in executing your commission respecting Linguet. Three numbers, containing the *Mémoires sur la Bastille*, had been published when your letter reached me; these I have sent to you by Lecointe, who will put them in the post at Geneva. I never was more completely disappointed in any book than in this. Before he enters upon his subject, he talks so much of the horrors, and of the unparalleled atrocities of the Bastille, putting his imagination and his language to the rack for the strongest images and expressions, that one is quite astonished, afterwards, to find only a narrative of a confinement, rigorous, indeed, but such as one would expect in almost every prison. He resembles the poet, his countryman, who began, —

> "Je chante le vainqueur des vainqueurs de la Terre;"

and one may very well say with Boileau, —

> "Que produira l'auteur après tous ces grand cris?
> La montagne en travail enfante une souris."

Even his motto is as injudicious as all the rest. "Non mihi si voces[1] centum sint," &c. After this mighty promise upon the cover, one opens the book, and behold it is with the utmost difficulty that the author is able to spin out three small pamphlets, of which his narrative does not occupy a third part. The memoirs are useful in one respect, as they serve to convince one that no account of the Bastille coming from a prisoner, can be at all interesting, and that the only men qualified to write a good history of the prison are the governor of it, or the *lieutenant de police*. Even with Linguet's exaggerated language, the horrors of the Bastille fall much short of what one's imagination had painted to one. I cannot agree with him "que jamais oppression n'a été si cruelle;" much less should I say, "que jamais elle n'a été reprochée avec tant d'énergie." I perceive, by your letter, that you are still inclined to think Linguet a good writer. It is to myself only I ought to make excuses for differing from you in opinion; but, indeed, upon this subject I do differ from you entirely. This, at least, I think certain: if Linguet is eloquent, we must not call Demosthenes so, or Cicero, or Rousseau, for no two things can differ more than their style of writing and his. We find all those great writers, in differ-

1 This word is *linguæ* in Virgil.

ent parts of their works, pleading their own cause, painting their own sufferings, and reproaching their enemies with the wrongs which they had done them. In doing this, we find that they content themselves with copying faithfully what passes in their own mind, with representing every thing exactly as it struck themselves, and with giving a voice, if I may so express myself, to nature. They keep the attention of their readers fixed upon the single subject they are treating of, because they know that all ambitious ornaments will only weaken its force. We never find them straining their imagination to find out metaphors and similes that were never imagined before. They invite, they even force us to think, but it is on the subject before us, not on the ornaments with which it is profusely covered; they do not oblige us to pause at every figure to consider its meaning; in a word, they do not sacrifice their subject to its ornaments: they seek to show us what they have suffered, and how they have been wronged, not what wit, imagination, and powers of language they possess.

I am not surprised that you were in such haste to sell out your stock after reading the author of the *Finances d'Angleterre*. However, French writers upon our government and politics deserve very little attention; they are commonly very ignorant of the subject on which they write, and very partial against the English. De Lolme, and perhaps Montesquieu, are the only foreigners whom I have read, who have written any thing worth reading upon our constitution. I can say nothing of Mably, for I have not seen his book; but the inaccuracies, to use no harsher an expression, of the French writers in general, are unpardonable. Who can imagine that the author of the treatise on *Lettres de Cachet* believed what he was writing, or that he had taken the trouble to inquire into the fact, when he tells the world that the trial by jury is falling into disuse amongst us, and that the *habeas corpus* can only be obtained with difficulty. A-propos of the *Lettres de Cachet*, that book has confirmed me in my opinion, that religion is necessary to excellence even in the arts; and I cannot doubt that, if the Comte de Mirabeau had been as devout as he was animated, he would have been infinitely more eloquent. With what energy might he have invoked the Author of his existence, and have called upon him to witness his veracity, instead of using that cold exclamation, "J'atteste l'honneur que tout dans mon récit est conforme à la vérité!" With how much more eloquence might he have committed his child to the care of Providence, and have implored its vengeance on his head, if ever he became a friend or an instrument of oppression, than have addressed those vows, as one may say, to aërial nothing, "Puisse la mort vous moissoner avant l'age," &c. &c. Swift has written a book[1] to prove the advantages of Christianity; but the work is ludicrous, and his principal argument is, that if Christianity was utterly destroyed, the wits would want a subject for pleasantry, and minute philosophers an enemy to combat. The subject, however, might, I think, very well be treated seriously; at least I know that when I was at

1 Entitled, *An Argument against abolishing Christianity*.

Paris, every thing I saw convinced me that, independently of our future happiness and our sublimest enjoyments in this life, religion is necessary to the comforts, the conveniences, and even to the elegances and lesser pleasures of life. Not only I never met with a writer truly eloquent, who did not, at least, affect to believe in religion, but I never met with one in whom religion was not the richest source of his eloquence. Cicero, sceptical as he is in his philosophical writings, in his orations always (except once or twice where it was his interest to shake the established faith of his country) appears to be a firm believer. He repeatedly invokes those "Dii immortales" who he knew did not exist, and is never perhaps so eloquent as where he adopts even all the absurdities of paganism : where, for instance, in his pleading for Milo, he attests the sacred hills and groves of Albania, its subverted altars, and the great Jupiter Latiaris, that they were roused to punish the infamous Clodius who had polluted all their holy rites : where, in his oration for Sextius, he invokes to his aid Jupiter Capitolinus, Juno, Minerva, and the Dii Penates, whose temples and shrines he had secured from destruction, and that maternal Vesta, whose priestesses he had saved from violation, and whose eternal fire he had preserved from being extinguished in the blood of his fellow-citizens, or lost in the general conflagration of the city : where, in his defence of Flaccus, he works upon the passions of his audience, by representing the sister of his client, a vestal, in the delirium of her grief, neglecting the sacred fire on which the existence of Rome depended, or likely to extinguish its eternal flames with her tears. But the instances are innumerable where the eloquence of Cicero owes all its wonderful force to the fables, the errors, and the superstitious rites of heathenism: and one cannot doubt that the same observations may be extended to the literature of France, when one reflects that her first orators are Bossuet, Massillon, and Flechier; and that the finest pieces of poetry, in the language, are *Athalie*, *Zaïre*, and Rousseau's *Odes*.

I suppose the *Courrier de l'Europe*, and all the gazettes, have proclaimed to you the scandalous alliance between Fox and Lord North. It is not Fox alone, but all his party; so much that it is no exaggeration to say that of all the public characters of this devoted country (Mr. Pitt only excepted), there is not a man who has, or who deserves, the nation's confidence. But that even these men may not be judged unheard, the apology for their conduct which they offer, or rather with which they insult the public, is this. They say the great cause of enmity between them was the American war, which being removed, there remains no obstacle to their now becoming friends: that this country has long been shamefully rent with party feuds and animosities, to which it is now high time to put an end, by uniting all the talents of the country in one administration: that their alliance implies no departure from their ancient principles; for, though each party consents to act with men whom they formerly opposed, yet neither gives up any of their political sentiments: that an administration formed of men holding contrary speculative opinions in politics is no novelty in this country: that even Lord Shelburne's administration was one of this kind, the Lord Chancellor and the Lord Advocate of Scotland being the warm advocates of the Crown, and of the present established Constitution, and the other Ministers being the zealous friends of the people, and the promoters of a reformation of the Constitution. These sophisms are not worth refuting.

Adieu; I make no apology for breaking off abruptly, since it is to procure you the pleasure of hearing from my father.

Yours most affectionately,

S. R.

Letter XXIX.

London, April 1. 1783.

To compensate, my dear Roget, for having of late written to you so little upon politics, I propose that it shall be the principal subject of the present letter. The peace has by no means deprived me of materials; on the contrary, it has rather increased them. To one who would acquire a knowledge of mankind, the political contests of this country offer much for reflection; unhappily the reflections they suggest, at least to an Englishman, and therefore to you, my dear Roget, as well as to myself, must be of a very melancholy kind.

The long-expected, and I will add, the much-dreaded, administration of Lord North and Fox has not yet taken place, though five weeks have elapsed since any of the late Ministers, except Pitt, have acted as Ministers, and this at a time when we are engaged in various negotiations of the greatest importance. What is the true cause of this delay I cannot inform you; some impute it to the averseness which the King entertains to the appointing of an administration so profligate; others to the same disposition in the Chancellor, and the influence he has over his Majesty. The week before last, Mr. Coke gave notice in the House of Commons that, if an administration was not formed before the following Friday (March 21.), he should move for an address to the King upon the subject. When the day came, he was informed that the new Ministry was settled. The Duke of Portland had arranged it, and it was (according to a list which appeared the next day in the newspapers) as follows: — The Duke himself, First Lord of the Treasury; Lord John Cavendish, Chancellor of the Exchequer; Lord North and Mr. Fox, Secretaries of State; Lord Keppel, First Lord of the Admiralty; Lord Stormont, President of the Council; Lord Carlisle, Lord Privy Seal. In a day or two, however, the project of this new Administration was laid aside; owing, as is pretended, to the King's having insisted upon having a list of the names of the persons who were to fill all the inferior departments before he would make any appointment, and the Duke of Portland and his party having absolutely refused to comply with that requisition.

On the following Monday, Mr. Coke made

his promised motion, for an address to the King, praying that he would be graciously pleased to form an administration entitled to the confidence of the people, and such as might have a tendency to put an end to the unfortunate divisions and distractions of this country. The motion was carried without a division, but not without debate; in which Fox inveighed against the Chancellor, once his boasted friend, and the subject of his panegyrics. He insisted upon the necessity, in order to our salvation from the dangers which threatened us, of an union of all parties, and of a general amnesty of all animosities and ancient prejudices. Divisions and opposition, according to him, would prove the destruction of the country; he would have it so, if possible, that there should be no difference of opinion in the nation; and to attain that desirable end of unanimity, he would consent to unite even with the Shelburne party, as well as with that of Lord North. That if any men could suppose that, in times so critical as the present, he, and those who acted with him, were actuated merely by motives of private interest, he would not condescend to remove their suspicions. Lord North was upbraided by some of his former friends with having abandoned them, and with having disgracefully made, not a coalition with Fox, but an humble submission to him; with having consented to accept a subordinate office, and to form part of a Cabinet in which there would always be a majority against him. Lord North treated these reproaches as the mere effects of disappointment in those who saw that, having less power and authority in the intended administration than he had when he was in office before, he would be less able to serve them. Mr. Pitt treated the offer of a coalition held out to him by Fox with all the scorn which it deserved: "He never would consent to call the abandonment of former principles a forgetting of ancient prejudices; nor would he be, by any consideration, induced to pass an amnesty upon measures which had brought his country almost to the verge of ruin; but he saw that his system of politics differed from that of his contemporaries, and he felt that his principles and his temper were not calculated for the times in which he lived." Since this debate it has been much reported that an administration will be formed from which both Fox and Lord North will be excluded, but to this I give no credit; and the only hope with which I endeavour to console myself is that such an administration cannot be of long duration, but must soon be put an end to, either by disputes among its own members, or by majorities of the House of Commons declaring against them; though, after what we have seen, we can hope for little good from the House of Commons. Fox seems already to have lost all his popularity; and it is almost a general wish that some man of character and credit may be opposed to him as a candidate for Westminster, at the election which his acceptance of a place will render necessary. Lord North has lost still more in the public estimation. Wonderful as it may seem, it is certain that he was growing into a kind of popularity. The tranquillity in which

doubt, the reflection which his speech produced in the minds of many of his hearers, was not unlike that which the usurer makes upon the preacher in the *Diable Boiteux*, " Il a bien fait son métier ; allons faire le nôtre."

We have lately had a very convincing proof that laws which contradict and (if I may so express myself) do violence to the general sentiments of a nation, never can be executed. Two officers quarrelled about a gaming debt; they did not fight till six months afterwards, when a duel ensued. One of the officers was shot through the lungs, and, though he could with difficulty stand, he insisted upon firing; he did so, and killed his adversary. The law is express, that to kill a man in a duel is murder. The coroner's inquest, however, which sat upon the body of the person killed, refused to bring in a verdict of murder; and the body was buried in Westminster Abbey, attended by the choir, and with a kind of military pomp. A few days afterwards the other officer died.

I have just got the newspaper with the account of the debate upon Mr. Pitt's motion. The motion was, that the House should come to the three following resolutions:—1. That it was the opinion of the House that measures were highly necessary to be taken to prevent bribery and corruption at future elections for Parliament. 2. That, in future, when the majority of voters for any borough should be convicted of gross and notorious corruption before a committee of that House, such borough should be disfranchised, and the minority of voters not so convicted should be entitled to vote for the county in which such borough should be situated. 3. That an addition of knights of the shire and of representatives of the metropolis should be made to the representative body. In his speech, he said that the addition he would propose should be of about 100 members. He spoke of a perfectly equal representation as a wild Utopian scheme which never could be realized, and gave as a reason for not proposing to strike off the corrupt boroughs and those which are the patrimony of particular families, that it would be an unjust and an unwarrantable invasion of private property. This is a kind of argument which, I confess, has no great weight with me; for I think the laws are not bound to protect men in the possession of such pecuniary advantages as they ought never to have obtained. If a man's having a pecuniary interest in a thing, no matter how acquired, is sufficient to make his property in it sacred, then may the laws become a shield to every species of fraud, iniquity, and immorality. The motion was lost (as you will, no doubt, have expected) by a majority of 293 against 149. Fox strenuously defended the motion; Lord North as warmly opposed it. Burke rose to speak; but it was late, and a great many members, dreading the length of his oration, quitted the House at the very same moment, which so much offended him that he sat down without speaking: this has happened to him more than once.

I am much obliged to you for giving me your sentiments on the question, whether any crime ought to be punished with death. The objection you make to the punishment of death, founded on the errors of human tribunals and the impossibility of having absolute demonstration of the guilt of a criminal, strikes me more forcibly than any argument I have ever before heard on the same side of the question. I confess, however, that to myself it seems absolutely impossible, even if it were to be wished (of which I am not quite sure), to omit death in the catalogue of human punishments; for if the criminal will not submit to the punishment inflicted on him, if he escapes from his prison, refuses to perform the labour prescribed to him, or commits new crimes, he must, at last, be punished with death. So it is, at least, in the *Utopia* of Sir Thomas More; and it is a very melancholy reflection, that some of the miserable victims of that excellent philosopher's compassion might, if his visions had ever been realized, have suffered years of miserable servitude in addition to the punishment of death, which would at last be inflicted on them as the consequence of crimes which they had been provoked to commit. One reason why I cannot think that death ought so carefully to be avoided among human punishments is, that I do not think death the greatest of evils. Beccaria and his disciples confess that it is not, and recommend other punishments as being more severe and effectual, forgetting, undoubtedly, that if human tribunals have a right to inflict a severer punishment than death, they must have a right to inflict death itself.

You will not, I hope, conclude from all this that I am perfectly satisfied with the penal codes that now subsist in Europe, and particularly with that in my own country, where theft (pilfering it should rather be called), forgery, and every description of the *Crimen falsi* are punished with death. The laws of our country may, indeed, be said to be written in blood; and we may almost apply to ourselves the words of Montaigne, "Il n'est si homme de bien qu'il mette à l'examen des loix toutes ses actions et pensées, qui ne soit pendable dix fois en sa vie."

Since you mentioned Locke on *Education*, I have read it. I have lent it, too, to Roustan, who exclaims with Mad[e] Genlis against the injustice of Rousseau, and wonders how he could dare to call his subject new, after Locke's treatise. But what there is in common between the moral system of the one and the other I leave you to judge, when Locke, according to his manner of education, would have curiosity in a child cultivated and encouraged, and all his questions answered to his understanding; would have the idea of God very early impressed on his mind, and have him taught to pray soon after he can speak; would have a disposition to generosity encouraged in a child, by making him sensible that it is his interest to be generous, and by taking care that more shall always be repaid him than he has given away; would have him stimulated to learning, by giving him dominion over his younger brothers and sisters, and making him their instructor; and when he relies so much upon the article of good-breeding, and repeats his instructions upon it so often, that he seems to have more remembered that he was educating a gentleman than a man. Rousseau was infinitely better acquainted with his subject than Locke; that is, with the dispositions, passions, capacity, and intelligence of children. Nevertheless, I admit that Rousseau owes a great part of his book to Locke; inasmuch as Locke directed the attention of Rousseau to objects which he might otherwise have overlooked, and that to some errors in Locke we owe some truths in Rousseau. The book is well written; not indeed with the elegance of an Addison, but with an energy of which Addison was incapable, particularly in those passages where the author inveighs against public schools, as seminaries of every pernicious principle; and where he reproaches the generality of parents with inculcating every vice in the tender minds of their children, not indirectly and by example only, but directly and by way of precept.

You have perfectly reconciled me to your plan of returning to England, and I now not only consent to it, but earnestly solicit its execution. Indeed, you do not know how painfully I resisted my own inclinations when, alarmed, though perhaps unreasonably, for your health, I started objections to your scheme. But one short truth will best show it. Of all my life, that short period which elapsed between your marriage and your being taken ill was infinitely the most happy. Let me then renew that happiness. Nor is it for my pleasure alone, but for a much better purpose, that I wish you were again in England. I have often lamented your absence, as depriving me of a very considerable assistance in my studies; but you are now to render me a more important assistance. I am soon to enter on a career which possibly (though I grant not very probably) may place me in important and critical situations, which will certainly give me partial and selfish interests, incompatible with the good of others, and which will throw me amidst mankind, and condemn me to hear the profession of dishonourable sentiments without opposing them, and to be a near spectator of selfish and degrading conduct without discovering any detestation of it. It will in part depend on you to save me from the contagion of such examples; for though my heart still recoils from them with an antipathy that seems quite insurmountable, I have I know not what kind of terror, which I cannot overcome, of the force of habit, of perpetual temptations, of being familiarized with a contempt for virtue, and, above all, of an habitual attachment to the miserable gold which one earns. The best shield against these is, I am convinced, the society and conversation of such a friend as yourself, whom one may consider as the pledge and deposit of all the sacred engagements which one has taken with God, one's self, and one's fellow-creatures. This very letter is some proof of what I say, for to whom should I venture to write thus but to yourself?

Adieu! Be assured of the sincere and invariable affection of your warmest friend and brother,

SAML. ROMILLY.

Letter XXXI.

My dear Sister, London, June 10. 1783.

I should not at this moment sit down to write to you, if I thought it would add to your misfortunes[1] to hear how much I share them; but, judging of you by myself, I do not fear increasing your grief. It were to no purpose not to speak of our affliction; it cannot but be always before us, nor can we wish it were not. What a loss I suffer, and how ill I am able to bear it, you know but too well. You know whether I have an affectionate heart; you know whether Roget did not, with yourself, engross almost all that affection. The anxiety for the health of our dearest friend, of which I never could divest myself, and the apprehension of the worst that could happen, which never quitted me when I had the least knowledge of his being ill, had made me suppose it impossible that any news from Lausanne could ever have surprised, how much soever it must afflict me. That news, however, which I had often formerly expected, and endeavoured to prepare myself to meet, came upon me at last the most unexpectedly. I had heard indeed of your last letter, but I had not seen it, and the most alarming circumstances in it were concealed from me.

Great as our loss is, my dear Kitty, (and I presume to place my loss nearly on a level with yours, when I reflect that I have lost the best and dearest friend I ever had, a better and a

[1] The death of Mr. Roget, which took place on the 23d May.

dearer than I ever shall have again,) still are we not without reason to be consoled, when we reflect that this great misfortune is ours alone, and reaches not our dear friend. It is we who are deprived of the society and friendship of the tenderest, the most amiable, the most virtuous of men; but our friend is happy, which in this life he never could have been; he was too good, too tender, too affectionate, for this life. It could not but be a source of misery to him as long as there were men in it who were unjust, and others who were unfortunate. Dissolution of life is not, in truth, a misfortune to any man who has lived well; to him it must have been less so than to any man I ever knew, for it was always present to his mind, and his whole life was a preparation for it. He is now assuredly rewarded for his virtues by that God in whom he has always firmly believed, and he now partakes of that immortality for which he showed, by the whole tenor of his life, that he knew he was created. But I feel that, however little reason there may be for our tears, it is hardly in our power to prevent them; and if we considered ourselves alone, what could we do better than indulge our sorrows to the utmost, and return, by our tears, the sentiments of affection which he always did and still does entertain for us? but it is in our power to make a better return, and it is our duty to do it. It is the duty of both of us to guard, to instruct, and protect the children which he has bequeathed to us; those dear children who have not lost, but only changed their father. We know how much our excellent friend had their happiness at heart; we know what a parent they would have experienced in him; and we will, my dear sister, take care that they shall not suffer by our misfortune, and that his fondest hopes shall not be disappointed. But to fulfil this sacred promise, it becomes us to take care that the excess of our grief do not put it out of our power to render them service. I entreat you then, my dear sister, not to indulge your grief, to be careful of your health, to think what would be the dreadful consequence of depriving your infants of that care and assistance which they have a right to expect from you. But it is not to your children alone, and to the memory of dear Roget, that you are bound to take the greatest care of your health, but for all your fond relations here in your native country; those relations who have deeply felt all your misfortunes, who have hardly ever dared, since you left them, to indulge any joy, whose greatest pleasures have always been damped with the reflection that one of those who was entitled to partake them was absent. Yes, indeed, my dear sister, you do owe us something. Hitherto your life has been most unfortunate; what remains of it you have the prospect of spending, not indeed joyfully, but unruffled with tears and anxieties, in a calm and pleasing melancholy. I have a thousand projects to mention to you; but when I reflect that it will be a month before I can have an answer, I dare not mention one of them. Pray write to us immediately. I thought it impossible any thing could add to my affection for you; but the more unfortunate you are, the more

I feel myself to love, to esteem, and respect you. That God may protect you under your misfortunes is the constant prayer of your most affectionate brother,

SAML. ROMILLY.

LETTER XXXII.

My dear Sister, London, June 13. 1783.

I could wish to be constantly with you, and, since that is impossible, at least to write to you every day; but the post, unfortunately, goes from hence but twice a week. What a consoling reflection must it be to you to think how much your tenderness alleviated the misfortunes of our dear friend! without you, how unhappy must have been the last years of his life! It is a comfort even to me to reflect, that if he had never known me, he would have been less happy than he was. Though his friendship has been to me a source of infinite uneasiness and affliction, I thank God that I was blessed with it; his life was happier, and mine, I am sure, will be better for it. I do not seek to divert my attention from the cause of my sorrows. I know that to be a resource as vain and ineffectual as it is unworthy. I rather consider what is the amount of my loss, and examine what is real and what imaginary in the terrors of death. I know that my dear brother's virtues had made him invulnerable to its sting. I know that he is immortal, I know that he still lives; and I carry the idea so far as to read over all his former letters. I think with myself he is still only in a foreign country, — we shall sòon meet again; not so soon, indeed, as we intended; but what can be late that is circumscribed by the limits of life, and what can be distant that lies no farther than the grave? I reflect that my dear brother is now more present with me than ever, that he looks down upon me from Heaven, is the witness of all my actions, knows all that passes in my mind, and sees the sincerity of my affection for him: that he will still be the guardian and director of my conduct; and that whenever I am doubtful how to act, I will consider how he would have acted in such a situation, and I shall then be certain always to determine for what is just and virtuous. It is a pleasure to me to reflect that by this means his will be the merit of the laudable actions which I may perform; and that perhaps it will be part of those joys which are to reward his good works, to contemplate their extensive effects, and to see the good fruits of the virtues which his friendship has inspired me with, and to behold his own virtues reviving again in his children, by the happy effects of that wise and judicious education which he had begun, and which he has taught you how to perfect. I do not exhort you, my dear Sister, to dismiss all sad reflections, but rather to turn them to another object. To think of your friends in this country, to think how your return among them will revive and cheer them. Think of our dear parents, and comfort them in their old age. Think of your sweet children, and bring them amongst protectors who are anxious to devote themselves to their care and service. When, my dear Kitty, will you set out upon your journey hither? To perform it alone must be painful; I will come to bear you company. I will be with you by the end of July, or sooner if you desire it, though it would be inconvenient to me. All the months of August, September, and October, shall be devoted wholly to your service. If you choose, we will return to London immediately; or if you prefer it, I will stay with you for some time at Lausanne or any other place, till the hottest weather has passed over. Above all things, let me entreat you to be careful of your health, think of your children, and remember that at their age the loss of a mother is much greater than of a father; think what endearing duties you have to discharge. We shall certainly join our dear friend again soon, (for what are a few years, what is a whole life compared to that eternity which we shall pass with him?) but let us endeavour, first, to have done all that we know will afford him pleasure, and not to leave unperformed those offices for which he would chiefly have desired to live. In the midst of our affliction, and under the hard lot which has befallen us, we will find out serious, nay melancholy pleasures, which might be envied by those who seem more the favourites of fortune. Once more let me entreat you to be careful of your health, and not to cause another affliction to your dearest friends, greater than they will be able to bear, — at least, if I may judge of their hearts by that of your most affectionate brother,

Saml. Romilly.

LETTERS FROM THE COUNT DE MIRABEAU AND OTHERS.

1783—1787.

LETTER XXXIII.

FROM MR. BAYNES.[1]

My good Friend, Paris, September, 1783.

Since you left me, I have not known what in the world to do with myself. The first morning,

[1] The following account of Mr. Baynes is extracted from a letter of Dr. Parr, dated March 2. 1820. See *antè*, p. 68.

"John Baynes was born at Skipton, in Yorkshire, where his father was a prosperous attorney. He was a member of Trinity College; and, at a time of life unusually early, he gained the highest, or nearly the highest honours, mathematical and classical. He had great ardour of mind, great singleness of heart, great variety of research. He was an antiquary as well as a scholar. He was for a time suspected of having written the celebrated Epistle to Sir William Chambers: he disclaimed the authorship, but confessed that he superintended the press. He had a very fine commanding person, the tones of his voice were impressive, his dress was at all times becoming, his manners were unaffected, and yet dignified. He was now and then fond of paradoxes, and would defend them resolutely, when they had all the properties of improbability and even absurdity. He was a steady advocate for civil and religious liberty.

"John Baynes was perhaps the most intimate friend Sir S. Romilly had in early life; and in consequence of their connexion, my own acquaintance at Warwick with Sir Samuel began at some assizes or sessions. Sir Samuel spoke of him with affection and admiration; and doubtless, if he had lived, he would have been a bright luminary in the literature and politics of England. He had not been called to the bar, but practised at Gray's Inn, I believe, as a conveyancer. He died, to my sorrow, of a fever; and his resignation at the approach of death was worthy of his intellectual, moral, and religious excellences. I wrote his epitaph in Latin."

I verily believe I should have been tempted to throw myself into the Seine, had I not, luckily, met with an acquaintance, who was at the Hôtel d'Espagne in the next street, at the Café Conti. I called on M. Romilly [1], and was very sorry to find Mad^e. Romilly was very ill ; so I did not stay, but promised to call the next day, which I did, and saw her much better, but he was not at home. The next morning I called at Passy, but Dr. Franklin was gone to Paris. I set off for Pontoise, and arrived there on Wednesday. I was much taken with the look of the place ; the bridge, the river Oise, the rising ground on which it stands, made me very much in love with it ; — began a copy of verses on the place. The next day I went to see the convents, and to make inquiries about a preceptor, but the devil a preceptor could I find ; did not like Pontoise quite so well. The third day, not meeting with any better success, I thought Pontoise a most horrible place indeed ; — burnt my verses, and set off for Paris again, where I now am *chez* M. Villa.

I went this morning to the Chambre du Parlement, where I understood rather more than I had done before. The subject of the cause was a suit between the sheriffs of a neighbouring town and the bakers, for enhancing the price of bread. But (would you believe it ?) the "avocats du Parlement de Paris" are as arrant squabblers as any of our King's Bench practitioners. I was not a little diverted with the dispute between a little dapper *avocat* with his own hair, and a great tall man in an

[1] See *antè*, p. 64.

enormous wig, both concerned in this cause: the tall man seemed to rely much on the prosecution being at the suit *de la ville;* "Ah," said the other, "on sait fort bien ce que c'est que la ville; ce n'est que deux ou trois officiers de la ville."

I have half read through M. Henault.[1] It is certainly a very useful book, and by a learned man; but he has two faults: 1. His principles of toleration in religion, and his ideas of government, are both very bad. 2. He is perpetually making very foolish and childish observations, *qui ne prouvent rien*, as he says himself. Pray tell me if you are not of the same opinion. His observations on the progress of customs, laws, manners, &c. are excellent, and show him to have been a great antiquarian in that particular line.

I saw St. Denis' church, a fine light building (I speak of the inside), the roof unornamented, the windows wonderfully rich and (*ut ita dicam*) *frequent*, the church being surrounded with windows which have hardly any space between them. The ornaments on the gate are very curious, being as old as Charlemagne. The lightness of the columns and windows pleased me much. This morning I went to see the Duchess of La Vallière at the Carmelites. Oh! I had almost forgot to tell you that, on Tuesday, I went to see the Duc de la Villière's library, which, for the number of rare and fine books, is well worth the trouble. I never saw such a magnificent collection for an individual; there are some volumes of drawings and paintings which I should think invaluable, immense numbers

[1] Probably *Abrégé Chronologique de l'Histoire de France.*

of ancient romances, printed and MSS., and a fine collection of the first printed books, all in excellent condition.

Pray tell me if you have already written to Pontoise. Write immediately; be full, explicit, nay, even be tedious; have no mercy on me.

Yours ever sincerely,

J. B.

Letter XXXIV.

FROM THE COUNT DE MIRABEAU.[1]

Mon Ami, [Londres,] Ce Jeudi [1785].

Je ne voulois plus vous écrire que je n'eusse une réponse de vous qui me dît, que ce n'est pas par simple tolérance que vous souffrez mon amitié et mes bavardages. L'extrait ci-joint d'une lettre de Franklin me force à un billet d'envoi. J'ai fait toutes les démarches nécessaires chez Johnson, pour remplir ses vœux de ce côté: du vôtre, je vous demande un avertissement bien

---

Letter XXXIV.

London, Thursday, 1785.

I had resolved, my dear friend, not to write to you again until I had had an answer from you, telling me that you did something more than merely tolerate my friendship and my idle talk; but the enclosed letter from Franklin obliges me to send to you. I have taken all the necessary steps with Johnson to fulfil his wishes on that side. From you I hope to receive a good introduction, in accordance with the very sensible

---

[1] Mr. Romilly became acquainted with Mirabeau in 1784. See *antè*, p. 78. This letter refers to the work on *The Order of Cincinnatus*, by Mirabeau, which Mr. Romilly was translating. (See *antè*, p. 79.) The translation was published by J. Johnson, St. Paul's Churchyard, in 1785.

fait dans le sens très-sage où il l'envisage, et je vous prie d'y dire un mot de l'ouvrage, si vous trouvez que cela convienne. Adieu, mon ami, car je ne veux pas rompre mon vœu; et, d'ailleurs, je suis très-occupé, soit par Madame de * * *, à qui il faut force instructions, soit par l'arrangement et le triage de mes papiers, que je fais avec autant d'exactitude que si j'allois me noyer. Vous trouverez ces deux rapprochemens de Madame de * * * et de la Tamise très-disparates; et cela vous rappellera peut-être ce temple, consacré à Vénus et aux Graces, dont parle Plutarque, sur le frontispice duquel étoient écrits ces mots, "*Il faut mourir;*" et cela vaut bien le "*libertas*" de la prison de Venise. Quoiqu'il en soit, soyez tranquille, mon ami; je ne me noyerai pas avant de vous avoir embrassé encore une fois. Peut-être, conviendroit-il à un homme d'un aussi grand et beau talent que vous, qui daigne traduire, de traiter, dans un discours préliminaire, le beau sujet de l'influence du bonheur de l'Amérique sur le reste du monde, ce

---

view of the subject taken by him; and I beg of you to insert in it a word or two about the work itself, if you think it right to do so. Farewell, my friend, for I will not break my vow; and, besides, I am much engaged, partly with Mad[e]. de * * *, who requires a good deal of instruction, and partly with the arranging and selecting of my papers, which I am doing with as much care as if I were going to drown myself. You will think the ideas of Mad[e]. de * * * and the Thames very incongruous: and this will perhaps remind you of that temple, sacred to Venus and the Graces, of which Plutarch speaks, upon the front of which were these words, "*We must die;*" a motto, which is at least as good as the "*Libertas*" of the prison of Venice. Be that as it may, do not be alarmed, my friend, I shall not drown myself before I have shaken hands with you once more. Perhaps it might suit a man of talents as great and noble as yours, who condescends to translate, to treat in a preliminary discourse that noble subject of the influence of the happiness of America upon the rest of the world, which would

qui vous feroit passer auprès de la *localité* de Maty.[1] Quoiqu'il en soit, envoyez-nous un averti sement, si non mieux.

Letter XXXV.

FROM THE COUNT DE MIRABEAU.

Mon cher Romilly, [Londres, ce 1. Mars, 1785.]

Vous me quittez aujourd'hui; et l'amie qui fait le bonheur de ma vie me quitte demain; ce concours de circonstances pénibles m'a fait sentir encore mieux combien je vous aime tous deux, et combien l'habitude est un lien étroit pour les bons cœurs.

> "Quel siècle jusqu'au soir; il mesure des yeux
> Le tour que le soleil doit faire dans les cieux:
> Il faut que sur ces monts ce grand astre renaisse,
> S'élève lentement et lentement s'abaisse."

---

place you near the *locality* of Maty. At all events, send us an introduction, if nothing better.

Letter XXXV.

My dear Romilly, London, March 1. 1785.

You leave me to-day, and she who makes the happiness of my life leaves me to-morrow; this concurrence of painful circumstances makes me feel still more forcibly how much I am attached to you both, and how closely habit binds together affectionate hearts.

> "Quel siècle jusqu'au soir; il mesure des yeux
> Le tour que le soleil doit faire dans les cieux:
> Il faut que sur ces monts ce grand astre renaisse,
> S'élève lentement et lentement s'abaisse."

---

1 Henry Maty, the editor of a monthly Review, the first number of which appeared in February, 1782.

C'est un très-mauvais poëte qui a fait ces quatre beaux vers, et la mémoire de l'amie me les rappelle au moment du veuvage. Eh! mon Dieu! nous vivons un jour: faut-il mutiler cette frêle journée par des privations de notre choix? des privations volontaires? Et quels sont donc ces tristes intérêts d'invention humaine pour lesquels cet être, si passager, malheureux par lui, par les choses, par ses semblables, cet être qu'on appelle homme, aggrave encore ses peines et diminue ses jouissances? En vérité cette pensée abat quelquefois mon âme, au point de m'ôter toute faculté d'écrire et de m'occuper.

Il fut heureux! disois-je un jour en parlant de Fontenelle. Ce mot, qui devroit retentir avec tant de joie dans les âmes honnêtes, à peine on ose le prononcer: la haine et l'envie ont toujours reproché son bonheur à Fontenelle; elles lui ont fait un crime de n'avoir point attiré sur lui la persécution des préjugés de son siècle, de n'avoir indiqué qu'à demi la vérité qu'il voyoit toute

---

These four lines were written by a very bad poet, and the recollection of my friend brings them to my mind at the moment of separation. Alas! we live but for a day! Shall we then curtail this one precarious day by privations of our own choice—by voluntary privations? And what, after all, are those pitiful objects of human invention, for the sake of which this short lived being, unhappy in himself, unhappy by his fellow-creatures and in the circumstances which surround him, this being, called Man, aggravates his sorrows and lessens his enjoyments? Indeed, this reflection at times so depresses my spirits, that it deprives me of all power of writing and of application.

"He was happy," said I, one day, in speaking of Fontenelle. These words, which ought to find a joyful echo in every good breast, alas! one hardly ventures to utter them. Hatred and envy have ever made Fontenelle's happiness a cause of reproach to him. They made it a crime in him that he did not draw down upon himself persecution from the prejudices of his age; that he showed to others only half of those

entière; de ne lui avoir ôté les voiles qui la cachoient que pour lui en donner d'autres qui la dérobent; d'avoir montré le génie tremblant devant les préjugés qui devoient trembler devant lui. Quelle passion que l'envie! elle poursuit sans relâche l'homme de génie, pour lui rendre tous les tourmens qu'elle en reçoit. S'il fait entendre des plaintes, elle prétend qu'il s'avilit par la vengeance; s'il se tait, elle assure qu'il est insensible à l'injure; si son âme impérieuse attaque à découvert les erreurs populaires, elle le peint comme un esprit séditieux, pour qui rien n'est sacré; si sa sagesse adoucit la vérité pour ne pas l'exposer aux outrages de la multitude, elle l'accuse de l'avoir étouffée dans sa pensée, d'avoir sacrifié les droits éternels du genre humain à quelques jours de repos. Sans doute, il faut bien admirer ces âmes fortes et intrépides qui annoncent la vérité avec l'éclat et la majesté qu'elle a prise dans leur génie, et, après la gloire de l'avoir découverte, veulent

---

truths of which he saw the whole; that he drew aside one veil from the image of truth, only to throw over it another; that he exhibited Genius trembling before Prejudice, which ought to have trembled before him. What a passion is envy! without relaxation she pursues the man of genius, throwing back upon him all the torment she suffers at his hands. If he utter a complaint, she says that he is lowering himself by retaliation; if he be silent, his silence is insensibility to insult; if his uncompromising spirit lead him to make popular error the object of his undisguised attack, she paints him as a factious spirit, with whom nothing is sacred; if his prudence soften truth, in order that it may not be exposed to the outrage of the multitude, she accuses him of having stifled it in its birth, and of having sacrificed the eternal rights of mankind to a few days of repose. Doubtless we must admire those vigorous and intrepid spirits who proclaim truth in all the splendour and dignity with which their own genius has clothed her; and who, not satisfied with the

obtenir encore celle de souffrir, et s'il le faut, de mourir pour elle. Je respecterai Fénélon écrivant le *Télémaque* dans la cour de Louis XIV. et Thomas Morus publiant *l'Utopie* dans le palais de Henri VIII. Ces âmes sublimes consacrent les siècles qui se sont déshonorés en les persécutant. Mais en versant des larmes d'attendrissement et d'admiration sur ces dévouemens héroïques, on regrette que l'esprit humain n'en ait pas retiré d'assez grands avantages. Mon ami, j'en viens à croire que l'on ne fait point triompher la vérité en s'immolant pour elle. La persécution qui étend les progrès de l'erreur, arrête ceux de la raison, et les philosophes ne se multiplient point, comme les fanatiques, dans l'exil, dans les prisons, et sous la hache des bourreaux. Peut-être il y a eu des pays et des siècles où la vérité la plus hardie, présentée tout à coup à un peuple souverain, persuadée à une multitude immense par l'ascendant de la parole, pouvoit faire une révolution aussitôt qu'elle étoit entendue; et il étoit beau de s'immoler

---

glory of discovering her, aspire to that of suffering, and, if need be, of dying for her. I shall always respect Fénélon writing *Telemachus* in the court of Louis XIV., and Sir Thomas More publishing the *Utopia* in the palace of Henry VIII. These noble spirits hallow the age, which dishonoured itself by persecuting them. But while one sheds tears of pity and admiration at the thought of such heroical self-devotion, one regrets that the human mind should not have benefited by them as it ought. I come, my friend, to the conclusion, that to sacrifice one's self for truth is not the way to ensure its triumph. Persecution, which spreads the progress of error, arrests that of reason; and philosophers do not, like fanatics, multiply in exile, in prison, and under the axe of the executioner. Perhaps there may have been a country and an age in which the boldest truth, announced on a sudden to a sovereign people, forced upon the attention of an immense multitude by all the powers of eloquence, might have given birth to a revolution at the very moment of its utterance; and it were noble to sacri-

à cette espérance. Parmi nous, ce n'est qu'avec le temps que la vérité peut vaincre les préjugés; il faut qu'elle règne non avec l'éclat d'une nouvelle création du génie, mais avec cette force invisible de la raison générale, qui a renversé les erreurs, sans qu'on ait entendu le bruit de leur chûte.

Voilà, mon cher Romilly, sous quels rapports ce Fontenelle, que j'ai si longtems méprisé, peut-être parceque c'est de tous les hommes d'esprit celui dont la nature m'a fait le plus dissemblable; voilà sous quels rapports Fontenelle me semble très-remarquable. Fontenelle paroît voir dans la vérité cette statue antique d'Isis, couverte de plusieurs voiles. Il croit que chaque siècle doit en lever un, et soulever seulement un autre pour le siècle suivant: il connoît les hommes et il les craint, non seulement parcequ'ils peuvent faire beaucoup de mal, mais parcequ'il est très-difficile de leur faire du bien; et il en a trouvé les moyens dans un art qui n'auroit jamais été, sans doute, celui

---

fice one's self to such a hope as this. But in our days, time only can give to truth the victory over prejudice; with us the reign of truth is not the dazzling sway of some new creation of genius, but it is the imperceptible influence of general intelligence, by which error is overthrown without the sound of its fall being heard.

This is the point of view, my dear Romilly, in which this Fontenelle, whom I have so long despised, only perhaps because of all men of genius he is the one to whom nature has made me the most unlike, appears to me to be so remarkable. Truth seems in his eyes to be like that ancient statue of Isis, which was covered with many veils. He thinks that every age should remove one veil, and only raise the next for the age which is to follow. He knows men, and he fears them, not only because they are capable of doing much harm, but because it is very difficult to do them any good: and he has found the means of doing them good by the practice of an art which would doubtless never have been the expedient of a more

Mais voilà beaucoup de bavardage pour vos yeux et peut-être pour votre esprit. Excusez-moi, mon cher Romilly ; j'ai besoin de distractions, et j'en cherche au sein de votre amitié, parcequ'elle m'est bien douce et bien chère. *Vale, et me ama.*

Ce Mardi.

Letter XXXVI.

FROM THE COUNT DE MIRABEAU.

Londres, ce Vendredi, 4 Mars, 1785.

Grâces à l'indicible étourderie de Baynes, dont je n'ai jamais vu l'égal dans un homme aussi sage et aussi studieux, vous avez à peine ma première lettre, mon bon ami, ou vous ne l'avez pas, et je suis cependant très-tenté de vous en écrire une autre ; car l'absence de Madame de * * * me laisse un mal-être auquel je ne puis échapper. Oh, combien les âmes sensibles éprouvent les besoins du cœur plus que les autres nécessités de

---

But your eyes, if not your head, will have had enough of this garrulity. Excuse it, my dear Romilly ; I want something to divert my thoughts, and I seek for it in the bosom of your friendship, because it is very pleasing and very dear to me. *Vale, et me ama.*

Tuesday.

Letter XXXVI.

London, Friday, March 4. 1785.

Thanks to the unspeakable thoughtlessness of Baynes, which I never before saw equalled in so steady and studious a man, you have hardly got my first letter, my good friend, or you have it not, and yet I am much tempted to write you another ; for Madame de * * *'s absence leaves me in a state of wretchedness which I cannot get rid of. Oh ! how much does an affectionate disposition feel the yearnings of the

la vie ! La mienne est une suite d'expériences sur les infirmités du cœur humain ; et je voudrois bien trouver le terme où il ne peut plus souffrir, afin d'être sûr du moins une fois d'avoir épuisé ma destinée.

J'aurois été vous chercher si vous eussiez été ici. J'ai été voir Baynes ; mais cet homme excellent d'ailleurs analyse toujours, et moi j'ai besoin d'être senti. Diriez-vous où, pressé de la nécessité de m'attendrir et d'être triste, j'ai été ? Dans les hôpitaux ; et en vérité je n'en ai pas été content, quoique Elliot m'ait montré les meilleurs comme les plus mauvais. J'aurois mille choses à dire ; mais je ne veux vous parler que d'une, qui, menant à des idées générales, vous fera mieux supporter mon bavardage.

Tous les hôpitaux, tous les lieux où l'on recueille les infirmes, les enfans trouvés, les mendians, les fols, &c. &c. ; toutes ces maisons sont établies dans les villes. Pourquoi ne les transporte-t-on pas des villes, qu'elles infectent, et qui les infectent,

---

heart more than all the other wants of life ! Mine is a succession of experiments on the infirmities of the human heart, and I would gladly find the period when it may cease to suffer, that I might, for once at least, feel sure of having exhausted my destiny.

I should have looked for you, had you been here. I went to see Baynes ; but that man, however excellent in other respects, is always analysing, and I want sympathy. Would you guess whither, impelled by the desire of indulging in my feelings of emotion and sadness, I went ? To the hospitals ; and, indeed, I was not pleased with them, though Elliot showed me the best as well as the worst. I have a thousand things to say, but I will keep to one, which, as it leads to general principles, will better enable you to bear with my tediousness.

All hospitals, all institutions for the reception of the infirm, of foundlings, beggars, lunatics, &c. &c. are established within towns. Why are they not removed from towns which they infect, and which

dans les campagnes, et surtout dans les campagnes les plus éloignées, dans les déserts; car tous les royaumes, et même l'Angleterre, ont des déserts?

1°. Les enfans, plus sensibles à toutes les impressions de l'air, prennent et communiquent les maladies contagieuses avec une extrême facilité; et chez eux, dans ces petits corps spongieux, pour ainsi dire, toutes les maladies sont contagieuses. Dans les hospices des villes, où on les amoncèle les uns sur les autres, il y a une contagion fixée parmi eux, et l'on peut dire qu'ils vivent toujours avec une maladie mortelle. Dans les campagnes, on les placeroit à d'assez grandes distances pour couper aisément toutes les routes de contagion à leurs maladies. De cela seul résulteroit trois grands biens: on en conserveroit infiniment davantage; l'air des villes seroit délivré d'un grand foyer de corruption; et l'entretien de ces maisons seroit soulagé des frais de tous les remèdes qu'on fait prendre à ces enfans continuellement malades.

2°. N'est-il pas étrange que ce soit dans les villes

---

infect them, to the country, and indeed to the most distant parts of the country, to deserts; for all kingdoms, even England, have deserts?

1°. Children, who are more susceptible to influence from the atmosphere, take and give contagious disorders with extreme facility, and with them, in their little spongy bodies, so to speak, all diseases are contagious. In town-hospitals, where they are huddled one upon another, contagion is settled amongst them; and it may almost be said that they live with a mortal disease. In the country they would be placed at distances from each other, sufficient to cut off with ease all access to contagion. From this alone would result three great advantages: the lives of many more would be preserved; the air of towns would be freed from a great hot-bed of corruption; and the funds of the establishment would be relieved from the expense of all those remedies which must be given to these children who are constantly ill.

2°. Is it not strange that it should be in towns, where luxury en-

où le luxe enchérit tout, où l'opulence même et l'industrie la plus active ont tant de peine à vivre, qu'on place des maisons qui doivent subsister de la charité du gouvernement ou de la nation? Qu'on les transporte dans les campagnes, où tout est à meilleur marché, leur entretien coûtera un tiers, une moitié, deux tiers de moins, suivant les lieux, et ce qu'elles consommeront sera une source de fécondité pour ces mêmes campagnes.

3°. Ici même, et peut-être autant ici que partout ailleurs, les employés à la régie de ces maisons dépouillent le pauvre des deniers donnés par la charité publique, et s'enrichissent en dérobant le pain à la faim dévorante, en volant à l'enfant qui se meurt le remède qui devait lui sauver la vie . . . . Le brigand couvre souvent la nudité du pauvre; le plus féroce assassin soutient l'homme qui tombe en défaillance, et dans ces administrations . . . . . C'est le crime qui accuse à la fois, qui outrage et qui révolte le plus l'humanite. Il

---

hances the price of every thing, where even opulence and the most active industry find it so difficult to live, that these establishments, which must subsist on the charity of government or of the people, should be placed? Let them be removed to the country, where every thing is cheaper, the cost of maintaining them will, according to the situation, be one third, one half, two thirds less, and what they consume will be a source of prosperity to the neighbouring country.

3°. Even here, and perhaps as much here as elsewhere, the officers of these establishments strip the poor of the pittance given by public charity, and enrich themselves in pilfering bread from those who are famishing with hunger, and in robbing from the dying child the remedies which were intended to save its life. . . . . The highwayman often covers the nakedness of the poor, the most ferocious assassin supports the fainting man, and in these establishments . . . . It is the crime which at once accuses, outrages, and most revolts humanity.

ne peut être commis que dans les lieux où les plus grands excès sont devenus des besoins, où les passions sans cesse irritées et toujours promptement satisfaites, font passer continuellement les âmes du délire, de la fureur des désirs, à cet assoupissement des voluptés et de la mollesse, dans lequel on n'a pas la force d'avoir un sentiment; où l'on est cruel et barbare par l'impuissance de recevoir les douces émotions de la pitié. Il ne peut être commis que dans les lieux où les objets de luxe vous cachent, pour ainsi dire, la nature; où la foule vous dérobe à chaque instant à vous-même; où le bruit des plaisirs étouffe et fait taire la voix intérieure de l'âme et de la conscience; où, vivant continuellement dans des spectacles qui ne sont qu'illusion, on finit par oublier qu'on est homme et qu'on vit avec des hommes. Un tel crime ne peut être commis que dans les villes à grand luxe. Dans les campagnes, où l'on ne sent guère que les besoins de la nature, où les passions sont moins séductrices, et moins énivrantes, on ne

---

It can only be committed in places where the greatest excesses are become necessities, where, from the constant excitement and prompt gratification of the passions, the minds of men pass continually from the delirium, the frenzy of desire, to that lethargic state of voluptuousness and effeminacy, which deprives men of the power of feeling, which makes them cruel and barbarous, from their inability to receive the soft emotions of pity. It can only be committed in those places where nature is in a manner concealed by objects of luxury, where the crowd every moment draws you away from yourself, where the sound of pleasure stifles and silences the inward voice of sympathy and of conscience, where living constantly amidst sights which are but an illusion, one ends by forgetting that one is a man, and that one lives with men. Such a crime can only be committed in towns of great luxury. In the country, where few desires but those of nature are felt, where passions are less seductive and less intoxicating, one sees nothing one is

voit rien qu'on soit tenté d'acheter par un si grand crime. Les administrateurs, restant continuellement près des enfans malheureux confiés à leurs soins, entendroient mieux à la fois, dans le silence des campagnes, et la voix de leur conscience et le cri de l'infortune. Ils seroient pitoyables et bons même par intérêt personnel.

Il se présente une objection, et elle est unique, à ce que je crois. On peut dire que des maisons éloignées des grandes villes, où sont aussi les grandes fortunes, ne seroient pas aussi bien placées pour attirer sur elles les bienfaits de la charité ; en les perdant de vue, la pitié s'affoibliroit peut-être ; elles ne s'enrichiroient plus des expiations du crime, et des dons généreux de la vertu. Mais, mon ami, je ne crois point que ce soient les mouvemens fugitifs et instantanés de la pitié qui attirent des bienfaits sur ces maisons. Elles sont très-peu connues dans les grandes villes au milieu desquelles elles sont placées; elles y sont aussi cachées qu'elles pourroient l'être dans les campagnes ; c'est

---

tempted to purchase at the price of so great a crime. The officers of the establishment remaining constantly with the unfortunate children intrusted to their care, would, in the silence of the country, be more alive both to the voice of their conscience and to the cry of misfortune. They would become kind and compassionate even from self-interest.

One objection presents itself, and one only, as I believe. It may be said that establishments at a distance from large towns where are also the large fortunes, would not be so well placed to attract the beneficence of charity; in losing sight of them, compassion would diminish, perhaps ; they would no longer be enriched by the expiations of crime, and the generous gifts of virtue. But, my friend, I do not believe that it is from momentary and fleeting emotions of pity that these institutions derive their benefactions. They are very little known in those large towns, in the midst of which they stand; they are there as much out of sight as they could be in the country; it is the matured

le sentiment réfléchi et constant de l'humanité qui leur portent des présens, et ces deux sentimens savent aller chercher loin les objets de leur libéralité. C'est communément par les dernières volontés de la vie, par les testamens qu'on leur laisse des biens, et la pensée d'un homme qui dispose de sa fortune pour les temps où il ne sera plus, n'est pas plus éloignée des malheureux qui sont à cinquante lieues de lui, que de ceux qui sont à ses côtés. Les réflexions, et les relations, et les lumières, en répandant au loin le sentiment de l'humanité, l'ont peut-être affoibli, mais elles l'ont singulièrement étendu. On pleure moins, on secourt davantage. La pitié prompte et passionnée est la générosité des siècles barbares; la générosité réfléchie et combinée est la pitié des siècles éclairés. Il ne faut donc pas croire que la source des charités particulières et publiques tarît dans les villes, si l'on en éloignoit les hospices des enfans trouvés ou des mendians; elle couleroit en refécondant dans sa route jusqu'aux lieux éloignés où l'on transporteroit ces maisons.

---

and the lasting feeling of humanity, which brings offerings to them, and these two feelings travel far in search of objects for their liberality. It is usually by the last dispositions of life, by wills, that property is left to them; and the thoughts of a man who disposes of his fortune for the time when he shall be no more, are not farther removed from the unhappy beings who are fifty leagues off, than from those who are by his side. Reflection, intercourse, and information, in spreading far the feelings of humanity, may perhaps have weakened, but have singularly extended them. Fewer tears are shed; more assistance given. Quick and impassioned pity is the generosity of barbarous ages; well considered and combined generosity the pity of enlightened times. It must not therefore be supposed that the source of public and private charity would be dried up in towns, if hospitals for foundlings or beggars were removed from them; it would flow on fertilizing in its course to the most distant spots in which these buildings might be placed. And

Et si tant d'avantages ne regardent que ces hospices mêmes, remarquez, mon ami, qu'il s'en présente de bien plus considérables pour la nation entière. On s'est plaint de tous temps, et depuis un demi siècle les plaintes ont singulièrement redoublé en Angleterre ce me semble comme en France, de ce penchant aveugle et funeste qui fait abandonner à tous les hommes les campagnes pour les villes, qui peuple les ateliers des arts et les manufactures, des hommes qui manquent à la culture des champs. L'établissement des maisons de charité dans les villes est très-propre à entretenir, à augmenter ce désordre. Les enfans qu'on y nourrit ne peuvent être élevés que pour les métiers et pour les villes; le travail sédentaire des métiers tue les enfans, dont le premier besoin est de courir, de sauter, et de s'ébattre. Et c'est là sûrement une des causes de la mortalité effrayante établie dans ces maisons. Si on les transporte dans les campagnes, les enfans que l'état y nourrit seront nourris et élevés pour les campagnes.

---

if these numerous advantages concern the hospitals alone, observe, my friend, that much more important ones result to the whole nation. Complaints have at all times been made, and for half a century they have wonderfully increased in England, as it seems to me, as well as in France, against the blind and fatal inclination which induces all people to abandon the country for towns, which peoples the workshops of art and manufacture with the men who are wanted for the cultivation of the fields. Charitable establishments in towns tend much to maintain and increase this evil. Children bred there can only be brought up for trade and for town; the sedentary employment of trades kills children, whose first want is to run, to jump, and play about; and this is no doubt one of the causes of the frightful mortality in these hospitals. If removed into the country, these children, fed there at the expense of the nation, will be fed and brought up for the country. Govern-

roit dans ce nouvel emploi des enfans et des hommes renfermés dans les hospices de la nation.

Voilà un beau rêve, n'est-ce pas, mon ami ? mais vous le trouvez trop long peut-être, et je finis. Pardon, mais il est doux de rêver au bonheur des hommes, tout méchans qu'ils sont, parceque ce n'est pas la faute du plus grand nombre s'ils le sont ; il est doux d'y rêver surtout quand on est très-malheureux et on craint de se réveiller. *Vale, et me ama.*

M.

LETTER XXXVII.

FROM THE COUNT DE MIRABEAU.

[Londres, ce 5 Mars, 1785.]

Vous saurez, mon ami, que je suis devenu si philosophe, si sage, si insouciant, qu'une conversion si prompte, si complète, est un vrai phénomène. Vous saurez que j'ai entendu hier M.

---

these means would be found in turning to this new account children and men now confined within the hospitals of the nation.

This is a fine dream, is it not, my friend? but you find it too long, perhaps, and I have done. Forgive me, but it is pleasing to make dreams for the happiness of men, wicked though they be, for it is not the fault of the greater number if they are so; it is pleasing to indulge in such dreams, above all when one is very unhappy, and when one fears to awake. *Vale, et me ama.*

M.

LETTER XXXVII.

London, March 5. 1785.

You must know, my dear friend, that I am become so philosophical, so rational, and so indifferent, that such a speedy and complete conversion is positively a phenomenon. You must know that yesterday

Gibbon[1] parler, comme un des plus plats coquins qui existent, sur la situation politique de l'Europe, et que je n'ai pas dit un mot, quoique dès la première phrase de M. Gibbon, sa morgue et son air insolent m'eussent infiniment repoussés. Vous saurez que pressé par votre candide ami le Marquis de Lansdowne de dire mon avis, je me suis contenté de proférer ce peu de mots : "Je n'entends rien à la politique, et surtout rien à celle de M. Gibbon ; mais je crois que je puis assez bien deviner les motifs des écrivains politiques, parceque, solitaire et studieux, j'ai l'habitude de démêler dans les écrits d'un homme de lettres ses principes, et les principes sont la clef de tout. Or, j'ai lu l'élégante histoire de M. Gibbon, et cela me suffit. Je dis son *élégante*, et non pas son *estimable* histoire, et voici pourquoi. Jamais, à mon avis, la philosophie n'a mieux rassemblé les lumières que l'érudition peut donner sur les temps anciens, et

---

I heard Mr. Gibbon[1] talk like one of the most arrant knaves in existence upon the political state of Europe, and that I did not utter a word, although I was infinitely disgusted with the air of insolent confidence which accompanied his very first sentence. You must know that, urged by your candid friend the Marquis of Lansdowne to give my opinion, I contented myself with delivering these few sentences : — " I understand nothing of politics, and especially nothing of Mr. Gibbon's politics, but I think I can pretty well guess the motives of political writers, because, solitary and studious in my habits, I am accustomed in the writings of a man of letters to make out his principles, and principles are the key to every thing. Now, I have read Mr. Gibbon's elegant history, and that is enough for me. I say his *elegant*, not his *valuable* history, and for this reason. Never, in my opinion, has philosophy more skilfully collected together the information which erudition can afford respecting ancient times, nor arranged it in a hap-

---

[1] This is a mistake of Mirabeau's. Gibbon was at this time at Lausanne. See *antè*, p. 85.

ne les a disposées dans un ordre plus heureux et plus facile. Mais, soit que M. Gibbon ait été séduit, ou qu'il ait voulu le paroître, par la grandeur de l'empire Romain, par le nombre de ses légions, par la magnificence de ses chemins et de ses cités, il a tracé un tableau odieusement faux de la félicité de cet empire, qui écrasoit le monde et ne le rendoit pas heureux. Ce tableau même il l'a pris dans Gravina, au livre *de Imperio Romano*. Gravina mérite indulgence, parcequ'il étoit excusé par une de ces grandes idées dont le génie surtout est si facilement la dupe. Comme Leibnitz, il étoit occupé du projet d'un empire universel, formé de la réunion de tous les peuples de l'Europe, sous les mêmes lois et la même puissance ; et il cherchoit un exemple de cette monarchie universelle dans ce qu'avoit été l'empire Romain depuis Auguste. Monsieur Gibbon peut nous dire qu'il a eu la même idée ; mais encore lui répondrai-je qu'il écrivoit une histoire, et ne faisoit pas un système. D'ailleurs cela n'expliqueroit point, et surtout cela

---

pier and more natural order. But whether Mr. Gibbon has really been led away, or has wished to appear to be so, by the greatness of the Roman empire, by the number of its legions, by the magnificence of its roads and of its cities, he has drawn an odiously false picture of the felicity of that empire, which crushed the world and did not make it happy. This picture too he took from Gravina, in his book *de Imperio Romano*. Gravina is entitled to indulgence, for he is excused by one of those great ideas of which genius especially is so easily the dupe. Like Leibnitz, he was taken up with the project of an universal empire, formed by an union of all the nations of Europe, under the same laws and the same authority, and he sought for an example of this universal monarchy in the Roman empire, from the time of Augustus. Mr. Gibbon may tell us that he entertained the same idea, but to this I should reply that he was writing a history, not founding a system. Besides, this would not explain, still less would it excuse, the

n'excuseroit pas l'esprit général de son ouvrage, où se montre à chaque instant l'amour et l'estime des richesses, le goût des voluptés, l'ignorance des vraies passions de l'homme, l'incrédulité surtout pour les vertus républicaines. En parcourant l'histoire du Bas Empire de M. Gibbon, j'aurois aisément deviné que, si l'auteur se montroit jamais dans les affaires publiques de la Grande Bretagne, on le verroit prêtant sa plume aux ministres, et combattant les droits des Américains à l'indépendance: j'aurois aussi deviné la conversation d'aujourd'hui; l'éloge du luxe et de l'autorité *compacte*, comme dit Monsieur. Aussi, je n'ai jamais pu lire son livre sans m'étonner qu'il fût écrit en Anglois. Chaque instant à peu près, comme Marcel, j'étois tenté de m'addresser à M. Gibbon, et de lui dire, '*Vous un Anglois! Non, vous ne l'êtes point. Cette admiration pour un empire de plus de deux cent millions d'hommes, où il n'y a pas un seul homme qui ait le droit de se dire libre, cette philosophie efféminée qui donne plus d'éloges au luxe et aux plaisirs*

---

general spirit of the work, which displays at every moment a love and respect for wealth, a taste for luxury, an ignorance of the real passions of man, and above all a disbelief in republican virtue. In reading through Mr. Gibbon's History of the Lower Empire, I should readily have guessed that, if the author ever came forward in the public affairs of Great Britain, he would be seen lending his pen to ministers, and contesting the right of the Americans to independence. I should also have anticipated the conversation of to-day, the praise of luxury and of '*compact*' authority, as he is pleased to call it. Accordingly I never could read his book without wondering that it should be written in English. At almost every moment, I was tempted, like Marcel, to address Mr. Gibbon, and to say to him, 'You an Englishman! No, that you are not. This admiration for an empire of more than two hundred millions of men, where there is not a single man who has the right to call himself free, this effeminate philosophy which bestows more praise upon luxury and pleasure than upon virtue,

qu'aux vertus, ce style toujours élégant et jamais énergique, annoncent tout au plus l'esclave d'un électeur d'Hanovre.'" Diriez-vous, mon ami, que des paroles si édulcorées ayent paru irriter M. Gibbon, et qu'il m'ait dit qu'il n'y avoit rien à répondre à des injures? et moi j'ai ri . . . . Oh ! je vous assure que je fais de grands progrès dans l'art de ménager les hommes.

Au reste, mon ami, notez deux choses que me dit hier le Marquis, qui a réellement beaucoup d'esprit et d'idées. La première, bien digne de remarque, c'est qu'on lit dans les *Mémoires de Bellecombe*[1] qu'un capitaine, dont il ne se rappela pas le nom, proposoit, avant le milieu de ce siècle, de conquérir le Bengale avec cinq cents hommes. On le prit pour un fol. Cela met bien à leur juste mesure les brigands postérieurs qui voudroient se faire passer pour des héros ; et cela prouve, ce que je pense

---

this style, always elegant but never energetic, proclaim, at the very best, the slave of an elector of Hanover.'" Could you have supposed, my friend, that words so softened down could have appeared to irritate Mr. Gibbon, and that he could have told me that he had no reply to make to abuse? As for me, I laughed. . . . . Oh ! I assure you I make great progress in the art of conciliating men.

In the mean time, my friend, observe two things which were said to me yesterday by the Marquis, who is really very clever, and very full of thought. The first, which is well worthy of remark, was, that in *Bellecombe's*[1] *Memoirs* it is said that an officer, whose name he did not remember, offered, before the middle of the present century, to conquer Bengal with five hundred men. He was taken for a madman. This places on their proper level the cut-throats of a later date, who aim at being thought heroes ; and it proves, what I have long thought,

---

[1] Probably Melcombe; see *Diary of G. Bubb Doddington, Lord Melcombe*, who, in 1751, relates a proposal by Colonel Milles, to conquer Bengal with 1500 men, p. 110. 4th edit.

depuis longtemps, que la révolution de l'Amérique s'est faite à Londres, et celle de l'Indostan dans le Bengale, *ex visceribus rei.*

La seconde chose porte sur une idée belle et profonde. "Je voudrois," dit le Marquis, "que l'on questionnât les scélérats convaincus, pour les étudier en philosophes, après les avoir interrogés en magistrats pour les condamner. On gouverne les hommes, et on ne les connoît point; on ne fait rien pour les connoître." Cette pensée m'a paru grande, vraie, et touchante.

Un malheureux, accusé d'un crime qui peut le mener à l'échafaud, est assis sur une sellette; on l'interroge, mais sur son crime uniquement, et, si son crime paroît établi, on l'envoie à la mort sans lui rien demander de plus. Chez nous, il se confesse à l'oreille du ministre de la religion, dans le sein du quel tous les secrets de sa vie doivent se perdre. On ne doit plus que de la pitié aux criminels même, lorsqu'ils ont entendu leur sentence de mort: car, dès ce moment, ils ont déjà

---

that the revolution of America was made in London, and that of Hindoostan in Bengal, *ex visceribus rei.*

The second thing involves a fine and profound thought. "I wish," said the Marquis, "that convicted criminals were questioned, in order that they might be philosophically studied, after having been magisterially examined with a view to their conviction. We govern men, and we do not know them, we do not endeavour to know them." This thought appeared to me important, true, and affecting.

An unfortunate man, accused of a crime which may bring him to the scaffold, is placed in the dock; he is examined, but with reference to his crime only, and if that appear to be proved, he is sent to death without another question being asked him. With us, he makes his confession in private to the minister of religion, in whose breast all the secrets of his life are to be buried. As soon as a criminal has heard his sentence of death, our only feeling towards him should be that of pity;

Letter XXXVIII.

FROM MR. BAYNES.

Dear Romilly, London, March 7. 1785.

I dined yesterday with your brother; we had, as usual, a very agreeable afternoon; he is to go in your stead with Mr. M. into the House of Commons, in case of your absence. It was your mother's birthday; they did not intend to tell me; but I happened to have found it out by accident previously, and, all on a sudden, I drank your mother's health, congratulating her on the occasion. They were all surprised, and we laughed most heartily, an art in which, if loudness and frequency are any merit, I surely excel. However, they soon guessed that I had got my information at Kensington, whither I had been on a walk with the Count.[1]

I dare say you are no more sorry than myself that the scrutiny is ended. Mr. Fox's party keep within no bounds of joy; they have illuminated two or three nights, and yesterday, the rabble drew Mr. Fox to the House of Commons.

The Count called upon me to-day, to desire me to write to Johnson to insist on his finishing the translation, and publishing it immediately.[2] Hardy has printed an English libel against him, apparently translated from the French of Linguet: — this, I trust, will be of no great service to H. if he should bring his cause to a trial. The Count

[1] Mirabeau. [2] See *antè*, p. 79.

complains bitterly of his hard fate, in losing Madame de * * * and you at once. By his letter to you, he seems to think my heart harder than adamant or Marpesian rocks, in being so insensible to his distress. For my part, as I well know that there are many persons who possess much finer feelings than myself, so, I trust, I am far from being that unfeeling philosophizing mass of clay which the Count seems to imagine me; and though I doubt not in the least the sincerity of his sorrow, yet I own I am, on this occasion, much more disposed to wish he had no greater cause of uneasiness. One reason why he seems to think thus of me is probably a certain reserve or backwardness (which, in other respects, I do not possess,) in expressing my affections either of pity or regard to any other person. This is perhaps a weakness, perhaps a fault, which I feel I possess, and which I cannot help attributing to the circumstance of my not meeting with a friend whose disposition exactly suited me, till very late in life. This, however, if a fault, will I trust be readily excused by you; particularly as, on many occasions, I cannot help fancying that I have seen you feel much more than you have ventured, or had the courage, to express. I do not know whether I am not much bolder on paper than in conversation, in expressing as well my own uneasinesses as my regards. I think I have observed the same in you. However this may be, I hope *you* will not think me the more insensible because I do not always express my sensations; nor insincere, when I assure you that I do really feel a great want of your company. I have even the pleasure to hope you will believe me, when I assure you that your friendship is the principal source of my present happiness; and that it is my greatest consolation to reflect that we shall never probably be far or long separated during our lives.

"Equidem ex omnibus rebus, quas mihi aut fortuna aut natura tribuit, nihil habeo, quod cum amicitiâ Scipionis possum comparare. In hâc mihi de republicâ consensus, in hâc rerum privatarum consilium; in eâdem requies plena oblectationis fuit" (I wish I might add, "nunquam illum ne minimâ quidem re offendi, quod quidem senserim"); "nihil audivi ex eo ipse, quod nollem. Una domus erat, idem victus, isque communis: neque solum militia, sed etiam peregrinationes rusticationesque communes."[1]

Yours, dear Romilly, ever sincerely,

J. B.

Tuesday, 8th.

Letter XXXIX.

FROM MR. BAYNES.

Dear Romilly, Gray's Inn, March 16. 1785.

The Count is delighted with your letter; he is determined you shall be a great man; and, from the conversation I had with him this morning in confidence, I have great reason to think that he has spoken of you in such terms to Lord Shelburne, as to induce Lord S. to offer you a seat in Parliament.[2] I doubt not but that you will be astonished at this information; it is, however, my

[1] Cic. de Amicit.

[2] See *antè*, p. 87.

firm opinion that some such plan is in agitation. I collect it only from what passed between the Count and me this morning. The terms offered will, I doubt not, be very liberal. Though my information is founded only on the Count's ideas, which are in general very sanguine, yet I see no reason to doubt his accuracy in this account. At all events, I thought it would be the best to tell you my suspicions; as it would be very unpleasant for you to be attacked unprepared upon so important a subject. I wish you would give me a line, immediately or as soon as possible, with the rough sketch of your ideas of this proposal. Pray consider it well. I will then tell you mine very freely.

Yours sincerely,

J. B.

Letter XL.

FROM THE COUNT DE MIRABEAU.

[Londres,] 18 Mars, 1785.

Mon Ami,

Je ne vous répondrai pas, parceque je suis écrasé d'ouvrage inattendu; mais je vous dirai du moins combien votre lettre m'a touché, combien elle porte l'empreinte d'un cœur tendre et d'une

---

Letter XL.

London, March 18. 1785.

My dear Friend,

I will not reply to you, because I am overwhelmed with unexpected business; but I will at least tell you how much your letter has touched me, how deeply it bears the stamp of a tender heart and an

âme honnête, et quel charme ce *dulcia sunto*[1] répand sur les plus grands talens et sur les plus fortes conceptions de l'esprit. Je sens comme vous avez senti dans votre lettre, quoique je ne pense pas sur ce sujet comme vous pensez; parcequ'il est impossible à ma raison de donner son assentiment à la seule émotion. *On ne me répond pas, mais peut-être on m'entend;* ces mots touchans proférés sur l'urne cinéraire d'un ami, m'ont toujours paru ce qu'on pouvoit dire de plus éloquent en faveur de l'immortalité de l'âme; et si je ne puis trouver à cette théorie qu'un attrait, et non pas une évidence portant conviction, ni même une probabilité entraînant persuasion, cet attrait m'a toujours semblé assez vif pour non seulement excuser, mais aimer et louer ceux qui admettent ce dogme, quoique leurs argumens me paroissent incomplets et défectueux. Et plût au Fabricateur des mondes, que le grand ressort qu'il a mis en nous,

---

honest mind, and what a charm these "*dulcia sunto*[1]" diffuse over the greatest talents and the most vigorous conceptions of the intellect.

I feel as you felt in your letter, although I do not think upon this subject as you think; because it is impossible for my reason to give its assent to feeling alone. "*I am not answered, but perhaps I am heard;*" these affecting words, uttered over the grave of a friend, have always appeared to me the most eloquent thing that could be said in favour of the immortality of the soul; and if in this theory I can find but a charm, and not evidence amounting to conviction, or even a probability carrying with it persuasion, still it is a charm which has always appeared to me attractive enough not only to excuse, but to make one love and praise those who admit this dogma, although to me their arguments appear incomplete and defective. And would that it had pleased the Creator of worlds that sensibility, the great elastic principle with

---

[1] Non satis est pulchra esse poëmata; *dulcia sunto*,
Et quocunque volent, animum auditoris agunto.
Hor. De A. P. 99.

la sensibilité, n'eût jamais entraîné notre espèce à des illusions plus dangereuses, à des paralogismes plus funestes! Quoiqu'il en soit, mon ami, si vous avez cru me faire un sermon, je vous dirai, sermonnez-moi toujours ainsi; la poësie de votre âme vaut mieux à la mienne que la logique de ma pauvre tête, qui, dans ce genre, après avoir bien travaillé, ne fait guère que substituer des difficultés à des difficultés.

Je vous attends avec impatience, mon bon ami, non pas seulement parceque vous voir et causer avec vous est devenu un des plus vifs et des plus précieux besoins de mon cœur et de mon esprit, mais parceque je suis très-trompé ou il s'ouvre une carrière digne de vous, et propre à donner l'essor à vos grands talens. On m'a fait des propositions à votre sujet qui ne blesseront pas votre délicatesse, puisqu'elles n'ont point effarouché la mienne, et qui vous présagent un nouvel ordre de choses. Je sais ce que votre damnable timidité et votre aimable modestie vont me répondre; mais, mon ami, je

---

which he has endowed us, had never seduced our species into more dangerous illusions, into more fatal paralogisms. Be that as it may, my friend, if you thought to read me a lecture, I will say to you, lecture me ever thus; the poetry of your soul is better for mine than the logic of my poor head, which, on such matters, after having laboured hard, does little more than substitute one difficulty for another.

I expect you impatiently, my good friend, not only because to see you and to converse with you is become one of the most lively and precious wants of my heart and mind, but because (unless I much deceive myself) a career is about to be opened to you which is worthy of you, and suited to the exercise of your great talents. Proposals have been made to me on your behalf, which will not offend your delicacy, since mine has not been alarmed by them, and which hold out to you the promise of a new order of things. I know the answer your insufferable timidity and amiable diffidence are going to make; but I

vous répéterai pour la millième fois qu'un homme fort doit avoir le sentiment de sa force, et que la sauvagerie n'est pas la modestie, ni la timidité la circonspection. Heureusement on a dans ce pays le très-bon esprit de mettre moins de prix aux graces que partout ailleurs; mais il est cependant une vacillation de contenance qui nuit partout, et le très-petit et frivole talent de costumer sa personne et son attitude ne se gagne que dans le monde. Si donc, par des raisons tirées de votre profession, ou de vos projets (car il n'est aucune autre objection admissible lorsqu'on vous appelle au rôle d'homme public sans conditions), vous ne voulez pas accepter les propositions qui vous seront faites, connoissez du moins, et voyez ceux qui veulent vous les faire. Répandez-vous, voyez, soyez vu, montrez-vous, formez-vous. Tout ce à quoi je me suis engagé c'est à vous amener, parceque je sais qu'un étranger ne peut pas conseiller dans les choses locales; mais je me suis engagé à cela, et vous ne m'en dédirez

---

will repeat to you, my friend, for the thousandth time, that a powerful mind ought to have the consciousness of its own power, and that shyness is not modesty, nor want of courage prudence. Fortunately, in this country, people have the great good sense to set less value upon external grace than in any other part of the world, but nevertheless there is a certain want of self-possession which is injurious every where; and the art of setting off the person and demeanour, petty and frivolous as it is, is only to be acquired in the world. If then, for reasons drawn from your profession or plans in life (for when, unfettered by conditions, you are called upon to take a part in public life, no other reason is admissible), you will not accept the proposals which will be made you, at all events know and see those who wish to make them. Mix in society, see and be seen, show what you are, form yourself. I know that in local matters a foreigner is not a safe adviser, and accordingly all that I have engaged to do is to bring you with me: to so much I am pledged, and you will not deny me; for, in

pas ; car, dans un pays libre, dans un pays où il y a une patrie, un citoyen doit conférence à quiconque la lui demande sur des objets d'utilité publique.

Tout ceci vous paroîtra peut-être du galimathias, mon ami, mais ce n'est rien moins qui cela, et vous en aurez la clef à la première vue. — *Vale, et me ama.*

Letter XLI.

FROM THE COUNT DE MIRABEAU.

[Paris,] 22 Mai, 1785.

Pour cette fois, mon bon et cher Romilly, et, sans tirer à conséquence, vous avez tort. J'arrive ce soir à minuit à Paris: j'y trouve votre lettre, arrivée de hier : et je n'ai que le temps de vous dire que je viens de faire 300 lieues, composer, imprimer, tirer, et brocher 300 pages à 2000 exemplaires ; que ce livre[1], bon ou mauvais, mais nécessaire pour sauver un bon ministre, et,

---

a free country, one which is truly a mother country, a citizen is bound to give audience to any one who may demand it of him on matters of public utility.

All this may, perhaps, appear jargon to you, my friend ; it is, however, nothing less, I assure you, and I will give you the key to it when we meet. *Vale, et me ama.*

Letter XLI.

Paris, May 22. 1785.

This time, my good and dear Romilly (but without any disparagement to you), you are in the wrong. I reached Paris, to-night, at twelve: I find your letter, which arrived yesterday ; and I have now only time to tell you, that I have travelled 300 leagues, composed, printed, struck off, and stitched 2000 copies of 300 pages each ; that this book[1], whether good or bad, — but which was necessary to save a good minister, and, what is more, to prevent a bank-

---

[1] The work alluded to was probably the one entitled *De la Banque d'Espagne, dite de St. Charles*, which was suppressed by the French government on the 17th of July, 1785.

qui plus est, une banqueroute de quelques centaines de millions, a été composé, imprimé en pays étranger, rapporté, et mis en état d'être distribué, en moins de cinq semaines, parcequ'il devoit paroître avant le 1er Juin: que ma tournée, un peu rapide comme vous voyez, se faisoit en pays où la moindre chose qui m'eût décelé me faisoit pendre ou empaler: que c'est là la raison unique qui m'a empêché d'écrire: que cela m'a si peu empêché de penser à mes amis que ma petite, qui ne m'a rejoint qu'à la fin, et quand j'ai eu besoin d'elle pour la contrebande, a dû écrire trois ou quatre fois; qu'enfin, en signe de souvenir, il est parti un paquet de cinquante exemplaires de ce livre, où je les rappelle aux ordres de leurs graces MM. Elliot, Romilly, Baynes, Vaughan, et Chauvet. La justification vous paroîtra complète, mon ami, si vous y ajoutez, que, le troisième jour après mon arrivée d'Angleterre, j'ai été saisi par cette besogne, le onzième en course, car de fait, mes matériaux une fois ramassés, le livre a été fait

---

ruptcy to the extent of some hundreds of millions,—has been written, printed in a foreign country (because it was essential that it should appear before the 1st of June), brought back, and got ready for distribution, all in less than five weeks; that my journey, somewhat rapid as you see, was in a country where the slightest thing which had betrayed me would have sent me to the gallows or the stake; that this has been the only cause of my not writing to you, and has so little prevented me from thinking of my friends, that my little dear, who only joined me towards the end of my expedition, when she was wanted for the smuggling, must have written not less than three or four times; that, to conclude, a parcel containing 50 copies of the book has been sent off, in token of remembrance, to Messrs. Elliot, Romilly, Baynes, Vaughan, and Chauvet, at whose disposal I beg to leave them. My justification will appear to you complete, my friend, if you add, that the third day after my arrival from England I was engrossed by this work; that on the eleventh I was on my journey (for, in truth, my materials once collected,

dans les auberges; que vos lettres ne me sont parvenues (sauf la vôtre) qu'après des circuits immenses; que deux me galoppent et ne me sont point encore parvenues; que je suis rendu de fatigue plus que motivée par une expédition d'une activité et d'une audace presque sans exemple; qu'enfin, si le prochain courrier je ne suis pas à la Bastille, vous aurez tous trois ou quatre une grande lettre de moi.—N. B. Que si j'y étois, Mde. de * * * le manderait, et qu'il ne faudrait pas beaucoup s'en effrayer.

Sur le tout, cher ami, aimez-moi comme je vous aime, et montrez sur-le-champ cette lettre à Elliot et Baynes, car il est temps qu'ils sachent ce qu'ils auroient dû deviner, que j'étois incapable d'une négligence si coupable, et qu'il falloit bien qu'il y eût un dessous de carte qu'ils ignoroient.—*Vale, et me ama*; car je tombe de sommeil, mais j'ai voulu saisir le courrier.

Justifiez-moi aussi auprès de M. Vaughan.

---

the book was written in inns); that all the letters of my English friends, with the exception of your own, made enormous circuits before they reached me, and that two of them are still in pursuit of me; that I am exhausted with fatigue more than accounted for by an expedition almost unexampled for its activity and boldness; and, finally, that, by the very next post, if I am not then in the Bastille, you shall all three or four have a long letter from me.—N.B. That if I were there, Mde. * * * would send you word of it, and there would be no great reason for alarm.

To sum up, my friend, love me as I love you, and show this letter, forthwith, to Elliot and Baynes, for it is time they should know, what they ought to have guessed, that I was incapable of such culpable neglect, and that of course there was an under-current of which they knew nothing. *Vale, et me ama;* for I am dropping from my chair with sleep, but I was resolved to save the post.

Set me right also with Mr. Vaughan.

Letter XLII.

FROM THE MARQUIS OF LANSDOWNE.

Sir, Bowood Park, Dec. 25. 1785.

I should have thanked you sooner for the favour of your letter, but deferred doing it till I had time to read the book[1], which accompanied it, with the attention which any thing coming from you will always command from me. The principles of penal law is the subject of all others upon which I am most ignorant, and most unread. However, your arguments, and the authorities to which you refer, incline me to think that a revision of our penal law is not only desirable, but necessary, for the purpose of making it agreeable to the spirit of the times, and such as can be executed.

Mr. Blackburne's plan was stopped during my time at the Treasury. I was assured that if the number of ale-houses could be lessened, the Vagrant Act inforced, and the general administration of justice as it stood invigorated, a great deal might be done without having recourse to any new institution. As Parliament was not sitting nothing could be done about the public-houses ; but a proclamation was issued, and every method tried to bring about the two last, and the effect answered the most sanguine expectation. I see by a late charge of Mr. Mainwaring's to the grand jury of Middlesex, that those most conversant in the police continue of the same opinion. Under these cir-

[1] Entitled *Observations on a late Publication, entitled "Thoughts on Executive Justice, by Madan."* See *antè*, p. 88.

cumstances, it was impossible for me to consent to so great an expenditure upon a plan which I plainly saw had been partially taken up, and the whole of the subject not properly considered. No man would do so in his private affairs; and I still think it would be inexpedient, in the double light of expenditure and punishment, till the measures, to which I allude, have had a fair and effectual trial. Upon the change of ministry these measures were dropped; and a number of persons confined under the Vagrant Act were immediately set at liberty; who have made, if I am rightly informed, a material part of those who have infested London since.

I propose to be in London in about a fortnight; when I shall be very glad of the pleasure of talking to you upon this or any other subject.

I am, with great truth and regard, Sir,

Your most obedient, humble Servant,

LANSDOWNE.

LETTER XLIII.

FROM SIR GILBERT ELLIOT.[1]

Dear Sir, Park Street, Feb. 10. 1786.

I thank you for the very excellent work[2] you have favoured me with. As I am writing to yourself I shall be more reserved than with any other man I can converse with on the subject; but you *must* just give me leave to wonder that you

[1] Afterwards Lord Minto.

[2] The work alluded to in the preceding letter.

should feel the least desire to conceal the name of the author. Your design is too honourable, I think, to leave you much anxiety about the performance, even if that were at all doubtful: but one is worthy of the other, and you know, from me, *c'est tout dire.* I do assure you, the perusal has given me the greatest pleasure, both from the certainty of the very high credit you must derive from it, and from the hope it affords me of seeing real and extensive good result, from our penal law and our administration of criminal justice being treated with your views, and by your pen. I entreat you to go on.

I send you the paper you desired, and some others which you may perhaps either have already or not want; but they may take their chance of serving you.

Believe me most sincerely, dear Sir,

Your faithful humble servant,

GILBERT ELLIOT.

LETTER XLIV.

FROM M. TARGET.

[Paris,] 19 Juin, 1786.

Recevez, Monsieur, tous mes remercîmens du bon ouvrage que vous m'avez envoyé. Je l'ai lu avec l'intérêt qu'inspire un grand objet social, et l'attendrissement que l'on ressent toujours à la

---

LETTER XLIV.

19 June, 1786.

Accept my best thanks, my dear Sir, for the excellent work you have sent me. I read it with the interest which a great social object must inspire, and with the feelings which must be always excited in read-

lecture d'un écrit dicté par l'amour de l'humanité. Ces sentimens s'accroissent de tout ce que peut y ajouter l'amitié que vous m'avez marquée, et dont je conserve un précieux souvenir. Ecrivez, combattez toujours, Monsieur, pour la bienfaisance et pour l'utilité publique; c'est le meilleur emploi d'une vie qu'on perd toutes les fois qu'on ne la consacre pas aux choses utiles.

Je suis délivré depuis peu de jours d'une affaire dont toute l'Europe a parlé: vous savez sans doute que par arrêt du 31 Mai dernier, M. le Cardinal de Rohan a été déchargé de l'accusation, et a obtenu une victoire pleine; les mémoires que j'ai faits pour lui sont à Londres; il y en a même une traduction Angloise, que je désirerois avoir si cela étoit possible.

Je ne recommande point à votre zèle la cause de Mad. de Rochard, qui me remercie à chaque occasion du présent que je lui ai fait en vous indiquant pour défenseur. Je n'ai sûrement aucuns

---

ing what is dictated by the love of mankind. Much is to be added to these feelings from the friendship you have shown me, the recollection of which is most valuable to me. Continue, Sir, to write and to labour in the cause of benevolence and of public utility; it is making the best use of a life which, when not devoted to usefulness, is thrown away.

It is only a few days since I have been set at liberty from a cause which has engaged the attention of all Europe. You, no doubt, know that, by the decree of the 31st of May last, the Cardinal of Rohan has been freed from the accusation against him, and has obtained a complete victory; the defence which I made for him is in London; there is even an English translation of it, which I should wish to have if possible.

I do not beg you to be zealous in the cause of Mad. de Rochard, who takes every opportunity of thanking me for the present I made her in pointing you out for her counsel; no exertions of mine are

efforts à faire pour vous engager à la servir de toute votre justice et de tous vos talens.

Ne m'oubliez pas, je vous prie, auprès de M. Baynes, que je remercie de sa lettre, et à qui je demande pardon de n'avoir pas répondu.

Jai l'honneur d'être avec un attachement respectueux et un dévouement inviolable,

Monsieur,
Votre très-humble
Et très-obéissant Serviteur,
TARGET.

LETTER XLV.

FROM MR. BAYNES.

My dear Friend, Trin. Coll. Camb., Oct. 3. 1786.

I should have been with you by this time, had not our Master and Seniors, by making the late election of Fellows exactly in the most improper as well as most unpopular manner possible, detained me in college a few days longer, for the purpose of endeavouring to effect some reform in the present mode of carrying on that business. How far we shall succeed, Heaven only knows. The particulars of what has passed I cannot now communicate, for many reasons.[1]

---

necessary to induce you to assist her with all your justice and all your talents.

Pray remember me to Mr. Baynes, whom I thank for his letter, and whose forgiveness I ask for not having answered it.

I have the honour to be, &c. &c.
TARGET.

---

[1] See the history of Trinity College, which is appended to Bishop Monk's *Life of Bentley*, vol. ii. p. 423. 2d edit.

My time has been, on the whole, very agreeably spent. Our juniors form a very pleasant party: Cautley and Hailstone and Popple have been with us pretty constantly; Mansell, the Momus of our Pantheon, supplies us as liberally with puns, as Harry Gordon, our Ganymede, with his nectarean port. Alas, poor Gordon! for our Seniors, the other day, thought proper to displace him, after Christmas next, for an insult on some of their own body. We are all unanimous, and facetious, and merry; what can I say more?

Our evenings are filled up by the exertions of two companies of comedians, one from Norwich, the other from I know not where; but the latter is under the management of W. Palmer, of the Theatre Royal, Covent Garden. Palmer and Edwin come down occasionally to W. Palmer's theatre. I am going thither, to-night, with some very handsome ladies; therefore, wonder not at my unusual brevity if I be obliged to conclude soon, as the hour is not far distant. Shakspeare and black letter muster strong at Emanuel. Farmer the master, Stevens, Isaac Reed, and Master Herbert, the editor of Ames, have taken up their quarters there. I have looked for Douce every day; but, alas! he does not come.

I shall come to law with redoubled fury. I have ransacked all the libraries here for manuscripts, but find nothing of much consequence except old readings, which are, mostly, very difficult to read. I have done a chapter of Coke on Fines, read a book of Cicero de Legibus, an oration in Greek, and newspapers and reviews "*sauns nombre.*" You seem all very dull in town, and want a certain person, who shall be nameless, to enliven you. I intend, therefore (provided I can accomplish my point by that time), to set off on Saturday next.

J. B.

Letter XLVI.

FROM MR. WILBERFORCE.

Dear Sir, Teignmouth, Aug. 20. 1787.

I loved and valued poor Baynes [1] more, almost, than I was warranted to do by the length of our acquaintance, or the time we had spent together; and, excepting one or two persons only, there is scarce any man living to whose future public services I looked forward with such good hope as I did to his. An understanding so solid as his, with such unaffected simplicity and honesty of heart, are indeed rarely to be met with in our days; and are a greater national loss than can well be estimated. Though a stranger to his father, it is impossible not to be deeply affected for his situation; I understand he had no other child. The book and ring I shall be much obliged to you if you will transmit to me at Exeter, or rather the latter of them only, and which may be sent in a letter, and will be forwarded to me wherever I may be rambling; the former you will have the goodness to reserve for me until my return to town.

[1] Mr. Baynes died in the summer of 1787. See *antè*, p. 94

I cannot lay aside my pen without expressing a wish, that I may be allowed to persuade myself that the connexion, which was formed between us through the medium of our deceased friend, will not be broken off; but that, though this bond of union exist no longer, we shall continue mutually to cultivate it, as opportunities may occur.

I am, dear Sir, yours, &c.
W. Wilberforce.

Letter XLVII.

FROM MR. MASON.[1]

Sir, Aston, near Rotherham, Sept. 15. 1787.

I was on a visit in South Wales, when the very afflicting news of our excellent friend's death was first communicated to me by the papers; and your letter of the 22d of August, directed to me at York, travelled almost half the kingdom after me, before it found me, only the last post day, returned to my parsonage. This, I trust, you will think a sufficient excuse for so late an answer, and will account for a silence which would, otherwise, have been highly culpable.

I should expatiate much on the character of him who is now lost to us and our country, did I not firmly believe that the person whom he selected for one of his executors, must have as true a sense and even more experience of his invaluable

[1] The poet.

qualities than myself; suffice it for me to avow, that, as youth is the season of virtue, I never saw youth more replete with moral excellence than his exhibited. The remembrance he was pleased to honour me with in his last moments, will make his, end only with mine. Let me intreat you, Sir, when you can do it with propriety, to make my tenderest expressions of condolence acceptable to his too justly afflicted parent, and I hope this will find both you and him somewhat recovered from so severe a stroke.

I am, Sir, with most true respect, your much obliged and obedient servant,

W. Mason.

CORRESPONDENCE WITH M. DUMONT AND OTHERS.

1788—1789.

Letter XLVIII.

TO MADAME D——.[1]

Gray's Inn, Oct. 14. 1788.

I profit very gladly of the liberty you have allowed me of writing to you, and of writing in that language in which I can most forcibly express the sentiments of affection and gratitude which I entertain for you and your family. The hours which I spent with them, were by far the happiest that I passed in France; and though my frequent visits to Passy must have shown that I thought them such, and have made this declaration unnecessary, yet I make it because I find a pleasure in doing so, and in transporting myself, though but in imagination, once again amongst you. If any thing could be wanting to make me feel how much I lost in quitting Paris, it was our unpropitious journey.[2] We had the misfortune to be kept six days by adverse winds at Boulogne; and, notwithstanding all the philosophy we could summon to

[1] These letters were written to a lady with whom and with whose family Mr. Romilly formed, during his stay at Paris, in 1781, a friendship which continued uninterrupted to the end of his life.

[2] Mr. Dumont accompanied Mr. Romilly on this journey.

our assistance, and a pretty large number of books with which we were provided, the contrast between our late residence at Paris, and our then condition, imprisoned in a miserable inn, and, to add to our mortification, with the coast of England full in our view, was too striking not to provoke very frequently our impatience. Our only resource was to talk of Paris and Passy, and in idea to live over again the time which was passed. A few hours more delay would have prevented the possibility of my arriving at Warwick in time for the sessions, and have totally disappointed the only object for which I was in so great a hurry to get from Paris. However, by travelling two nights, and not stopping in London even to unpack my trunks, I arrived time enough: and the only misfortune produced by this delay (but which, indeed, I feel as no small one) is, that I have been prevented delivering Miss D——'s letters till my return from Warwick.

With respect to public affairs, I interest myself so much in them, that I am as impatient to read the foreign gazettes as if the preservation of our liberties depended upon the recovery of those of France. I have found Mr. Seguier's speech (for which I return you many thanks) much more curious than edifying. What has most shocked me in it, even more than his legislative *volonté du Roi*, is the doctrine which he takes so much trouble to enforce, that *les abus naissent du sein des innovations;* because it appears to me to be a doctrine which is pernicious every where, but which in France is destructive not only of all public good, but even of every hope of good; for the people to be happy and free would certainly be, in France, the greatest of all innovations.

Permit me, Madam, to beg that you would present my most affectionate compliments to all your family, to Mr. Guyot and to Mr. Gautier, to whom I hope to have the pleasure of writing by the next post. I have the honour to be, with the sincerest respect and affection, Madam,

Yours, &c.

Saml. Romilly.

Letter XLIX.

TO THE SAME.

Madam, London, Feb. 27. 1789.

Miss D—— does me great injustice in supposing that the late situation of our affairs, or indeed any possible situation of them, could make me forget your family. It has not been forgetfulness, but the fear of tiring you, which has prevented my writing sooner. Perhaps I may still have that to fear, but even at so great a risk, I cannot any longer delay telling you the pleasure I always feel in hearing from you.

Our situation in England begins to wear a very happy appearance. The King, if not quite recovered, is very nearly so. There will be no regency, and consequently no change of ministry. The joy which has taken place throughout the nation is very sincere and very general: it is not, however, universal. A number of persons had made themselves sure of coming into great and lucrative offices, and of long enjoying them : these have now waked from their dream of grandeur, and find themselves condemned still to toil on in an unsuccessful opposition.

I quite concur with Miss D—— in her judgment of the King of Prussia's letters. It is certain that the King every where gives his philosophical correspondents indirect lessons of toleration and forbearance. The historical parts of his works, though certainly not written in the proper style for history, are very instructive. The description he gives of his own desolated dominions at the end of that war of seven years in which he reaped so much glory, seems better calculated to inspire mankind with a detestation of war than any arguments or any eloquence.

Gray's letters I have never read since they were first published; but I remember at that time being very much delighted with them; and particularly with some fragments of poems which are nearly equal to his finished performances. I cannot say that I am acquainted with the Abbé de Mably's *Observations on the History of France*, although I have bought them, for I have not yet had time to look into them. I entertain much more respect for the Abbé de Mably's memory on account of his private character, than his literary talents. I have never much admired any thing I have read of his, not even his famous *Entretiens de Phocion*. If this letter were by any accident to fall into Mr. Gautier's hands, I fear it would quite ruin me in his good opinion. May I beg of you, Madam, when you see him, to assure him that however erroneous my judgment may be with respect to others, it is very just with respect to himself, and that I always entertain the warmest friendship for him.

But it is time for me to put an end to this letter; permit me to do it with the most earnest assurances of the respect and attachment with which I am, &c.

SAML. ROMILLY.

LETTER L.

TO THE SAME.

Abergavenny, April 18. 1789.

I write to you, Madam, from a place, the name of which is, I fancy, hardly known to you. It is a little town on the borders of Wales, which I have hurried to from the circuit in order to pass a week with my sister. She has lately come hither for the sake of her children's breathing the pure air which blows from the Welsh mountains, and enjoying the pleasures which this beautiful country affords. It is the most beautiful that I have seen in England, or any where else, except in Switzerland. Indeed, it very much resembles some parts of Switzerland, but every thing is on a smaller scale; the mountains are less high, the rocks less craggy, and the torrents less rapid. The valleys are perfectly Swiss, and are enchanting: scattered over with villages and farm houses, and portioned out into a multitude of small fields, they bespeak a happy equality of property, and transport one back in idea to the infancy of society. You will easily imagine that, at this time of the year, I cannot have seen this country to its greatest advantage. We have had a very long winter; it has quitted us little more than a week ago, and though the summer has burst upon us all at once, yet the trees are but just beginning to put out their leaves; and, though the outline of the landscape may be seen, all its colouring, except the rich verdure of the fields, is wanting. But the most beautiful objects in this country, and which are in a great degree independent of the season, are the health, the cheerfulness, and the contentment which appear on the countenances of the inhabitants.

The poor people here have a custom which I never knew observed any where else, and which is very poetical, and very affecting. Once a year (on Palm Sunday) they get up early in the morning, and gather the violets and primroses, and the few other flowers which at this season are to be found in the fields, and with their little harvest they hasten to the churchyard, and strew the flowers over the graves of their nearest relations. Some arrange their humble tribute of affection in different forms with a great deal of taste. The young girls, who are so fortunate as never to have lost any near relation or any friend, exert themselves that the tombs of the strangers who have died in the village, at a distance from all who knew them, may not be left unhonoured; and hardly a grave appears without some of these affectionate ornaments. I came here soon after this ceremony had been observed, and was surprised on walking through a churchyard, to find in it the appearance of a garden; and to see the flowers withering each in the place in which it had been fixed. I have been the more delighted with my excursion hither, from the contrast it forms to the noise, the hurry, the crowd, and the contentions of the courts I have just quitted. What would I not have given to have been able to transport your family hither; to have enjoyed their company in this charming spot; and to have had the pleasure of introducing my sister to you! But all that is impossible.

I am very much indebted to Miss D—— for the news which she sends me respecting French politics, in which I take the greatest interest.

The question respecting the abolition of the slave trade is to be discussed, in about ten days' time, in the House of Commons; and I am happy to find that those who are concerned in the trade begin to be very seriously alarmed. The society, which has so strenuously exerted itself to procure the abolition of the trade, wrote a letter some time ago, to Mr. Necker, to entreat that he would endeavour to procure the concurrence of the French government with that of England in so laudable an enterprise. Mr. Necker's answer was very flattering to them, but gave them so little reason to hope for the concurrence of France, that they thought it advisable not to publish it. The King of Spain is giving additional encouragement to the trade; and the argument which is used with most force here, and indeed the only argument from which any thing can be feared, is that, by our abolishing the trade, we shall give no relief to the negroes, but only transfer to our neighbours the advantages which we derived from that commerce. I believe that argument admits of a very easy refutation; but, if it did not, I should have no objection to making such a transfer, when I must at the same time transfer all the guilt of so abominable a traffic.

I hear my friend, M. Dumont, is gone to Paris, and I make no doubt he will have the honour of waiting on you. There is no pleasure I envy him so much, as that of seeing you and your family. I beg to be remembered very affectionately to them all, and have the honour to be, &c.,

SAML. ROMILLY.

LETTER LI.

TO M. DUMONT.[1]

Dear Dumont, Gray's Inn, May 15. 1789.

My conscience reproaches me for having sent you so shabby a letter as my last, in return for yours, which was so long and so very entertaining.[2] I was quite delighted with it. You transported me into the midst of the assembly of your district, and I was as much amused as if I had been present. I took the liberty of reading parts of your letter to Trail and Wilson. We all agreed in admiring it, and in abusing you, first for not employing your talents in writing some useful work, and secondly, if you wo'n't do that, for not writing me more letters.

[1] Mr. Romilly became acquainted with Mr. Dumont at Geneva, in 1781 (see *antè*, p. 58.), and an intimate friendship was maintained between them up to the close of Mr. Romilly's life.

[2] In this letter, dated April 28., Mr. Dumont had given a very long and detailed account of the proceedings connected with the election of deputies to the states-general.

I was in the House of Commons last Tuesday, when Wilberforce opened the business of the slave trade. He did it in an admirable speech, which seemed to make a great impression on the House. What he proposes is, that the trade should be totally and immediately abolished. Pitt, Fox, Burke, and Grenville (the Speaker of the House), all declared that they were for a total abolition, and seemed to vie with one another who should express in the strongest terms his detestation of the trade. Fox says, that it will certainly before long be abolished, and the only question is, whether England shall have the honour of setting so noble an example, or shall wait to follow it in others: that he made no doubt that the French would soon abolish the trade: that, though he had often talked of the rivalship of France, and professed himself a political enemy to that country, yet God forbid that he should not do justice to their national character; and he did not believe that there was any nation on earth who would be more quick to catch a spark of such noble enthusiasm, even from those whom they might consider as their enemies, or who would be more eager than they would to imitate our example. Wilberforce, among other reasons which he gave for believing that the trade which we abandoned would not be taken up by the French, relied much on the character of M. Necker, and particularly on the passage in his book on Finance, where he says that the only obstacle to the abolition of the trade is that, if one nation abolished it, another and perhaps a rival nation might take advantage of their generosity. For, when once England has abolished the trade, France cannot have to fear any thing from her rivals by abolishing it; and it is impossible to suppose that any man, much more M. Necker, would consent to become so infamous as he must, if, after having published this work, he should attempt to take advantage of us, because we had abolished the trade. But what gives us better security than these arguments is, that the trade cannot be carried on by France, but under much greater disadvantages even than those under which it is carried on by us; for the commodities proper for the African market are (at least the greater part of them) manufactured better and cheaper in England than any where else. A part of Wilberforce's speech which I thought admirable was, where he showed that the present barbarism of Africa was to be ascribed principally, if not solely, to this trade; which, by making it the interest of the native princes to wage war perpetually with one another, and to plunder and carry away their own subjects, and which, by destroying all mutual confidence among the native subjects, and encouraging men to enslave their neighbours and parents to sell their children, prevented any improvement in manners or civilisation. Burke, in speaking of this trade, described it very truly, very concisely, and with great energy. He said that it was a trade, which began by violence and war, was continued by the most dreadful imprisonment, and ended in exile, slavery, and death. Among the speakers, none did more service to the cause which we have so much at heart, than those who spoke against it. All they did was to use invectives, to insist that the statements which had been made were misrepresentations, to call Wilberforce's propositions reveries, and to rely on objections which had been answered and on arguments which had been refuted. A few days before this debate came on, a petition was presented to the House of Commons by a great many of the manufacturers of Sheffield, stating that they were greatly interested that the slave trade should not be abolished, the principal manufactures employed in that trade being made by them; but declaring that they were desirous that no regard might be had to their interests, but that they might be readily sacrificed and the trade abolished. There seems the greatest probability that the Bill for the abolition will pass the Commons; but it is to be expected from the enemies to it, that they will throw every obstacle they can in the way of it; and that, by bringing a multitude of witnesses to the bar of the House, they will delay the business till the next session, when all will be to begin again. What opposition may be made to the Bill when it gets into the House of Lords cannot be foreseen; however, I think it is certain that in three or four years to come, at farthest, this trade will no longer disgrace England.[1]

Mr. Frazer, is, or will very soon be, at Paris. He will call on you. If Rousseau's *Confessions* are published by that time, pray do not fail to send them to me by him. I wish much too to see Necker's speech to the states.

[1] It continued, however, till 1806, when it was abolished by the Whig administration.

Have you read Voltaire's posthumous letters? What do you think of them? We talk of you very often in Frith Street, and long to see you. If you don't come back soon, pray write me another of your long letters. I am sure you would conquer your idleness, if you knew how much pleasure they give me. I write to you in a very great hurry.

Pray give my compliments to Mr. Clavière, and to all his family, to M. de la Roche, and to M. and Mad[e]. Mallet. The family of Mad[e]. D—— I fear have quitted Paris.

Yours most sincerely,

S. R.

Letter LII.

FROM M. DUMONT.

Paris, 22 Mai, 1789.

Je viens de recevoir votre lettre, mon cher Romilly, et je suis charmé qu'un scrupule de conscience m'ait valu l'intéressante relation de ce qui s'est passé dans la Chambre des Communes relativement à la traite. J'avois oublié de vous dire que je m'étois fait agréger à la Société des Amis des Noirs à Paris, pour voir par moi-même de quel esprit elle étoit animée, et de quoi l'on pouvoit

---

Letter LII.

Paris, May 22. 1789.

I have just received your letter, my dear Romilly, and I am delighted that a scruple of conscience should have procured me the interesting account of what took place in the House of Commons on the subject of the slave trade. I had forgotten to tell you that I had joined the Society of the Friends of the Negroes at Paris, that I might myself see the spirit which animated them, and what might be expected from them.

se flatter. C'est un foible commencement ; elle a environ cent souscripteurs, et la plupart de ceux qui la composent sont des grands seigneurs ou des hommes de lettres, qui peut-être ne désintéressent pas assez leur amour propre, et ne s'occupent pas assez de la chose elle-même. Tout est formalité dans l'assemblée ; leur manière de recueillir les opinions est si mauvaise que la moindre question traîne durant des heures, et l'ennui m'en a toujours chassé avant la fin de la discussion.

Cette société, toute foible qu'elle est, a causé de l'ombrage à des planteurs, qui l'ont dénoncée au Roi, mais ils ont été bien désappointés. "Tant mieux," a-t-il répondu ; "je suis charmé qu'il y ait dans mes états quelques honnêtes gens qui s'occupent du sort de ces pauvres nègres." Ce mot a donné un peu plus de vigueur à nos philanthropes. Il faut espérer qu'on fera ici par émulation ce qu'on aura fait en Angleterre par principe.

Les *Confessions* de Rousseau ne paroissent pas ;

It is a small beginning ; there are about a hundred members, most of whom are men of rank or men of letters, who perhaps do not sufficiently set aside their personal vanity, and do not attend sufficiently to the object itself. All is formality at their meetings ; their mode of collecting the opinions of the members is so bad, that the most trivial question drags on for hours together, and I have always been driven away by ennui, before the end of the discussion.

This society, feeble as it is, has given umbrage to some of the planters, who have complained of it to the King, but they have had little reason to be pleased with his answer. "So much the better," he replied ; "I am delighted to hear that there are some honest men in my kingdom, who have taken up the cause of these poor negroes." This answer has infused a little more spirit into our philanthropists, and it is to be hoped that emulation will do here what in England will have been done on principle.

Rousseau's *Confessions* are not yet published. I hear nothing more

je n'en ai plus entendu parler, mais ce que je vous ai mandé à cet égard est certain. J'ai lû quelques unes des lettres posthumes de Voltaire; elles ne sont pas fort intéressantes; il faut en acheter une bonne par vingt mauvaises. Le règne de Voltaire est passé, excepté au théâtre. Rousseau s'élève à mesure que l'autre s'abaisse. La postérité sera bien étonnée qu'on les ait regardés comme rivaux.

Mes complimens à MM. Trail et Wilson; ils devroient bien venir passer l'été à Paris; je crois qu'ils y passeroient six semaines d'une manière fort agréable.—Adieu, mon cher Romilly; aimez-moi comme je vous aime.

Et. D.

Letter LIII.

TO M. DUMONT.

Dear Dumont, London, June 9. 1789.

I return you many thanks for your long and very entertaining letter of the 3d of this month. It has given me as much pleasure as I could possibly have received from the scenes themselves which

---

said about them; but what I wrote to you on the subject is correct. I have read some of Voltaire's posthumous letters; they are not very interesting; it is at the expence of twenty that are bad that one has to get at one that is good. Voltaire's reign is over, except at the theatre. Rousseau rises in proportion as the other sinks, and posterity will be much astonished at their having been considered as rivals.

My compliments to Messrs. Trail and Wilson; they should come and pass the summer at Paris; I think they would spend six weeks there very agreeably. Farewell, my dear Romilly, &c. &c.

Et. D.

it describes, if I had been present at them. The inconveniences of debating in so tumultuous a manner are terrible; they render me quite impatient that the papers I sent the Count de Sarsfield should be published.[1] Perhaps they would do no good; but, however, there is at least a chance of their doing good.

Mirabeau is probably so much engaged with the politics of the day, that you must not speak to him of any other subject. If you may, I wish you would tell him, that, upon my return last autumn from Paris, I told Mr. Vaughan and Sir Gilbert Elliot that he said he would send each of them a copy of his *Monarchie Prussienne*, and that they have neither of them received one. I wish Mirabeau may be induced by the noble opportunity which he now has of making the most distinguished figure, and rendering a most essential service to mankind, — I wish he may be induced to avoid provoking so many enemies as he has hitherto done. He should remember that he at the same time makes them enemies to his principles, and consequently to the good of mankind.

I dined a few days ago at Mr. V.'s. Lord W. was there. The abolition of the slave trade was the subject of conversation, as it is indeed of almost all conversations. I was sorry to find that Lord W. is not a friend to it. I make no doubt that he looks upon me as a mad enthusiast; and, to speak the truth, I cannot boast of having shown much coolness in the conversation: but I every day hear

[1] An account of these papers is given at p. 101. They consisted of a statement of the rules and forms of proceeding of the English House of Commons, and were intended to serve as a model for the French Assembly, which met at Versailles on the 5th of May.

such arguments used upon the subject as no human patience can endure. You have seen the representation of a slave-ship. Can you believe it possible, after having seen that representation, the truth of which it is easy to ascertain with a pair of compasses, that any man should be found capable of giving such an account as I here transcribe of an African voyage? "In the interval between breakfast and dinner, the negroes are supplied with the means of amusing themselves, after the manner of their country, with musical instruments; the song and dance are encouraged and promoted; the men play and sing, whilst the boys dance for their amusement; the women and girls divert themselves in the same way, and amuse themselves with arranging fanciful ornaments for their persons with beads. . . . . When tired of music and dancing, they go to games of chance. The women are supplied with beads, which they make into ornaments, and the utmost attention is paid to the keeping up their spirits, and to indulge them in all their little humours." Such is the evidence which two African captains have not been ashamed to give before the Privy Council. Some other witnesses however are examined; one, a surgeon, who speaks of what he himself saw. "It was usual," he says, "to *make* the slaves dance, in order that they might exercise their limbs, and preserve health. This was done by means of a cat-o'-nine tails, with which they were driven about among one another, one of their country drums beating at the same time; on these occasions they were compelled to sing, the cat being brandished over them for that purpose. He sometimes heard the women among themselves singing, but always at those times in tears. Their songs contained the history of their lives, and their separation from their friends and country. These songs were very disagreeable to the captain; he has sometimes flogged the women, for no other reason than this, in so terrible a manner, that the witness has been a fortnight healing the incisions." It appears by the Report of the Privy Council that the crimes for which men are made slaves in Africa are frequently those of witchcraft, and that for witchcraft the punishment involves the whole family of the person convicted.

Trail and Wilson desire their compliments to you; they will thank you to inquire which is the best French Journal that they can take in, in order to have an account of the proceedings of the States. Is Mirabeau's [1] regularly continued? the last number you sent me comes no lower down than the 11th May. It was reported here that even these letters to his *commettans* were suppressed.

Your friends in Frith Street, not forgetting your little niece, desire to be very affectionately remembered to you.

[1] *Lettres de Mirabeau à ses Commettans,* which afterwards attracted great attention under the name of the *Courrier de Provence.* See *Souvenirs sur Mirabeau,* by Dumont, chap. vi.

Letter LIV.

FROM M. DUMONT.

Surène, près Paris, 21 Juin, 1789.

Je vous envoye, mon cher Romilly, un exemplaire de la *Traduction*[1], &c.; vous en aurez d'autres que je vous porterai moi-même, car je ne reste plus ici que pour voir deux ous trois séances des trois ordres réunis, et juger s'ils s'inspireront mutuellement assez de respect ou de terreur pour s'assujettir à la discipline, et si, de l'émulation entre les ordres, résultera le bien public. Quant à votre ouvrage, il sera utile, les bons esprits le lisent avec attention, mais son effet sera lent: ils ont tant de vanité nationale, tant de prétention, qu'ils aimeront mieux toutes les sottises de leur choix, que les résultats de l'expérience Britannique. Le temps seul les éclairera sur les absurdités du réglement de police qui est en projet, et ils s'accoutumeront

---

Letter LIV.

Surène, near Paris, June 21. 1789.

I send you, my dear Romilly, one copy of the *Translation*[1], &c.; I will myself bring you others; for I shall only remain here to see one or two meetings after the union of the three orders, and to determine whether they will inspire each other with sufficient respect or fear to submit to control, and whether, from emulation between the different orders, public good can arise. As to your work, it will be useful; the well-disposed read it with attention, but its effect will be slow. The French have so much national vanity, so much pretension, that they will prefer all the follies of their own choosing to the results of English experience. Time alone will enlighten them on the absurdities of the police regulations which are in contemplation, and will

---

[1] A translation of the papers mentioned in the preceding letter.

à l'idée, qui les révolte, d'emprunter quelque chose de votre gouvernement qui est ici respué comme un des opprobres de la raison humaine : quoique l'on convienne que vous avez deux ou trois belles loix ; mais il est insoutenable que vous ayez la présomption de dire que vous avez une constitution. Cependant il faut convenir que la jalousie nationale a été clairvoyante, et leur a très-bien fait découvrir qu'il y avoit une grande distance de la théorie de Montesquieu et de De Lolme à la pratique réelle, à l'état vrai des choses. J'ai revu la traduction, mais ce fut un travail fort rapide, une révision avec l'homme dont vous connoissez la turbulente impatience ; vous ne serez juge que des fautes qui restent, et non de celles que j'ai fait disparoître, et cette comparaison seule pourroit me mériter un peu d'indulgence.

Mille amitiés, je vous prie, à nos amis communs. Je suis fort pressé pour finir.

Aimez-moi comme je vous aime.

Et. Dumont.

---

accustom them to the idea now so revolting to them, of borrowing any thing from your government, which is here repudiated as a reproach to human reason. It is, indeed, admitted that you have two or three fine laws ; but then you have the unwarrantable presumption to assert that you have a constitution. Nevertheless, it must be allowed that the national jealousy has been clear-sighted, and has very properly made them discover that there is a wide difference between the theory of Montesquieu and De Lolme and actual practice — the real state of things. I have gone through the translation ; but revising, with a man whose boisterous impatience you well know, was hurried work. You can only judge of the faults which remain, and not of those which I have struck out ; and yet this comparison alone can entitle me to any indulgence. Best remembrances to our mutual friends.

Yours, in haste, &c.

Et. Dumont.

Letter LV.

TO M. DUMONT.

Dear Dumont, July 28. 1789.

I sit down to write a few lines to you as fast as I can, before I set out on the circuit, which will be early to-morrow morning. I shall return in about a fortnight, and how I shall dispose of myself during the vacation is yet uncertain. It is true that you have written me some very long letters, but that was long ago. Since affairs have been in such a state in France as must make every man who has the least humanity impatient for news, you have not let me hear from you once.

I am sure I need not tell you how much I have rejoiced at the Revolution which has taken place. I think of nothing else, and please myself with endeavouring to guess at some of the important consequences which must follow throughout all Europe. I think myself happy that it has happened when I am of an age at which I may reasonably hope to live to see some of those consequences produced. It will perhaps surprise you, but it is certainly true, that the Revolution has produced a very sincere and very general joy here. It is the subject of all conversations; and even all the newspapers, without one exception, though they are not conducted by the most liberal or most philosophical of men, join in sounding forth the praises of the Parisians, and in rejoicing at an event so important for mankind.

Pray congratulate Mirabeau on my behalf; tell

him that I admire and envy him the noble part he is acting. The force of truth obliges me to say this, though I am really offended with him (and I wish you would tell him so), for having very wantonly bestowed on me a very undeserved panegyric.[1] The book in which it is contained is certainly, upon the whole, well translated; but there are some errors in it which I would correct, and send you or him the corrections, if I thought there were any probability of its passing through a second edition.

You have never sent me the third and fourth letter of Mirabeau to his constituents; I wish you would get them for me to complete my set. When is Mr. Clavière's great work to appear? I don't know whether I told him not by any means to use the name of Dr. Price as an authority for the information he communicated to him through me. Be so good, therefore, as to tell him that Dr. Price begs he may not be named.

My brother and sister beg to be very affectionately remembered to you. They think we should all be happier, sitting in their little parlour in Frith Street, than being spectators of the revolutions in France, and the tragedies which attend them. We have just heard the news of the murder of Foulon and his son-in-law, which no doubt every body, and chiefly the friends of the people, must

[1] The following is the passage alluded to: — "Je dois ce travail, entrepris uniquement pour la France, à un Anglais qui, jeune encore, a mérité une haute réputation, et que ceux dont il est particulièrement connu regardent comme une des espérances de sons pays. C'est un de ces philosophes respectables, dont le civisme ne se borne point à la Grande Bretagne," &c. See Dumont's *Tactique des Assemb. Législat.* vol. i p. 285. 2d edit.

consider as a very unfortunate event. Adieu! Believe me to be, with unalterable affection,

Yours, &c.

S. R.

Letter LVI.

FROM Mlle. D——.

Paris, 27 Août, 1789.

Si vous avez pu croire que c'étoit par oubli ou par négligence que nous n'avons pas répondu à vos dernières lettres, Monsieur, et que nous avons gardé un si long silence, vous nous avez fait une grande injustice. La multitude de scènes, d'idées, d'évènemens, par lesquels nous avons passé, nous ont causé tant d'agitations, que, même en pensant plus que jamais à nos amis, il étoit impossible de leur écrire. Combien de fois, Monsieur, vous avez été présent à mon esprit, pendant ces trois mois qui feront époque dans ma vie, par tant de raisons. C'est à *vous*, Monsieur, que j'ai besoin de parler de la Suisse; personne ici ne m'entend, et je sais bien que *vous* m'en-

---

Letter LVI.

Paris, August 27. 1789.

If you can have believed that it has been through forgetfulness or neglect that we have not answered your last letters, Sir, and that we have so long been silent, you have done us great injustice. The multitude of scenes, of ideas, of events through which we have passed, has thrown us into a state of so much agitation, that whilst we have thought more than ever of our friends, we have found it impossible to write to them. How often have you been present to my mind, during the last three months, which, for so many reasons, will form an epoch in my life! It is to *you*, Sir, that I must turn when I would talk about Switzerland; no one here understands me; and I

tendrez, me comprendrez, car vous connoissez ce pays favorisé du Ciel, et vous étiez digne de le parcourir. Je n'ai été que dans une bien petite partie de la Suisse, mais j'en ai vû assez pour juger de tout ce que la nature y a accumulé de grand, de beau, de sublime, pour l'admiration des âmes sensibles. J'ai éprouvé là des sensations qui m'étoient inconnues, et en vérité *trop* délicieuses ; car elles m'ont laissé beaucoup trop de regrets d'être destinée à vivre si loin des objets ravissans qui les causoient. J'ai visité cette île[1] où Rousseau a joui de quelques mois de bonheur, du seul qui étoit fait pour lui, auquel il étoit accessible, celui qu'il trouvoit dans la contemplation de la nature et de lui-même. Nous y avons retrouvé encore ce même calme dont il a sû si bien jouir, qu'il a sû si bien peindre, et qu'il a si vainement recherché depuis. J'ai vû Genève, encore dans une ivresse, ou, si vous voulez, une illusion de bon-

---

am well aware that *you* will, and will feel with me on this subject; for you know that country, so favoured by Heaven, and you were worthy to know it. I have only been in a very small part of Switzerland; but I have seen enough to form an idea of all the grandeur, the beauty, the sublimity which nature has there thrown together for the admiration of men of feeling. I there felt emotions to which I was before a stranger, and which, indeed, were *too* delightful; for they have left behind them too much regret that I should be destined to live so far from the enchanting scenes which called them forth. I visited that island[1] where Rousseau enjoyed a few months of happiness, the only happiness which was made for him, and to which he was accessible, that which he found in the contemplation of nature and of himself. We found there the same tranquillity which he knew so well how to enjoy and to describe, and which he has so vainly sought for since. I saw, Geneva, which was still in an intoxication, or, if you will, a dream of

---

[1] L'île de Saint Pierre, in the middle of the Lake of Bienne.

heur, qu'il seroit cruel et barbare de détruire et de troubler. J'ai vû dans le canton de Berne, sous un gouvernement haïssable par ses formes, mais doux dans ses effets, un peuple tranquille et heureux, garanti par son aisance et sa prospérité, encore mieux que par ses montagnes, des orages et des révolutions qui désolent d'autres contrées. C'est au milieu de ces vallées fortunées, où le bonheur doit être bien plus facile, puisqu'il y est dépouillé de tant de biens factices, c'est là où il seroit si doux de vivre et d'oublier le reste du monde, que la nouvelle des désastres de la France est venue m'atteindre. Quoique la succession la plus inconcevable d'évènemens inespérés ait ensuite un peu calmé nos alarmes, nous avions un trop grand besoin de venir rejoindre tout ce qui nous étoit cher, pour continuer paisiblement notre voyage. Nous l'avons donc précipité, et nous sommes depuis peu de jours de retour au sein de notre famille, encore émues du bonheur d'avoir

---

happiness, which it would be cruel and barbarous to destroy or disturb. I saw in the canton of Berne, under a government hateful in its forms, but gentle in its effects, a happy and contented people, sheltered by the comfort and prosperity of their condition, still more than by their mountains, from the storms and revolutions by which other countries are laid waste. It was in the midst of those favoured valleys, where happiness is the more accessible that it is there stript of so many factitious pleasures, — it was there, where it would be so delightful to live and to forget the rest of the world, that the news of the disasters of France reached me. Although the most inconceivable succession of unhoped-for events has since, in some degree, allayed our fears, we felt too strongly the want of being reunited to all that was dear to us, to continue our journey in peace. We accordingly hastened our return, and have now been some days at home in the bosom of our family, and are still under the joyful emotion of having found so

retrouvé tant d'objets chéris, préservés de tous maux, au milieu de tant de dangers.

Je ne vous dirai aucune nouvelle, Monsieur; vous êtes mieux informé sûrement que peut-être je ne le suis moi-même. L'inquiétude est encore le sentiment dominant, et surtout sur l'objet des finances. Mais les biens dont nous allons jouir, ne sauroient être trop achetés; on se fera gloire même des soucis et des peines dont on les payera. Et vous, Monsieur, qui seriez si digne de voir de près le spectacle intéressant qu'offre la France dans ce moment, celui d'un grand peuple qui veut rentrer dans ses droits naturels que les institutions sociales avoient effacées depuis si longtems, ne viendrez-vous point? Jamais de plus grands motifs n'attirèrent sur le Continent, et, en vérité, si vous y résistez, je ne sais à quelle hauteur je placerai ce degré de vertu. J'attends au moins, Monsieur, de votre amitié, une lettre de vous. Je n'en ai jamais si vivement souhaité, pour savoir votre opinion de ce qui se passe ici. Veuillez nous faire part de quelques

---

many objects of our love, preserved from all harm in the midst of so many dangers.

I shall send you no news, Sir, for you are, no doubt, as well informed, perhaps better than I am myself. Anxiety is still the prevailing feeling, especially on the subject of finance. But the blessings which we are going to enjoy can scarcely be too dearly purchased; we shall even glory in the cares and privations by which we shall have paid for them. And you, Sir, who are so worthy to be a near spectator of the interesting spectacle which France exhibits at this moment, that of a great people re-assuming their natural rights, which social institutions had so long obliterated, will not you come? Never was there a stronger motive to draw men to the Continent; and, in truth, if you resist the temptation, I know not at what height I shall place this degree of virtue. At least, Sir, I trust to your friendship for a letter; I never before so strongly wished for one, that I may hear your opinion on what is passing here. Pray impart to us

unes de vos réflexions; j'ai encore bien plus d'envie de vous entendre sur la France, que je n'avois de besoin de vous parler de la Suisse.

Recevez, Monsieur, &c.

Letter LVII.

FROM MR. TRAIL.[1]

Dear Romilly, Paris, Oct. 18. 1789.

You will see that Mirabeau has proposed a law for the suppression of riots, similar in many respects to our Riot Act. It is intended by him to be much milder; and Dumont wishes extremely to have an accurate statement of the English law on that subject. I believe he has the Riot Act; but I think there are many cases in which the civil magistrate employs force, and military force where he has it, without going through the forms prescribed by that statute. If the mob are actually committing a felony, may not the magistrate, or even any person whatever, disperse them by force? In 1780, immediately after the riots, Lord Mansfield stated the law in the House of Lords, which appeared to many to give more power to the magistrates than it was supposed did legally belong to them; but the Chancellor approved of every thing

---

some of your reflections; I have a still greater desire to hear from you about France, than I had to write to you about Switzerland.

I am, &c.

---

[1] For an account of Mr. Trail, and the origin of Mr. R.'s intimacy with him, see *infrà*, note to letter of Sept. 21. 1791.

he said: and if you could transmit to Dumont a copy of that speech, which you will find in the *Parliamentary Register*, he will be greatly obliged to you. The sooner you do it the better.

I have seen but little of the National Assembly, and I am afraid that I shall see little more. It is supposed the members will not venture to regulate the admission of strangers by tickets, or in any other way; but will permit the vacant space to be filled by such as come first. I was in the assembly on Tuesday evening, all Wednesday, and on Thursday forenoon, when they adjourned till Monday at Paris. Mirabeau spoke a few sentences with great precision, and like a man of business: he has an imposing and dictatorial manner, with an air of superiority and self-sufficiency. I heard a short speech from Volney, which I liked on account of the temper and delicacy with which he reproached the Assembly for changing, inconsiderately, the order of the day. The sudden departure of the Duke of Orleans is the only topic of conversation among all ranks, ages, and sexes, so far as I know. The most prevailing report is, that the Ministry got evidence of his being engaged in some conspiracy, and offered him the alternative of a trial, or a pretext for withdrawing out of the kingdom. The object of his plot, according to some, was to put himself upon the throne by the most violent and sanguinary means; according to others, to get himself declared Regent, in case the King should withdraw, or should, by any other means, be removed from the government. It is confidently asserted that they can prove his having distributed large sums of money among the people: perhaps from this single fact the other reports have arisen. For my own part, having no authority for any of the stories, I believe none. I am the more inclined to scepticism, that I perceive every body suspecting a plot in every accidental circumstance that occurs. It is difficult to decide which of the parties are most credulous and suspicious. I have read almost all the printed accounts of the late excursion [1] to Versailles, and have conversed with several persons who were about the palace at the arrival of the Parisians, and, after all, I cannot make out a consistent story. It is certain the Paris militia, preceded by several hundred women, went to Versailles; that a few of the *Gardes du Corps* were killed, and one or two women; and that they prevailed on the King to come with his family to reside in the capital. It is equally certain that the officers of the *Gardes du Corps* gave, some days before, a great entertainment to a great number of military people at Versailles; that the King permitted them to use the Opera House, and he and the Queen and Dauphin visited them after dinner, and conversed familiarly with them; and that during this entertainment, some rash and violent expressions were used, the national cockade laid aside, and the black one resumed. This example was beginning to be followed hy some military men at Paris; and, added to this, bread became unaccountably scarce, and for a day or two was hardly to be got at all. The removal of the National Assembly will bring things, I should imagine, to a

[1] On the 5th and 6th of October.

crisis. If the people do not disturb their deliberations, all will go well; if they do, the King and they must, with the support of the municipality, endeavour, once for all, to restore energy to the laws; and if they fail, it is in vain to conjecture the consequences. This morning I saw his Majesty walking in the Champs Elysées, without guards. He seemed easy and cheerful. He passed along the line of 5000 or 6000 of the Paris militia, who are reviewed there every Sunday. Dumont is at the Hôtel Royal, Rue Neuve St. Marc. I have not seen him since he came from Versailles, although we have been in search of each other.

Yours,

J. T.

Letter LVIII.

FROM M. DUMONT.

Paris, 19 Octobre, 1789.

Eh bien, mon cher Romilly, vous l'aviez prévu; nous le disions ensemble; rien n'étoit fini; l'horizon étoit *trouble*. Vous avez vu un insipide entr'acte, et à peine étiez vous parti [1] que la scène est devenue très-intéressante et très-animée. Vous

---

Letter LVIII.

Paris, October 19. 1789.

Well, my dear Romilly, you foresaw it. We both said so; nothing was concluded; the horizon was overcast. You saw an insipid interlude, and you were hardly gone [1] when the scene became very interesting and very animated. You do not ask me for details;

---

[1] Mr. Romilly had spent the greater part of the months of August and September of this year at Paris. See *antè*, p. 104—112.

ne me demandez pas des détails ; ceux qui peuvent être publiés sont partout ; ceux qu'il faut dire en confidence, il ne faut pas les envoyer par la poste.

Vous me demandez mon opinion sur la révolution. Hélas ! mon ami, que puis-je vous dire ? Cette terre-ci est tellement volcanique, les mouvemens sont si soudains, l'autorité si foible, qu'on a lieu de redouter ce séjour [1] pour l'Assemblée Nationale. Plusieurs provinces sont blessées de la conduite de Paris, et regardent les quinze mille ambassadeurs armés, envoyés à Versailles, comme un attentat qui intéresse tout le royaume. Les autres croyent que la capitale est *l'œil de la France*, comme le dit M. de Warville, et que sa vigilance a sauvé la liberté d'une conspiration plus hardie que la première. L'une de ces conspirations est aussi bien prouvée que l'autre ; et vous savez mon avis sur la précédente. Des mécontens, des imprudens,

---

indeed, those which can be published are to be had every where, those which must be told in confidence must not be sent by the post.

You ask me my opinion of the revolution. Alas ! my friend, what can I say ? The ground on which we stand is so volcanic, all our movements are so sudden, all constituted authority so weak, that one cannot but dread the present abode [1] for the National Assembly. Several of the provinces are offended at the conduct of Paris, and look upon the march of the 15,000 armed ambassadors to Versailles as an outrage which concerns the whole kingdom. The other provinces look upon the capital as "the eye of France," to use M. de Warville's expression, and believe that its vigilance has preserved our liberty from a much bolder conspiracy than the *first*. The evidence upon which both conspiracies rest is of the same value, and you know my opinion of the first. Discontented men, imprudent ones, ill-disposed

---

[1] The National Assembly had removed from Versailles to Paris after the 5th and 6th of October.

des malveillans, des ennemis de la liberté, des courtisans corrompus, des gens qui voudroient bien avoir assez de moyens pour mal faire — assez de caractère pour être dangereux — il y a de tout cela; mais des conspirateurs, des chefs, des projets suivis, une marche souterraine, une réunion d'efforts, de vues, de personnes, voilà ce qui n'existe pas, ou du moins ce qui n'est pas prouvé. La conduite future de Paris, le sentiment des provinces, voilà deux données qui me manquent pour asseoir mon jugement. Si les députés sont insultés, s'ils ne sont pas libres, vous prévoyez bien qu'ils fuiront les uns après les autres. La désertion est déjà très-considérable, et ils n'ont vu qu'avec la plus vive douleur leur translation à Paris. Les plus zélés républicains en ont pensé à cet égard à-peu-près comme les autres.

Dès que je verrai M. de Mirabeau, je lui rendrai fidèlement votre commission. Vous pouvez compter que Trail vous portera ce que vous demandez, excepté les deux cahiers arriérés du *Courrier de*

---

people, enemies of liberty, corrupt courtiers, creatures who long for ability enough to do mischief—determination enough to be dangerous, —all this we have; but as for conspirators, leaders, settled designs, deep-laid plots, a concert of efforts, views, or persons, nothing of this exists, or, at least, nothing is less established by evidence. The future conduct of Paris, and the feeling of the provinces, are data without a knowledge of which it is difficult to form a judgment. If the deputies should be insulted, if they should not be free, it is clear that they will desert their post, one after the other. This desertion is already very considerable, and it was with the deepest sorrow that they beheld their removal to Paris. On this subject the most zealous republicans have thought much like the others.

As soon as I see M. de Mirabeau, I will faithfully deliver to him your commission. You may rely upon Trail's bringing you what you ask for, excepting the two numbers of the *Courrier de Provence* in arrear, be-

Provence, parceque ma maudite mémoire a laissé échapper les Nos.; mais cette omission sera bientôt réparée.

L'affaire des nègres n'est pas mûre, mais je vous assure qu'elle n'est point négligée; et il me paroît encore probable qu'elle sera traitée même dans cette session. Le Duc de la Rochefoucauld est très-instant là-dessus. Nous avons les papiers dont vous parlez entre les mains, et ils iront à leur destination première, ou retourneront dans les vôtres.

L'Evêque de Chartres et l'Abbé Sieyes m'ont prié de vous faire leurs amitiés.

Et. D.

Letter LIX.

TO MADAME D——.

London, Oct. 20. 1789.

It was with great concern and anxiety, Madam, that I learned the events which passed at Paris and Versailles, soon after I left them. Those events were related here with circumstances so alarming, that it was impossible not to feel great uneasiness for those dear friends whom I had left

---

cause my confounded memory has allowed the numbers to escape me; but the omission shall be soon repaired.

The question of the negroes is not yet ripe, but I assure you that it is kept alive; and I still think it likely that it will be discussed even this session. The Duke de la Rochefoucauld is very earnest about it. The papers of which you speak are with us, and they shall either go to their original destination, or be returned into your hands.

The Bishop of Chartres and the Abbé Sieyes have begged that I would remember them to you.

Et. D.

at Paris, and of whom none are so near to my heart as your family. It is astonishing how formidable dangers appear at the distance of above two hundred miles, and when one sees them through that cloud of uncertainty which attends all the early accounts we have from Paris. I endeavoured to comfort myself with supposing that those accounts must be greatly exaggerated; and so they have proved to be. Still, however, I own that I am much concerned at what has passed. I cannot but think that the removal of the National Assembly to Paris may be a source of great mischief; and I fear for the freedom of debate in the midst of a people so turbulent, so quick to take alarm, and so much disposed to consider the most trifling circumstances as proofs of a conspiracy formed against them as the Parisians seem to be, and, indeed, as it is natural to suppose a people, so new to liberty, would be. At any rate, I am vexed at seeing even the possibility of new obstacles arising to the establishment of a free constitution in France; not that I suppose it possible that any obstacles can prevent such a constitution being established; but they may delay it, and that alone, under the present circumstances of France, would be a dreadful evil.

I find the favour with which the popular cause in France is considered here, much less than it was when I quitted England. We begin to judge you with too much severity; but the truth is, that you taught us to expect too much, and that we are disappointed and chagrined at not seeing those expectations fulfilled.

Our ministers have lately held a council on the affairs of France, the result of which was, that England should in no way interfere in them.

S. Romilly.

Letter LX.

TO M. DUMONT.

Dear Dumont, Gray's Inn, Oct. 23. 1789.

I this morning received Trail's letter, in which he says that you desire to be informed of our law respecting the suppression of riots; and I sit down immediately to comply with your request, though I believe Trail could have given you a better account of it from his memory, than I can from books. The Riot Act, he says, he believes you have, and that Mirabeau has in some degree taken it for his guide. I am much surprised that he has, for that act has always appeared to me to be a very useless law. It makes the offence of persons being riotously assembled together for the space of an hour after proclamation has been made for them to depart, punishable with death. This severity was certainly never meant to be executed against all who should expose themselves to it: the only object was to hold out a terror; although it ought to have been foreseen that the circumstance of the law not being executed would prevent its inspiring terror. The effect of the law, certainly, has not been to prevent riots, which have been at least as frequent and as mischievous since as before the passing of it. One great absurdity in the act is, that it is not calculated to disperse a mob immediately, and that nothing can be done under it for an hour, although in that space of time the mischief may have increased a hundred times. It is true that the magistrates in England do not wait patiently for an hour before they take any steps to suppress a riot; but every thing which they do before that time, they do by virtue of the powers which they derive from older statutes, or from the common law, and not from the Riot Act.

The powers which the justices have, independent of the Riot Act, are these. Two justices of the peace and the sheriff may, in order to suppress riots which happen in their own county, either within their own view or of which they have credible information, raise the power of the county; that is, they may command all persons whatever within the county, except women, clergymen, and children under fifteen, to attend them and assist in dispersing the rioters, arresting them and conducting them to prison: and all persons who refuse or neglect to give such assistance are punishable by fine and imprisonment. And if the justices or the sheriff neglect to call for such assistance, when it is necessary, they too are punishable in the same manner. The persons so called on to assist are to arm themselves; and if they kill any of the rioters who make resistance, they are justifiable. Besides this, all persons whatever may act of their own accord, and without the authority of any magistrate, to suppress riots which they are themselves witnesses of. Neither the Riot Act nor any other statute declares on what occasion the magistrates may call military force to their assistance; nor, indeed, is it anywhere said that the magistrates may upon any occasion call in military force; which I mention, because it is generally supposed that the justices have a right to call in the soldiers, after they have made proclamation for people to depart. The fact is, that the justices have power to command the assistance of all the king's subjects, and consequently they may command the assistance of soldiers, who are subjects like the rest; and this they may do after proclamation by the Riot Act, and before it by the older statutes.

This doctrine of soldiers being to be considered as other subjects was heard by many persons with great dissatisfaction when it was advanced by Lord Mansfield and the Chancellor, in 1780. During the riots of that time no proceedings whatever were had under the Riot Act; proclamation was not anywhere made for the people to disperse, and the soldiers acted without the direction of any magistrate. Lord Mansfield and the Chancellor asserted (and there can be no doubt that the law is) that all persons *might* act to suppress riots, and that, where felonies were being committed, such as the burning of houses, &c., it was *the duty* of all persons to do every thing in their power to prevent those felonies, and to resist the persons committing them, and that soldiers had this power and were bound by this duty as well as other men. I do not send you a copy of their speeches, because they are long, but they amount to no more than what I have told you.

There is one part of the Riot Act which seems very wise; it is that which makes the district in which the riots have been committed liable to be sued, by the persons whose houses or property have been destroyed, for the amount of the loss; and which directs how, when that loss has been so recovered, it shall be raised by a tax on the district. The effect of this is to make it the interest of the inhabitants of every district that the peace shall be preserved, and to render them more active than they would otherwise be in suppressing riots.

It is possible I may be mistaken on some of the information I send you, for I write in great haste: if, therefore, you mean to make any use of it, show my letter first to Trail, and he will probably be able to correct my errors.

Pray, if you ever see the Bishop of Chartres and the Abbé Sieyes, say a great many civil things to them from me. I leave full seope to your genius.

I am quite impatient for the numbers of the *Courrier de Provence* subsequent to 44.

Mirabeau promised me Helvetius's *Letter on Montesquieu;* pray torment him for it, and send it me if you can. I think the Address to the Constituents on the Tax of the fourth part of the Income admirable. If Trail be still at Paris, tell him that I am much obliged to him for giving me some account of French politics; and that I don't write to him because no news can be worth receiving from so dull a place as London, where the Duke of Orleans is feasting with the Prince of Wales in ignominious safety. Yours sincerely,

S. R.

Letter LXI.

TO M. DUMONT.

Dear Dumont, Nov. 17. 1789.

As we cannot yet see you, I wish you to make your stay at Paris as profitable as possible. If it is not very profitable, I think your bookseller must certainly cheat you. The *Courrier de Provence* is become very fashionable in London; and though the booksellers here make a profit of cent. per cent. (for they charge half a guinea for a month's subscription), yet I saw the other day, in De Boffe's shop, a list of forty-five subscribers to it. Among them were some persons of the first rank: the Duke of Portland, Lord Loughborough, Mr. Grenville the Secretary of State, Lord Mountstuart, and many others whose names I don't recollect. Elmsly has it too, and is a more fashionable bookseller than De Boffe. From all this I conclude that there will very soon be a long list of subscribers in London alone.

You know my opinion about the Ministers being in the National Assembly; I need not tell you therefore, what I think of the question[1] which has been lately carried on that subject. They seem to suppose the eloquence of a minister to be more dangerous than that of any other man; but the

[1] The decree passed by the National Assembly on the 7th of November, 1789, to the effect that no member of the representative body should be capable of holding the situation of a Minister, as long as the Assembly to which he belonged should be in existence. See *Choix de Rapports, &c.* vol. v. p. 177.

fact is that it is much less dangerous, because he always speaks under the disadvantage of being supposed to be interested in every question, and all his words are weighed with peculiar distrust. Upon the supposition that seems prevalent in France, that a minister is, by virtue of his office, an enemy to the public good, they ought to rejoice at having him in the Assembly, and that he may fight against them in the face of day.

I was very sorry to see that large rewards had been offered at Paris to persons who would make discoveries of the conspirators in the plot supposed to have been formed against the nation. If France contains in it any such men as Bedloe and Titus Oates, I fear that it is likely to be disgraced with such scenes as were acted in England in the reign of Charles II., when a Popish plot was supposed to have existed, when discoveries of pretended conspiracies were every day made, and the most infamous false accusers grew rich upon the public terror and credulity, and the worst men in the nation made some of the best instruments in the foulest judicial murders.

I very much fear that the nation will follow the example we have set them as to the support of the poor; and, having taken the possessions of the clergy into their hands, and by that means deprived the poor of that resource, will establish in the place of it a certain provision. If that provision is to be distributed according to the discretion of persons in whom that trust may be reposed, it is very well; but if, as with us, any poor person shall be enabled to demand support as a matter of right, and not be made dependent for it on the judgment of other men, I am well satisfied that it will be there, as it has been with us, a source of much greater mischiefs than any it is intended to prevent; that it will prove a great check to industry; and will, in the end, produce greater misery than would arise from the poor being left to depend entirely on the casual bounty of the charitable.

Don't you think the invention of having *suppléants* a very injudicious one? The people should form their judgment of a man at the moment he is about to discharge a public duty, and not a long time before. A man may enjoy the public confidence when he is named a *suppléant*, and may have lost it totally long before he takes his seat in the Assembly. Surely there is great inconvenience in such a man sitting as a new representative of the people. With us, whenever the King appoints a man to any office, his seat in Parliament is vacated, and an appeal is in some sort made to the people, whether the honour or the trust has been properly bestowed; and the people are called upon to say whether, notwithstanding their representative is under personal obligations to the King, they have confidence enough in him to continue him their Minister. So appeals are sometimes made from the House of Commons to the people: as, where the House expels a Member, the people, if they please, may re-elect him, and the House must then receive him. This has been decided in the case of Wilkes: but nothing of this kind can ever happen in France; for the moment a seat in the National Assembly has by any means become vacant, the *suppléant* succeeds to it.

I have not time to make this letter as long as I intended, but I send it you; for I don't know when I shall have time to write again.

Yours affectionately,

SAML. ROMILLY.

LETTER LXII.

TO M. DUMONT.

Dear Dumont, 1st Dec. 1789.

After receiving so many letters from me, you will no longer, I hope, pretend that I have not as good a right as everybody else to reproach you with your idleness.

Trail, who subscribes to the *Courrier de Provence*, lends me the numbers of it as he gets them. I am very much rejoiced that the law excluding the children of bankrupts from voting for representatives in the National Assembly was not carried in the manner it was proposed[1], notwithstanding that you and Duroveray seem so warmly to have espoused it. Surely it is gross injustice to punish a man for not paying a debt which he has not the

[1] The proposition was that the children of bankrupts, who should not, in the course of three years, have discharged that portion of their fathers' debts with which they would have been chargeable in case they had inherited property from him, should not be eligible to any council or assembly, municipal, provincial, or national, or capable of exercising any judicial or municipal office. (See *Moniteur*, 1789, No. 78.)

means of paying, and which he never contracted. That that law has produced all the happy effects which were seen at Geneva, requires, I think, to be proved. It might be very true that that law existed, and that the people of Geneva were happy and virtuous, without one being the cause of the other; and one might just as fairly conclude, because in England we have a very unequal representation of the people in Parliament, and yet the perfect enjoyment of civil liberty, that these are to each other cause and effect. I think you talk a great deal too much of Geneva, and that you are likely to prevent, rather than to promote the freedom of the Republic, by so often dinning it in the ears of the French. They will soon be as tired of hearing you talk of your Geneva as they are of hearing M. Necker talk of his integrity.

We have lately had an account of a most terrible insurrection at Paris. The martial law was held, we were told, in the utmost contempt; every body was under arms, and many lives had been lost. The newspaper, called the *World*, went so far as to say, that the streets of Paris were streaming with blood, and it concluded the account with saying, that the King and Queen were yet alive. It appears now that there is not a word of truth in all this, except the conclusion. It is supposed to have originated with the aristocratical refugees here, who have great influence over our newspapers. Calonne has the *Times* entirely to himself. It was in allusion to that circumstance that one of the Miss Norths the other day said of the report of the insurrection, that it was *une Calomnie;* a saying which you have too pure a taste for puns not to admire.

I hope you are seriously thinking of writing the History of the Revolution, and preparing materials for it. You will be unpardonable if you do not. I assure you with the utmost sincerity that I don't believe there is any man living capable of doing it so well as yourself; and it certainly must be the fault of the historian if it is not one of the most interesting works that ever was composed. Pray undertake it, and collect all the materials for it that you can.

There seems to be an end of Joseph the Second in the Low Countries to my inexpressible joy.[1] It has been said in our newspapers that L—— discovered the Brussels plot to the Government, and was seized to conceal his treachery. To judge by the character of the man only, one would think this probable. I have just received, from Lord Lansdowne, the *Courrier de Provence*, from No. 56. to 68. inclusive, for which I return you many thanks. I have just received, too, the sequel[2] of Rousseau's *Confessions*, and am so impatient to read them that I must conclude thus abruptly.

Yours very affectionately,

S. ROMILLY.

[1] In the January following the Emperor lost all remains of authority in the Low Countries, and an independent confederacy was formed under the title of the United Belgic States.

[2] The second part of the *Confessions of Rousseau*, containing the account of his life subsequent to the year 1741. The first part, which embraced only the twenty-nine first years of his life (from 1712 to 1741) was published (with the omission of the more objectionable passages) in 1781, three years after Rousseau's death.

LETTER LXIII.

FROM M. DUMONT.

[Paris,] Dec. 1789.

J'attendois une occasion pour vous écrire, mon cher Romilly; car, sans avoir des secrets à vous communiquer, l'idée de ces trahisons des postes gâte le plaisir de la causerie, et retient toujours au fond du cœur quelque chose vui voudroit en sortir.

Mirabeau est tombé dans l'Assemblée, soit par un effet des manœuvres de ses ennemis, soit par le déluge des libelles, soit enfin par les fautes perpétuelles où l'entraine ce caractère violent, cette fureur de domination, et cette ambition impatiente qui s'est trahie elle-même. On n'a pu souffrir l'idée de le voir ministre. Au lieu de donner aux inimitiés le temps de se calmer, de se refaire une réputation à neuf, de prendre une marche lente et

---

Letter LXIII.

Paris, December, 1789.

I have been waiting for a private opportunity to write to you, my dear Romilly ; for, without having secrets to impart, the notion of post-office treachery spoils the pleasure of conversation, and keeps buried in the heart one thought or other which is longing to escape.

Mirabeau has lost ground in the Assembly, whether from the intrigues of his enemies, or from the torrent of libels poured forth against him, or from the continual faults into which he is drawn by his impetuous disposition, his rage for domination, and that impatient ambition which has been its own betrayer. The idea of seeing him minister could not be endured. Instead of allowing time for enmities to subside, for his own reputation to be formed anew; instead of

mesurée, dont l'effet eût été infaillible, il a tout brusqué et tout détruit. Pendant plus d'un mois, sa tête étoit comme altérée par les convulsions de ses passions. Sa motion pour le rétablissement des exilés Corses [1] a eu beaucoup de succès, mais tel est l'effet du décri personnel, ce qui feroit beaucoup d'honneur à d'autres ne lui en fait point. Je ne sais s'il pourra reprendre de l'ascendant, mais je suis bien sûr, qu'à moins d'une refonte totale, il n'aura jamais que des éclairs de succès dont la lueur ne tarde pas à l'égarer, et ranime les efforts de ses ennemis. Quelle carrière il aura manqué ! . . .

La motion de Duroveray sur les faillis fut très-applaudie. Je ne veux pas entrer en polémique avec vous sur l'extension de l'exclusion jusqu'aux enfans ; si je me trompe à cet égard, c'est de bonne foi, mais je ne crois pas être dans l'erreur :

---

pursuing a slow and measured course, the effect of which would have been infallible, he has risked and ruined every thing. For more than a month, his head was, as it were, disordered by the convulsions of his passions. His motion for the restoration of the Corsican exiles [1] has had great success ; but such is the effect of his loss of character, that he gains no credit by what would have conferred much on any other man. I do not know whether he will be able to recover his ascendency ; but I am sure that, unless his whole conduct be remodelled, he will never have more than flashes of success, the glare of which is sure to lead him astray, and revive the efforts of his enemies. What a career he will have missed !

Duroveray's motion with respect to bankrupts was received with great applause. I will not enter into a controversy with you as to the exclusion being extended to the children. If I am mistaken on this point, I am at least sincere ; but I cannot think that I am wrong :

---

[1] The decrees of the Assembly, constituting Corsica a part of the French empire, and permitting exiled Corsicans to return to France as French citizens, were passed on the 30th of November, 1789.

les faits sur cette matière valent mieux que les abstractions. J'en ai mille à vous citer où l'exclusion prononcée a fait réparer des torts, des malheurs, ou des crimes ; je n'en connois pas un seul où elle ait entraîné une injustice. La loi n'est pas encore absolument et irrévocablement décrétée, puisqu'elle l'a été sauf rédaction, et que la rédaction est à faire.

Je n'ai pas perdu de vue le recueil des matériaux pour écrire quelque chose sur cette révolution, et si rien au monde peut vaincre le profond sentiment de la disproportion de mes forces avec une telle entreprise, c'est l'encouragement de votre amitié ; au reste, la moisson même des évènemens est encore en herbe ; il faut au moins une seconde législature pour compléter l'ouvrage de la première, et le temps seul peut faire des révélations sans lesquelles ils seroit impossible de donner un corps d'histoire. Mais il faut en causer au coin du feu, et surtout à la promenade. Le petit essai que je fais

---

facts, in a matter of this kind, are better than abstractions. I could quote you a thousand in which this exclusion enforced has brought about the redress of injuries, of misfortunes, nay, of crimes ; and I do not know one where it has led to injustice. The law is not yet absolutely and irrevocably passed, but it was so, with the exception of the wording of it, which is still to come.

I have not lost sight of the collection of materials with a view of writing something on the Revolution ; and if any thing in the world can overcome the deep sense I entertain of the disproportion between my own powers and such an undertaking, it is the encouragement which your friendship gives me. However, the harvest of events is not yet ripe ; there must be a second legislature at least to complete the work of the first, and time alone can bring to light those facts, without which it would be impossible to form the groundwork of a history. But we must talk the matter over by our fireside, and especially in our walks. The slight attempts which I am now making in the lighter ranks of

dans les fantassins de la littérature me montre tous les jours davantage combien j'ai peu de goût pour ce métier. Vous dites que nous ennuyerons de Genève à force de répétitions, autant que le vertueux Necker de son integrité ; cependant c'est le plaisir de parler quelquefois de Genève qui nous donne le courage d'aller en avant. Nous en disons trop pour nos lecteurs, mais pas assez pour nous ; et je ne vous promets pas de me corriger là-dessus, quoiqu' assurément je sente bien que vous avez raison.

Vous avez donc lu les *Confessions de Rousseau*[1]; on voit combien son style dépendoit de l'état de son âme. On y cherchoit l'histoire de ses sentimens, on n'y trouve guère que celle de son ménage. La première lecture m'a désappointé ; la seconde m'a fait plus de plaisir. Il est si bon homme, si naïf ; il se montre avec tant de vérite ; ses sentimens sont toujours si près de la nature. Cet ouvrage a fait

---

literature, show me every day more and more how little taste I have for this vocation.

You say that we shall tire out people by our repeated allusions to Geneva, as much as the virtuous Necker does by descanting on his integrity ; nevertheless, it is the pleasure we feel in sometimes talking of Geneva, which gives us the courage to go on. We say too much about it for our readers, but not enough for ourselves ; and I make no promise of amendment, although I quite feel that you are right.

So you have read Rousseau's *Confessions*.[1] One sees how much his style depended on the state of his mind. One seeks in it for the history of his feelings and opinions, and one finds only that of his domestic life. The first reading disappointed me ; the second gave me more pleasure. He is so good — so simple ; he describes himself with such truth ; his feelings are always so close to nature. The work has

---

[1] See note, p. 379.

peu de sensation, mais cette sensation n'a pas été défavorable à Rousseau. Cerutti a eu beau imprimer des injures dans le *Journal de Paris;* il n'a persuadé personne.

Mille petites occupations m'empêchent de causer avec vous aussi longuement que je me l'étois promis. En relisant ma lettre, je m'aperçois que je n'ai presque rien dit de ce que je voulois vous dire. Je m'en console en pensant que le peu que j'ai dans mon répertoire nous fournira matière à conversation. Dites beaucoup de choses de ma part à nos amis de Frith St.; je me promets tant de plaisir de nos paisibles soirées qu'il redouble mon impatience de me débarasser de mes liens. Le *Courrier de Provence* ne m'enrichit pas, nous ferons banqueroute avánt que nous ayons sauvé les débris de cette sotte entreprise.[1]

---

made little sensation, but that little has not been unfavourable to Rousseau. Cerutti might have spared his abuse of it in the *Journal de Paris;* he has convinced no one.

A thousand little occupatious prevent me from talking with you as long as I had wished. In reading over my letter, I perceive that I have scarcely said any thing of what I had intended. I console myself with thinking that the little which remains of my budget will furnish us with matter for conversation. Say many kind things for me to our friends in Frith Street. I promise myself so much pleasure from our quiet evenings, that it makes me doubly impatient to throw off my fetters. The *Courrier de Provence* is not making my fortune; we shall be bankrupts before we have saved any thing from the wreck of this foolish undertaking.[1]

---

[1] See note, p. 353.

Letter LXIV.

TO MR. VAUGHAN.[1]

Dec. 29. 1789.

I am very much obliged to Lord Lansdowne for sending me the *Domine Salvum*[2], &c.; and am very grateful for his goodness towards Dumont in feeling any solicitude on his account. I cannot, however, entertain the least doubt of Dumont's being perfectly safe at Paris, notwithstanding his being named in that libel. A work so contemptible and so malignant, replete with notorious falsehoods, can hardly have made impression on any body. I believe the only person who has thought it deserving of any notice is the aristocratical editor of the *Leyden Gazette*. You may recollect my speaking to you about the book, near two months ago, when I dined at your house with Mr. Dugald Stewart. Perhaps I did not say that Dumont was named in it; indeed, I thought it of little consequence. However, my friendship for Dumont could make me wish, if himself alone were to be considered, that he were no longer at Paris; for it is impossible not to feel the utmost indignation, when one sees that the services which he has rendered to the French nation, and which are certainly not much less considerable than those of any one man in the National Assembly, have

[1] See *antè*, p. 85.

[2] This was a political pamphlet, which had been published some weeks before at Paris, and in which M. Dumont had been mentioned as the principal writer of Mirabeau's journal (the *Courrier de Provence*).

no other reward than the calumnies of the most malignant libellers. I believe it is no exaggeration to say that all the good which Mirabeau has done was suggested to him by Dumont, or Duroveray, and that they have prevented him from doing nothing but what was mischievous. It is hardly necessary to say that Dumont has acted with the purest disinterestedness, and that he has never had any other object in view than that of being useful, He has done what few people could have had magnanimity enough to do; he has seen his compositions universally extolled as masterpieces of eloquence, and all the merit of them ascribed to persons who had not written a single word in them; and he has never discovered that he was the author of them but to those from whom it was impossible to conceal it. Of every thing that he has written, the advantages have been shared between Mirabeau and his bookseller, the one taking the glory, and the other the emolument. It is true, that, with respect to the *Courrier de Provence*, Dumont ought by agreement to receive a share of the profit; but the honest bookseller always manages so well that though the book is in every body's hands, there never are any profits to divide.

S. R.

1790—1791.

Letter LXV.

TO M. DUMONT.

Dear Dumont, Jan. 26. 1790.

I sit down to answer your letter of the 18th of this month; but it will give me great pleasure if the answer does not reach you, and if you have quitted Paris before my letter gets there. I assure you I am much more impatient for your return than you are yourself. I trembled lest you should set out for Geneva; but you say nothing about any such intention, and therefore I trust you have given it up. I still fear, however, that you will again get involved with the *Courrier de Provence;* but, indeed, you ought not, through good-nature, thus to sacrifice yourself to others. I shall not be easy till I see you quietly established in Berkeley Square, writing the History of the Revolution, and giving me a sheet at a time to translate. Positively you must undertake it. Your objections, which amount only to this, that you will not be able to attain an ideal perfection which you have painted to yourself, are good for nothing. With all the defects which even your severity may imagine, it will still be the most useful work that has been published for a century, and will be infinitely better executed by you than by any other person that attempts it. Once more, you must undertake it. Make it a work for posterity, but make it a work for the present generation too; and prepare for yourself the sublimest of all pleasures, that of contemplating the extensive good which you will have effected. Indeed, I am serious in thinking that you cannot renounce the idea of writing the work I have mentioned to you, and be exempt from all criminality.

My only commissions are to beg you would bring me the Bishop of Autun's[1] book on *Lotteries*, a copy of my *Règlemens of the English House of Commons*[2], *Helvetius' Letters*, and to inquire the date of the Abbé Sieyes' pamphlets. At least I don't, at present, recollect any others.

I grieve beyond measure that the National Assembly does nothing respecting the slave trade. The question has been revived, here, the first day that the House met on business. If there were any prospect of the French giving up the trade, I think it certainly would be abolished here. I cannot conceive why it is delayed. If the subject were merely introduced, and the temper of the French seen, it would be sufficient.

I write in great haste,

Yours, affectionately,

SAML. ROMILLY.

[1] Talleyrand.

[2] See *antè*, p. 101.

Letter LXVI.

TO MADAME G——.

Gray's Inn, Jan. 26. 1790.

I was very sorry, Madam, that I could not send you my congratulations [1] at the same time that you received those of your other friends. I am sure that you will have received none more sincere, and that no one has formed more ardent wishes for your happiness than I have. All those wishes, indeed, are now comprehended in one — that of long life; for length of life to both of you must be to both a prolongation of the greatest happiness. I long to pay you both a visit, and to see you in your *ménage*, which I cannot express in English, because we have no word for it; although there is no country, I believe, where the domestic comforts which it imports is more felt and valued than ours. As I cannot visit you in reality, I do it often in idea, and transport myself from my solitary chambers in Gray's Inn, to the cheerful fireside of my dear friends in the Rue des Capucines. I accompany you too in many of your frequent visits to Mme. D——, and enjoy the satisfaction she feels at being surrounded by her happy and virtuous family.

We, in England, are surprised and rejoiced that so great an operation as the division of the Kingdom should have been accomplished in France without any thing that deserves the name of oppo-

[1] On her marriage.

sition. So convincing a proof of the unanimity and public zeal of the whole country, makes it impossible, even for the most incredulous, to doubt any longer of the success of the Revolution. I was present in our House of Commons on the first day of the session, and blushed for our legislators when I heard Lord Valletort's observations on the French Revolution, and found that they passed without animadversion. However, it was a very thin House; none of the considerable men of opposition were there, and the friends of the ministry were probably unwilling to disconcert their young aristocratical friend in his first essay at public speaking; but this, I admit, is a very bad excuse.

I am disappointed and vexed beyond measure at the turn which affairs seem likely to take in Flanders. One would have thought it impossible that one of the first measures of a people who had just recovered their independence, and who had such examples before them, would be to sanction their old government, with all its abuses, and that one of the worst governments on the face of the earth; and that in all their manifestoes they should complain of the Emperor's tolerating other religions as an insufferable grievance. Indeed, one can hardly rejoice at their success. It is of little consequence that they have thrown off the yoke of Joseph II., since they willingly submit to the double yoke of a proud aristocracy and a persecuting superstition. Pray assure M. G—— of my most affectionate regard; and believe me, &c.

SAML. ROMILLY.

Lettte LXVII.

FROM MADAME G——.

[Paris,] 7 Février, 1790.

Si nous écrivons rarement à nos amis, Monsieur, nous y pensons bien souvent, et rarement un jour se passe sans une occasion de prononcer votre nom entre nous : tantôt un événement politique, tantôt la lecture d'un de vos grands poëtes, nous ramène à vous ; et sûrement il y a bien peu de pensées intéressantes, auxquelles votre idée ne puisse être liée. Vous voulez nous affliger en nous présentant comme si peu probable l'espérance de vous voir en France ; mais l'avenir est si incertain, il amène si souvent des maux et des biens sur lesquels on ne comptoit pas, que nous ne voulons point désespérer du plaisir de vous voir au milieu de nous, et nous nous reposons pour cela sur le temps et les circonstances.

Letter LXVII.

[Paris,] February 7. 1790.

If we seldom write to our friends, Sir, at least we very often think of them, and scarcely a day passes without there being some occasion to mention your name : at one time a political event, at another the perusal of one of your great poets, brings us back to you ; and, indeed, there are very few interesting thoughts with which you are not associated in our minds. You seem bent on distressing us, by holding out so little prospect of our seeing you in France. But the future is so uncertain, it brings with it so often both good and evil, upon which one did not reckon, that we are resolved not to despair of having the pleasure of seeing you amongst us, but to trust for it to time and circumstance.

Nos affaires ici vont bien, et la venue du Roi à l'Assemblée a produit un excellent effet.[1] On est à présent tout occupé de prêter *serment*. Vous trouverez peut-être quelque ridicule dans cette idée, et qu'on se presse trop de jurer de maintenir une constitution qui n'est qu'ébauchée. Tout cela a été produit par une effervescence, qui ne permettoit pas la réflexion, mais qui aura de bons effets. L'Assemblée travaille avec ardeur, et paroît bien disposée. Les finances sont toujours notre côté malade, et c'est cependant le point important ; mais les biens du clergé seront notre salut, et on va s'occuper très-incessamment de mettre en vente ceux qui en sont susceptibles. La France offre dans ce moment un beau spectacle, et je ne doute pas que vous n'y fixiez avec complaisance vos regards, d'autant plus qu'actuellement tout est calme et tranquille, et qu'il n'est plus question des

---

Our matters go on well here, and the King's visit to the Assembly has produced an excellent effect.[1] Every one is now busy in taking the oath. You will perhaps think this notion somewhat ridiculous, and that people are in too great a hurry to swear to maintain a constitution of which nothing exists but a mere outline. All this has been brought about by an ebullition of feeling which allowed no time for reflection, but which will do good. The Assembly is earnest in its labours, and appears to be well disposed. Finance is still our weak point, and yet the most important; but the church property will be our salvation, and steps are about to be taken to offer for sale that portion of it which can be so disposed of. France affords at this moment a noble spectacle, and I have no doubt that you contemplate it with pleasure ; the more so, that at present all is calm and tranquil,

---

[1] On the 4th of February the King came to the Assembly to accept the constitution formed by them ; and on the following days the oath of fidelity to the constitution was taken by the Assembly and other public bodies.

horreurs qui ont tant révolté, et avec raison, les étrangers.

La division de la France[1] paroît achevée ; mais ce n'est pas sans peine, et il est difficile d'imaginer le travail du comité de constitution. Les réclamations ont été innombrables, et il n'y avoit pas de petit village qui n'eut de fortes raisons à alléguer pour être choisi pour chef-lieu de district ou de département. Les municipalités sont formées en grande partie ; les élections sont assez bonnes, et dans trois endroits on a élu pour maire l'intendant, et dans beaucoup des privilegiés.

Excusez, Monsieur, ma précipitation, mais je ne veux pas manquer encore ce courrier. Croyez à notre amitié.

M. D. G.

---

and that there is an end of the horrors with which foreigners were so greatly and so justly shocked.

The division of France[1] appears to be completed, but not without difficulty; and it is not so easy to form an idea of the labours of the constitution-committee. The claims set up have been numberless, and there was no little village which had not strong reasons to urge for its selection as the capital of the district or department. Most of the municipalities are formed. The elections are tolerably good ; in three places the intendant has been elected mayor, and in many others persons of the privileged class.

Excuse haste, but I must not again miss the post. Believe me, &c.

M.D.G.

---

[1] The Act which decreed a division of France into eighty-three departments was passed on the 15th of January, 1790; and the letters patent of the king relative to this new division of the kingdom were issued on the 4th of March. See *Moniteur* for 1790, No. 17.

Letter LXVIII.

FROM MADAME G——.

Paris, 4 Mars, 1790.

M. Dumont vient de nous faire dire, Monsieur, qu'il partoit pour l'Angleterre, c'est à dire, qu'il alloit vous revoir et vous rejoindre; on ne peut se refuser à le charger d'un petit mot pour vous. Nous avons reçu les pamphlets et votre lettre qui en indique la destination, qui a été aussitôt fidèlement remplie. Nous avons lu, avec beaucoup d'intérêt, *Thoughts on the Influence*[1], &c. dont l'auteur se cache si soigneusement qu'on n'ose pas le deviner, quoiqu'on en ait pourtant bien envie. Ce sera un bien beau spectacle, que l'émulation de ces deux nations pour parvenir au bien et au perfectionnement dans leurs gouvernemens, et qui rendra bien méprisable et bien puérile celle

---

Letter LXVIII.

Paris, March 4. 1790.

Mr. Dumont has just sent us word, Sir, that he is setting out for England; in other words, that he is going to see and join you. We cannot deny ourselves the pleasure of giving him a few lines for you. We received the pamphlets you sent us, and immediately forwarded them to their destination, according to the directions contained in your letter.

We have read, with much interest, *Thoughts on the Influence*[1], &c., the author of which conceals himself so carefully, that we do not venture to guess who he is, although we are very anxious to do so. It will be a very noble spectacle to behold the rivalry of these two nations vying with each other in their endeavour to increase the measure of human happiness, and to perfect their respective governments; which

---

[1] *Thoughts on the probable Influence of the French Revolution on Great Britain*, printed in 1790. See *antè*, p. 103.

d'un genre bien différent qui a existé depuis si longtems entr'elles. Je souhaite bien vivement que cette émulation soit bientôt établie à juste titre, et que le moment où l'Angleterre aura quelque chose à envier à la France ne soit pas trop éloigné. Notre position, à l'envisager philosophiquement et moralement, est grande, belle, et faite pour animer et exciter tous les sentimens nobles et élevés. Mais le règne de l'imagination ne subsiste pas toujours, et nous avons bien des maux réels. Au reste, il nous sied fort mal de tenir ce langage, car nous sommes du nombre de ceux auxquels la révolution ne procurera que de grands et nombreux avantages, et à qui elle ne coûtera presque rien. Je plains foiblement aussi ceux qui ne sont attaqués que dans leurs préjugés les plus chers, qui perdent des places, des pensions même, quoiqu'une grande révolution de fortune soit souvent bien pénible à supporter. Mais je gémis sur la cessation d'ouvrage de tout genre, de manufactures de toute espèce, qui se fait sentir

---

will place in a justly puerile and contemptible light that very different rivalry which has so long subsisted between them. I fervently hope we may soon see this spirit of emulation in operation on proper principles, and that the moment is not far distant when France may possess something which may be justly envied by England. Our position, looking at it in a philosophical and moral point of view, is great and noble, and calculated to animate and excite every fine and elevated feeling. But the reign of imagination will not last for ever, and we are suffering under many real evils. However, it ill becomes me to hold this language; for our family is of the number of those to whom the revolution will bring many and great advantages, without imposing upon us any important sacrifice. I have but little sympathy either for those who are attacked only in their darling prejudices, who lose places, and even pensions; although a great reverse of fortune is often very hard to bear. But what I do lament is the cessation of every kind of work, and of every sort of manufacture, which is felt from one end

d'un bout du royaume à l'autre, et qui cause une misère aussi difficile à imaginer qu'à décrire; heureusement que la belle saison qui s'approche, va beaucoup adoucir sa rigueur. C'est vraiment le côté triste de la révolution, celui qui fait désirer avec une bien vive ardeur que l'ordre et la confiance, qui feront tout revivre, renaissent bientôt. Il est peu probable que la France donne à l'Angleterre l'exemple de l'abolition de la traite et de l'esclavage des nègres : on craint d'ouvrir une nouvelle plaie, et peut-être pour l'honneur de notre humanité le craint-on trop.

Je désire ardemment que vous conserviez votre bonne opinion de notre révolution ; et je souhaite bien que nous la justifions : c'est sûrement un des suffrages qui lui fait honneur, et je me le cite souvent pour ranimer mes espérances.

Recevez, &c.

M. D. G.

---

of the kingdom to the other, and which creates an amount of misery as difficult to imagine as to describe ; fortunately, the summer is coming on, and will greatly mitigate its severity. This is indeed the melancholy side of the revolution, and makes one long very ardently for what would give new life to every thing, the restoration of order and confidence. It is little likely that France will set England an example by abolishing the slave trade and slavery : people are afraid of opening a fresh wound, and too much so perhaps for the honour of humanity.

I fervently wish that you may retain your good opinion of our revolution, and I much hope that it may be justified. Your good opinion is one of those which does us honour ; and I often recall it to my mind for the sake of reviving my hopes. Believe me, &c.

M. D. G.

Letter LXIX.

FROM MADAME G——.

Paris, 2 Mai, 1790.

Nous sommes depuis quelque temps privés du plaisir de vous écrire, monsieur, et cependant nous avons reçu plusieurs marques de votre souvenir. Nous avons envoyé, dès le même jour qu'il nous est parvenu, l'ouvrage[1] de M. Bentham à un membre du comité de constitution, qui sait parfaitement l'Anglois; et certainement si ces messieurs l'ont voulu, ils ont eu assez tôt connoissance de cet intéressant travail, pour pouvoir en profiter. L'Assemblée est sérieusement occupée de l'ordre judiciaire dans ce moment. On craint beaucoup qu'elle ne fasse qu'à moitié bien; peut-être auroit-il été plus sage de ne faire que des changemens provisoires, et de renvoyer à quelques années ce travail important, qui pourroit bien se ressentir de l'agitation

---

Letter LXIX.

Paris, May 2. 1790.

We have for some time been deprived of the pleasure of writing to you, sir, although we have received several tokens of your kind recollection of us. We forwarded, on the same day that it reached us, Mr. Bentham's work[1] to a member of the constitution-committee, who knows English perfectly; and certainly if the committee had wished to profit by this interesting work, they have been in possession of it quite long enough to have done so. The assembly is at this moment earnestly engaged on the judicial establishment. It is greatly feared that what it does will only be half done; and perhaps it would have been wiser if none but temporary alterations had now been made, and the permanent execution of this important work had been postponed some years,

---

[1] *Emancipate your Colonies.*

des esprits, de l'exaltation des têtes, &c. Je redoute quelquefois, monsieur, que vous ne nous trouviez bien *François* dans la plupart des choses que nous avons faites. On s'échauffe, on dispute, on discute avec esprit de parti; on décide promptement, parcequ'on est pressé par les circonstances, et quand le décret est rendu, on se persuade qu'il étoit impossible de pouvoir rien faire de mieux. Il y a une fermentation plus vive que jamais dans l'Assemblée depuis quelques jours. Les derniers décrets sur les biens du clergé ont causé une irritation chez ceux qui en sont les victimes, qui va jusqu'à la rage. Dans leur désespoir ils se portent aux dernières extrémités. Heureusement que leur influence sur les esprits est très-foible, et que leur protestations et toutes leurs démarches ne servent qu'à les rendre moins intéressans, et à gâter leur cause. Je crois que si vous étiez au milieu de nous, vous auriez souvent des momens pénibles, et que vous souffririez de la licence effrénée qui

---

to a period when it would be less likely than it now is to suffer from the agitation and enthusiasm of men's minds.

I sometimes fear that you must think most of the things we have done very *French*. We get heated, we dispute, we discuss with party-spirit; we decide precipitately, because we are pressed by circumstances, and when the decree is passed, we persuade ourselves that it was not possible to do better.

For some days past the Assembly has been in a more violent state of ferment than ever. The last decrees respecting the property of the church have caused an irritation amongst those who are sufferers by them, which amounts to a state of phrenzy; and, in their despair, they would carry matters to the last extremity. Happily their influence on men's minds is very slight; and all their protestations and proceedings serve only to lessen the interest with which they are regarded, and to injure their cause. If you were in the midst of us, I think you would have many painful moments, and that you would grieve at the unbounded licence which pervades all writings and all conversations. Every

règne dans les écrits, dans les propos. Toute idée de décence, de retenue, est foulée aux pieds, et il est à craindre qu'on n'ait de la peine à se raccoutumer à obéir aux lois qu'on se sera imposées. Au reste, ce qui peut rassurer, c'est que les provinces sont beaucoup plus calmes et raisonnables; que la milice nationale est partout fort bien composée et disposée à faire exécuter les décrets de l'Assemblée.

Nous avons, au milieu des agitations de la révolution, passé un hiver très-heureux et paisible, fort réunis en famille, prenant l'intérêt le plus vif à la révolution, et nous affligeant quelquefois de voir les deux partis aller trop loin. Toutes les fortunes ont été pendant quelque temps en grand danger; mais l'opération des assignats semble réussir, et probablement nous sauvera. Recevez, Monsieur, mille choses de vos amis de Paris, qui s'occupent bien souvent de vous, et qui vous sont bien sincèrement attachés.

M. D. G.

---

idea of decency and of restraint is trampled under foot; and it is to be feared that men will not easily return to a habit of obedience to the law, even though it be the law of their own creation. In the meantime one may derive some confidence from the fact, that the provinces are much more tranquil and reasonable, and that the national militia is every where formed of good materials, and is well disposed to give effect to the decrees of the Assembly.

In the midst of all the agitations of the revolution, we in our family circle have passed a calm and happy winter, taking the deepest interest in the revolution, and grieving sometimes to see both parties going too far. All private property was, for some time, in great danger; but the operation of the *assignats* seems to succeed, and will probably prove our salvation.

I have many kind messages to send you from your friends at Paris, who think of you very often, and are very sincerely attached to you.

M. D. G.

Letter LXX.

TO MADAME G——.

Madam, Gray's Inn, June 4. 1790.

You are apprehensive that I shall think a great deal of what has been done in France is very *French*, and I guess that you allude to an observation which I remember to have made on young Vernet's picture at your exhibition; but though your countrymen have acquired a manner in the fine arts which is peculiarly their own, it may be doubted whether they have been legislators long enough to have given their name to any peculiar mode of legislation. I assure you, however, that if I were to venture to call any species of law-making *French*, I should use that expression as a term of great honour, and not of reproach. The National Assembly are better judged of at a distance than near at hand, because they should be judged by what they do, and not by their manner of doing it. I find this by experience; and I have, I assure you, much more respect for the National Assembly now that I am at London, than I had while I was at Versailles. I am far from approving of every thing that they have done; but one finds so much to admire, that one is not willing to dwell upon the few things which one would wish were otherwise than they are.

I congratulate you on the decision of the National Assembly [1], on the King's right of making

[1] The decree of the National Assembly on this subject was made on the 22d of May, 1790, and was in substance as follows:—"The right

war. I hope it has given you as much pleasure as it has me. I consider every difficulty thrown in the way of making war as so much gained to humanity; and if a project of universal peace can ever be established, I am satisfied it must rather be by disarming kings than by the Abbé St. Pierre's congress of regal deputies. I know that many very warlike republics have existed, and that it is easy to cite the example of the Romans, the Carthaginians, and so forth: but I hope the French Revolution has put those kinds of historical arguments quite out of fashion. I know, at least, that by such arguments I could have proved to demonstration, eight months ago, that the districts of Paris, — those sixty republics, as they were called, — with their senates and their demagogues, would never have submitted to be annihilated; which, however, has since happened without opposition (as far as we have heard here, at least,) even of a single individual.

I am afraid, though I should not call any thing that has passed with you very *French*, you would, if you had been here at the first news of a Spanish war, have thought us very, very *English*. The discovery of the grand elixir, which would efface pain and disease out of the list of human calamities, could not have given a man of humanity more pleasure than some persons felt here at the prospect of plundering foreign merchants, and burning and

---

of making peace and war belongs to the nation. War can only be decided on by a decree of the legislative body, passed on the formal proposal of the king, and sanctioned by him." See *Moniteur* for 1790, No. 144.

sinking Spanish ships. It is very fortunate for France that her National Assembly does not meet in a city where they can be much influenced by the barbarous prejudices of persons concerned in privateering, or in particular branches of commerce. The situation of our parliament has more than once made an unjust and impolitic war have the appearance of being popular. I had the mortification, a few days ago, of finding myself considered as a maintainer of the most extravagant paradoxes, because I asserted that a war of any kind must be to England a calamity; but that a victorious war would be the greatest of calamities. And this is thought a paradox; after the experience of the glories, as they are called, of Lord Chatham's administration, — glories which procured no one solid advantage to this country; which did not add one single moment's happiness to the existence of any human being, but which were purchased by an immense debt, by infinite bloodshed, and, what was worse, which gave us false notions of our honour, and our dignity, and our superiority, of which we cannot be corrected but by the loss of much more treasure, and more blood! But I beg your pardon for troubling you with my observations on these melancholy subjects. I would have talked with you of subjects more pleasing to us both, but it is now too late to correct my error, for I have got to the end of my paper, and it is impossible for me at this moment to command time enough to begin another letter. Pray remember me very affectionately to Mr. G., &c. &c.

Letter LXXI.

TO THE SAME.

London, August 20. 1790.

The first use, Madam, to which I devote the leisure that the long vacation affords me, is to return you many thanks for the translation of Mr. Bentham's book on *Usury* [1], which you did me the favour to send me. I have read it with very great pleasure. It appears to me to be extremely well done, and the omissions and alterations which have been made in the order of the work I think very judicious. I have given a copy of it to Mr. Bentham, who is exceedingly pleased with it, and returns many thanks to his unknown translator, for so ably assisting him in propagating opinions which he hopes will prove useful to mankind.

I very gladly seize the opportunity of M. De la Roche's departure to send you the new edition of Adam Smith's *Theory of Moral Sentiments*. It was published only a few months before the author's death, and contains many passages and some whole chapters not published in any of the preceding editions. These will afford you entertainment if you should be, as I suppose you are, already acquainted with the rest of the work. If that should not be the case, you will receive great pleasure from the whole of it. Not, indeed, that I think his theory perfectly solid: but the speculations of an ingenious man on such a subject are always interesting, and those of Adam Smith would render any subject in-

[1] *Defence of Usury.*

teresting. I have been surprised, and I own a little indignant, to observe how little impression his death has made here. Scarce any notice has been taken of it, while for above a year together, after the death of Dr. Johnson, nothing was to be heard of but panegyrics of him. Lives, Letters, and Anecdotes, and even at this moment there are two more lives of him about to start into existence. Indeed one ought not, perhaps, to be very much surprised that the public does not do justice to the works of A. Smith, since he did not do justice to them himself, but always considered his *Theory of Moral Sentiments* as a much superior work to his *Wealth of Nations.*

The French Revolution seems to be growing popular, where one would last expect it, even in our Universities. One of the questions proposed this year by the Vice-Chancellor of Cambridge, for a Latin prize dissertation was, "Whether the French Revolution was likely to prove advantageous or injurious to this country;" and the prize was given to a dissertation [1] written to prove that it would be advantageous to us.

I was very agreeably surprised to hear from my friend Mr. Vaughan that he had spent part of one of the very few days which he passed at Paris in your company. I have been importuning him with questions about you, and have made him tell me where he saw you, and when, and for how long, and how long he walked in the garden at Passy, and every thing which could assist me to transport myself to the same scene, and to make one of the company.

[1] This dissertation was written by Mr. Whishaw.

Pray assure Mr. G—— of my warm and unalterable friendship. I mention him less frequently in my letters than I should do, if I did not consider the whole of them as being addressed to him at the same time as to you.

Letter LXXII.

TO M. DUMONT.

Dear Dumont, September 25. 1790.

After reading Duroveray's letter with the greatest attention, I cannot say that I find in it sufficient reason to induce you to undertake the journey which he proposes. If he does not deceive himself as to the situation of affairs at Geneva, your presence seems quite unnecessary; and matters are likely to be settled without you, if not in the best manner possible, at least in the best that can be expected; and if he does deceive himself, and considers matters with too sanguine hopes, it must be at least doubtful what can be done, and how distant may still be that crisis which he supposes has already arrived. I cannot conceive how Duroveray can persuade himself that the people of Geneva ought to be careful not to let the present opportunity pass unimproved. That opportunity (if it ought to be called by that name) is what the French Revolution has offered them, and seems likely to be an opportunity which will last for ages. A counter-revolution is impossible; and, if there were degrees of impossibility, it would be still more impossible that France should again exercise any control over the government of Geneva. The most essential thing, therefore, at Geneva is to do nothing precipitately; the making a constitution is a work of reason, not of enthusiasm. Argument and discussion may be of great use at the present moment at Geneva; but I do not see what good is to be done by eloquence; and argument and discussion may as well be communicated to them from London as at Geneva. I can easily conceive, indeed, that, if you were on the spot, you might be able to induce them to do more for the natives than they would otherwise do; but I own I should dread the effects of what they might be induced to do merely from a sudden movement, with which they would be inspired, and which, in cooler moments of selfish reflection, they might repent of. It is easy to foresee the jealousies which might arise from hence, how the seeds of future divisions might by that means be sown, and how the most generous conduct on your part might in the end receive no other reward than the complaints and dissatisfaction of your countrymen. With all this, however, I cannot in my conscience tell you that I think you would be of no use at Geneva. I have too high an opinion of your talents and your virtues to think that you could ever be useless where any good was to be done. But, of whatever use your journey might be to your countrymen, I am sure it would be of none to yourself: and a person destined to do as much good as I sincerely believe you are, ought to be allowed a little to consider what effect any measure he may take is likely to have on his own character. A person who sets out on such a mission as that on which our friends desire you to go to Geneva assumes to himself a degree of importance which, however well you may be entitled to it, it is not in your temper to assume, and which, if such an expedition prove fruitless, cannot fail of covering him with ridicule. I admit, however, that all this and much more ought to be risked, if there were a prospect of rendering any important service to your country; but I cannot persuade myself that this is the present case. The disinclination you have to going to Geneva is alone sufficient to convince me that you would be of little service there; and though I cannot blame the zeal of your friends, who importune you to surmount that disinclination, and to sacrifice your own ease to an object which they think important; yet, in fact, it is much easier to recommend sacrifices than to make them. The truth is, that we never know what the sacrifices are which we recommend; and that which we look upon as only a slight inconvenience, may be to the person whom we would persuade to submit to it a very serious evil. I say all this merely to convince you that you alone are the proper judge what you ought to do. Trust to your own judgment alone. Regard no part of the letters which you receive from Geneva but the facts they contain, and the opinion which is entertained of your abilities and your virtues, and from those data decide whether you ought to go or not. To undertake such a journey, on such an occasion, merely from deference to the opinions and wishes of others, is a weakness hardly excusable. Trust to yourself, and I have no doubt of your doing right.

I dined two days ago with Trail, who was in town for a day. He is very much pleased with Mirabeau's two speeches on the family compact and the assignats [1], and has conceived a higher opinion of him than he ever had before, at finding he can do so much when deprived of the assistance to which he owed so great a part of his former reputation.

Erskine is returned from Paris a violent democrat. He has had a coat made of the uniform of the Jacobins, with buttons bearing this inscription, "Vivre libre ou mourir," and he says he intends to wear it in our House of Commons.

Yours affectionately,

SAML. ROMILLY.

LETTER LXXIII.

TO M. G——.

Dear G——, Gray's Inn, Oct. 29. 1790.

I thank you for your good news, and congratulate you upon it most cordially. I will venture to cast the nativity of your little daughter, and to pronounce that she is infallibly destined to be happy; for the education she will receive cannot fail of rendering her so. You promise me that she is by and by to be my very good friend; in the meantime, however, I foresee that the little damsel will do me a great deal of mischief, and will

[1] See *Moniteur* for 1790, Nos. 240. and 241.

engross moments that otherwise perhaps would be employed in writing some of those letters which I always expect with so much impatience, and read with so much pleasure. Pray tell Mad^e. G——, however, that I shall never admit the validity of such an excuse ; and since she has received her morality from me, tell her that I hold it to be an indisputable principle in morals, that there are no incompatible virtues, and that therefore she may be a good mother and a good correspondent too ; and much as I wish well to my little new-born friend, I cannot consent to sacrifice to her the very few hours in the year which I have any claim to. In short, tell her that I shall not believe she is perfectly recovered, till I see a letter from her under her own hand.

At the same time that you tell me you won't speak of public affairs, you let me discover very easily what your opinion of them is ; but I really think that if you are disappointed at the turn which the Revolution has taken, it is because you expected too much. I will admit all the violence, and, if you will, even the interestedness of the leaders in the National Assembly ; but that men should act from the pure motive of procuring good to others, without any regard at all to themselves, is, I am afraid, more than one is entitled to expect, even under the most perfect government that human wisdom could desire, much more under such a government as that under which the characters of all the men who are now acting any public part in France has been formed. Notwithstanding the vanity and ambition of some individuals, and notwithstanding the injustice which the Assembly itself has been guilty of in several instances, it must be admitted that no assembly of men that ever met since the creation has done half so much towards promoting the happiness of the human species as the National Assembly. Don't imagine that I judge of what is passing in France merely from the accounts in our English papers; I constantly read four French papers; and among them the *Gazette Nationale*, and the *Journal des Débats et des Décrets*. Our English papers indeed affect to treat every thing which is done in the National Assembly with contempt; but it is the contempt of the contemptible.

Our parliament is to meet on the 25th of next month; and we shall then learn, it is to be hoped, why we have been making such expensive preparations for war. There are, I think, about 150 or 160 new members in the parliament; some of them certainly will take part in the debates. Erskine is, I think, the most remarkable of these; though his eloquence, which certainly is very great, was not displayed to much advantage when he was formerly in parliament. Another new member, who will probably speak, is Sir Elijah Impey, the East India Judge, the friend of Mr. Hastings, and the man against whom the last parliament were very near voting an impeachment. As to Mr. Hastings himself, his partisans pretend that the dissolution of the parliament has put an end to his impeachment; and it is said that even the Chancellor maintains that opinion. It is an opinion, however, for which the principal members of the House of Commons insist there is not the least foundation, and there will probably be some violent debates on the subject in both houses. If, on the pretence of a dissolution, an end should be put to the trial, I should not be at all surprised to see Mr. Hastings dignified with a peerage, and taking his seat among his judges; as his friend Sir Elijah Impey has taken his among his accusers.

Pray remember me very affectionately to Mad^{e}. D———, and to all her family.

Yours, &c.

SAML. ROMILLY.

LETTER LXXIV.

FROM MADAME G——.

Paris, 3 Nov. 1790.

Nous venons de recevoir, Monsieur, votre obligeante lettre, et je ne laisserai pas partir M. Smith sans quelques lignes qui vous prouvent mon parfait rétablissement, puisque vous ne voulez y croire qu'à cette condition.

Nous sommes bien aises que vous considériez encore notre révolution et notre position sous un aspect un peu favorable. Votre opinion nous redonne du courage. Peut-être notre différence de manière de voir tient-elle à ce que vous ne

---

LETTER LXXIV.

Paris, Nov. 3. 1790.

We have just received your obliging letter, and I cannot allow Mr. Smith to leave us without a few lines which may satisfy you as to my complete recovery, since you will believe it on no other condition.

We are very glad that you still view our revolution, and the posture of our affairs, in a somewhat favourable light. Your good opinion gives us fresh courage. Perhaps, the difference in our mode of viewing

voyez que les résultats des opérations de l'Assemblée, et que nous qui sommes sur le lieu de la scène, nous sommes blessés du spectacle du jeu des passions dans tous leurs excès, des fureurs de la cabale, de l'intrigue, uniques ressorts qui conduisent dans ce moment nos affaires. Quelquefois on ne peut s'empêcher de craindre qu'une si grande dépravation, dans les esprits et dans les caractères, ne nuise et n'empoisonne totalement tout le bien qu'on avoit lieu d'espérer de la révolution. Voilà la cause du découragement des honnêtes gens, qui gémissent de voir tous les jours se reculer davantage l'époque du retour de l'ordre et de la paix ou milieu de nous.

M. D. G.

Letter LXXV.

FROM THE SAME.

Paris, 18 Février, 1791.

Nous aurions dû répondre bien plutôt, Monsieur, à votre obligeant envoi, et à la lettre qui

---

arises from your seeing only the results of the proceedings of the Assembly, whilst we, who are on the spot, are shocked by beholding the working of passions in all their excesses, and the raging of cabals and intrigues, the only springs which now direct our movements. Sometimes one cannot help fearing lest so great a depravation of mind and disposition should neutralise, or entirely poison, all the good one had reason to expect from the revolution. This it is which discourages right-minded men, who lament to see the time when order and peace may be restored to us becoming every day more distant.

Letter LXXV.

Paris, Feb. 18. 1791.

We ought, Sir, to have acknowledged much sooner your obliging packet, and the letter which accompanied it, and which M. Dumont

l'accompagnoit, que M. Dumont nous a remise. Nous nous sommes procuré le plaisir de parler beaucoup de vous avec lui : nous avons tâché d'arranger que vous fissiez bientôt un voyage ici, et nous trouvons que vous ne pouvez pas vous en dispenser. Pensez bien, Monsieur, au plaisir que nous aurons à vous voir, à tous les objets d'intérêt que la France peut vous offrir, et vous serez de notre avis. Nous vous rendons mille graces des pamphlets que vous nous avez envoyés : ils nous sont fort agréables ; car on met ici un très-grand intérêt à ce que vous dites et pensez de nous. C'est à dire, que quand vous blâmez quelques-unes de nos opérations, les aristocrates triomphent, et se font gloire de votre autorité, tandis que les démocrates disent que vous êtes *reculés*, que vous n'êtes pas encore à *notre hauteur*, et que vous ne connoissez pas encore les principes. Quand vous nous admirez, alors c'est différent ; car pour le blâme et la louange, les Jacobins sont hommes comme pour plusieurs autres petites choses. Mira-

---

delivered to us. We indulged the pleasure of talking much of you with him. We endeavoured to settle for you the plan of a journey to Paris, which we really think it is incumbent on you to put into early execution. Consider well the pleasure we shall have in seeing you ; all the interesting objects which France offers to you, and you will agree with us. We return you many thanks for the pamphlets you have sent us : they were very welcome ; for we feel a strong interest in all that you say and think about us. That is to say, when you blame any of our proceedings, the aristocrats triumph and glorify themselves on the strength of your authority ; while the democrats say that you are gone backwards, that you have not risen to our height, and that you have not yet any knowledge of principles. When you admire us then the case is altered ; for, in so far as blame and praise are concerned, the Jacobins are much like the rest of mankind ; as, indeed, they are in many other small matters. Mirabeau has lately met with a

beau a éprouvé un échec, dernièrement; il était en concurrence avec M. Pastoret, pour être Procureur-Syndic de notre département. Danton a fait un discours pompeux, pour prouver aux électeurs qu'il devoit être élu, mais cette fois l'éloquence a eu le dessous, et M. Pastoret l'a emporté.

Vous avez mille choses de tous les individus de notre famille. Notre petit enfant prospère à merveille, et nous procure déjà beaucoup de bonheur. Recevez l'assurance de la sincère et inviolable amitié de mari et femme.

Letter LXXVI.

TO M. DUMONT.

Dear Dumont, London, April 5. 1791.

I make you no apology for not writing sooner, because you deserve none. I own I have been much disappointed, after all your promises, to have received only one letter from you since your departure. The only way in which I can account for it is by supposing that you intend to return very shortly,—the end of this month or the begin-

---

rebuff; he was opposed to M. Pastoret as candidate for the place of Procureur-Syndic of our department. Danton made a pompous speech to prove to the electors that he ought to be elected; but, for this once, eloquence had the worst of it, and M. Pastoret carried the election. Every member of our family unites in kind regards to you. Our little child thrives wonderfully, and is already a source of much happiness to us.

Yours, &c.

ning of the next, as you at first intended. The politics of Geneva at least will not delay you, as I understand every thing is finally settled. I cannot give you my opinion of that settlement, as I am not sufficiently informed of the circumstances that relate to it.

Kirkerbergher[1], I am afraid, is quite forgotten by you. I have written a few letters for him since you went, but he will not be able to go on with spirit till you return. We have been anticipated in our design by a real Kirkerberger. A man of the name of Wendeborn, who has published a book in two volumes 8vo., entitled, *A View of England towards the Close of the Eighteenth Century.* I have only seen the accounts which the Reviews give of it, and it seems accurate, and not devoid of merit; but I do not believe that we shall find he has often taken the same ground as we take. I thought K. had been a name of our own invention, but I find Rousseau, in his *Confessions,* mentions a Bernese of that name who made him a visit at the Isle de St. Pierre.

There have been several answers to Burke since

[1] It appears from preceding letters that Mr. Romilly had been very urgent with M. Dumont to write a History of the French Revolution. This suggestion was never acted on to the extent which Mr. Romilly had hoped that it might; but a series of historical letters on the events of the four months from April to September, 1789, of which he had been an eye-witness, were written by M. Dumont, and translated into English by Mr. Romilly. To this translation were added several original letters of Mr. Romilly, on subjects connected with the manners and institutions of England, and the whole was published in one small 12mo. volume, in 1792, under the title of *Groenvelt's Letters,* which name was substituted for that of Kirkerbergher, which they had at first intended to give to this work. It is afterwards referred to under the letter K. Various circumstances, which it is unnecessary to state, prevented the intended continuation of this work.

you left us, but none that have much merit, except one by Paine [1], the author of the famous American *Common Sense*. It is written in his own wild but forcible style; inaccurate in point of grammar, flat where he attempts wit, and often ridiculous when he indulges himself in metaphors; but, with all that, full of spirit and energy, and likely to produce a very great effect. It has done that, indeed, already; in the course of a fortnight it has gone through three editions; and, what I own has a good deal surprised me, has made converts of many persons who were before enemies to the revolution. As you are not likely to see it soon, I will give you a specimen of his manner. He is speaking of the law of primogeniture. "The nature and character of aristocracy shows itself to us in this law. It is a law against nature. Establish family justice and aristocracy falls. By the aristocratical law of primogeniture, in a family of six children, five are exposed. Aristocracy has never more than one child; the rest are begotten to be devoured. They are thrown to the cannibal for prey, and the natural parent prepares the unnatural repast. All the children which the aristocracy disowns (which are all except the eldest) are in general cast, like orphans, on a parish, to be provided for by the public, but at a greater charge. Unnecessary offices and places in governments and courts are created, at the expense of the public, to maintain them." He speaks of titles of nobility with true republican contempt, and says that "they afford no idea," that

[1] *Rights of Man*.

"no such animal as a Count or an Earl can be found any where but in imagination."

Bentham leads the same kind of life as usual at Hendon: seeing nobody, reading nothing, and writing books which nobody reads. His brother, who is a colonel in the Russian army, and a great friend of Potemkin's, is on his road to England, on a visit. My brother and sister desire to be remembered to you.

Yours sincerely and affectionately,
SAML. ROMILLY.

LETTER LXXVII.

FROM MADAME G——.

Paris, 7 Avril, 1791.

Nous avons reçu ces jours derniers encore un paquet de vous, Monsieur, contenant les réflexions de M. Bentham sur notre ordre judiciaire, une esquisse du règne de George III., et une réponse à M. Burke. Nous vous rendons mille grâces de ces marques d'attention, fort agréables en elles-mêmes, et qui ont de plus le mérite de nous assurer de votre souvenir. Vous devez trouver

---

LETTER LXXVII.

Paris, April 7. 1791.

We have received within the last few days another packet from you, containing the observations of Mr. Bentham on our judicial establishment, a sketch of the reign of George III., and an answer to Mr. Burke. We return you many thanks for these marks of attention, very agreeable in themselves, and which have the additional merit of assuring us that we are not forgotten by you. You must think that

que nous y répondons bien mal, car nous n'avons pu vous envoyer aucune brochure ni nouveauté qui fût digne de vous. Nous avions pensé un instant à vous faire parvenir les *Mémoires de Franklin*, dont nous avons ici une traduction informe et incomplète, mais nous avons présumé que vous connoissiez, peut-être, déjà le manuscrit, et qu'ils ne devoient pas tarder à paroître en original à Londres. Nous avons lu l'ouvrage de M. Paine en réponse à M. Burke ; c'est la folie inverse ; cependant il y a des idées assez piquantes, et assez neuves, et qui sont assez au niveau de celles qui remplissent les têtes Françoises, actuellement.

Vous aurez sûrement pris part à la perte que la France vient de faire par la mort de Mirabeau.[1] L'impression que cet évènement a produite seroit seule une preuve suffisante que la révolution est complète et achevée jusques dans les dernières classes de citoyens ; que les titres, les rangs, les places ne

---

we make a very poor return, for we have not been able to send you any pamphlet or new publication worthy of you. We had at one moment thought of sending you *Franklin's Memoirs*, of which we have here an imperfect translation; but we presumed that you were, perhaps, already acquainted with the MS., and that the original would shortly be published in London. We have read Mr. Paine's work in answer to Mr. Burke ; it is the opposite extreme of madness; it contains, however, ideas somewhat new and striking, and which are pretty much on a level with those which at present fill the heads of Frenchmen.

You will, no doubt, have felt for the loss which France has just suffered by the death of Mirabeau.[1] The impression which this event has produced, would alone be sufficient proof that the revolution is complete, and that its effects extend even to the lowest classes of the people ; that titles, rank, and office no longer dazzle us; and that

---

[1] Mirabeau died on the 2d of April, 1791.

nous éblouissent plus, et que le talent seul sera désormais l'objet des regrets et des honneurs. La carrière de Mirabeau ne pouvoit pas finir dans un moment plus propice pour sa gloire : six mois plutôt sa mort auroit été considérée comme heureuse pour la chose publique, et il y a seulement deux mois qu'elle auroit été vue généralement avec indifférence. Mais depuis quelques semaines il avoit tellement embrassé le bon parti, et on sentoit si bien qu'il devoit faire réussir tout ce qu'il voudroit, que tous les honnêtes gens avoient mis leur espoir en lui, pour le retour de l'ordre et de la paix, et le regardoient comme la terreur des factieux et le soutien de la constitution ; aussi, sa perte cause-t-elle des craintes exagérées peut-être. Il faut se flatter que les vrais amis de la chose publique se rallieront avec plus de fermeté encore, en proportion de ce qu'ils sentent que sa mort peut leur ôter. Nous n'avons plus rien à apprendre, je crois, des républiques Grecques et Romaines, pour les honneurs

---

talent alone will henceforth be the object of our regret and of our homage. Mirabeau's career could not have come to an end at a moment more propitious for his own fame ; six months earlier, his death would have been considered as a happy event for the public; and only two months ago it would have been looked upon with general indifference. But for some weeks past he had so entirely taken up the right side, and it was so strongly felt that he could not but accomplish whatever he wished, that all well-disposed people had placed in him their hopes for the restoration of order and peace, and looked upon him as the terror of the factious, and the prop of the constitution. Accordingly, his loss has raised fears, which are, perhaps, exaggerated. We must hope that those who have the public good at heart will rally with a degree of vigour proportioned to their sense of the loss they have sustained by his death. We have nothing more to learn, I believe, from the Greek and Roman republics, with respect to the honours to

à décerner aux grands hommes. Les spectacles, les divertissemens publics, ont été fermés: tous les corps, à l'envi, ont décidé de porter le deuil et de se rendre à son convoi. L'Assemblée Nationale, les électeurs, la municipalité, le département, les ministres, plusieurs clubs, une grande partie de la garde nationale, &c. formoient le cortège le plus imposant et le plus lugubre ; un concours innombrable de peuple était sur son passage ; un morne et profond silence régnoit dans cette multitude immense, qui paroissoit frappée d'un sentiment nouveau et extraordinaire. C'étoit seulement grand dommage que quelques vertus ne pussent pas se trouver dans le nombre de choses qu'on regrettoit dans cet homme illustre, et qu'au contraire, le talent s'y trouve obscurci par tout ce qu'il y a de dégoûtant dans la nature humaine. Son corps a été présenté à St. Eustache, où s'est fait le service funèbre, et ensuite déposé à l'ancienne église de Ste. Geneviève, en attendant qu'il puisse être placé dans la nouvelle église à côté des grands hommes que

---

be decreed to great men. The theatres and other places of public amusement were closed, and all public bodies vied with each other in their zeal to put on mourning, and to attend the funeral. The National Assembly, the electors, the officers of the municipality and the department, the ministers, several clubs, and a large portion of the national guard, formed a most imposing and mournful procession; an immense concourse of people attended it on its passage; a deep and solemn silence reigned throughout the countless multitude, which seemed to be overwhelmed by some new and extraordinary feeling. What a pity it is that no virtues are to be found among the things for which this illustrious man is regretted; and that, on the contrary, talent was in him obscured by all that is most repulsive in human nature. His body was taken to St. Eustachius, where the funeral service was performed, and it was afterwards deposited at the old church of St. Geneviève, where it will remain till it can be placed in the new church, by the side of the other great men whom the Assembly has thought worthy of

l' Assemblée jugera digne d'y admettre. Mirabeau a conservé une très-grande présence d'esprit et un grand sang-froid jusques dans ses derniers momens. Il fait par son testament un grand nombre de legs. Il possède une terre, une maison, et l'aperçu de sa fortune est d'environ un million, mais on croit qu'il en doit *deux*. M. de la Marck, son ami, a promis de suppléer à ce qui pourroit manquer, pour que ses dernières volontés puissent être remplies, mais M. de la Marck est endetté au-delà de ce qu'il possède. Il laisse quelque chose à Mad. le Jay, à ses enfans, puis à un fils naturel, ensuite à une de ses sœurs, et à ses nièces.

Mon mari n'a pas le temps de vous écrire ; il vous adresse mille choses.

Agréez, &c.

---

being admitted there. Mirabeau retained great presence of mind and composure up to the last moment. He leaves, by his will, a great number of legacies. He possessed an estate and a house, and his fortune is estimated at about one million, but it is believed that he owes *two*. His friend, M. de la Marck, has promised to make good what may be wanting to carry into effect his last wishes; but M. de la Marck himself owes more than he is worth. He leaves something to Madame le Jay, to her children, to a natural son, to one of his sisters, and to his nieces.

My husband has not time to write to you. He desires many kind regards.

Believe me, &c.

Letter LXXVIII.

FROM M. DUMONT.

Sacconex [1], 9 Avril, 1791.

Voilà donc Mirabeau éteint au milieu de sa carrière! Est-ce un malheur pour la révolution? Je le crois, sa maison étoit un foyer de liberté. S'il ne travailloit pas lui-même, il faisoit travailler; il excitoit les talens, et donnoit un appui considérable au parti qu'il embrassoit. Il étoit dangereux, sans-doute, à cause de ses passions, qui le gouvernoient absolument; mais on pouvoit les diriger au bien, et il avoit l'amour de la gloire. J'ai senti, aux regrets que sa perte m'a fait éprouver, qu'il avoit bien plus gagné mon affection que je ne le savois moi-même. On ne pouvoit pas le connoître et n'être pas séduit par son esprit et

---

Letter LXXVIII.

Sacconex [1], April 9. 1791.

So Mirabeau is extinguished in the midst of his career! Is it a misfortune for the revolution? I think it is; his house was a focus of liberty. If he did not work himself, he made others work: he stimulated men of talent, and was a strong prop to the party whose cause he espoused. He was dangerous, no doubt, from his passions, which exerted absolute dominion over him; but even these might be directed to good ends, and he had a love of glory. I felt from the grief that I experienced at his loss, that he had acquired a stronger hold on my affections than I had been myself aware of. It was impossible to know him, and not be fascinated by his talents and his engaging manners.

---

[1] Near Geneva.

ses manières caressantes. Combien de fois il m'a fait déplorer qu'il manquât à ses moyens la puissance que donne une réputation intacte! Il a été consumé par ses passions; s'il avoit su les modérer, il avoit pour cent ans de vie. Nos aristocrates le déchiroient, et ils le regrettent. C'est une perte pour eux que celle d'un homme qui soutenoit le crédit public.

Je compte partir du 20 au 25 de Mai pour Paris, et du 10 au 15 Juin pour Londres; ainsi j'arriverai vers le milieu de Juin, et je me remettrai d'abord pour m'égayer et me distraire à la correspondance de Kirkerberg. Il faut renoncer à faire un nom Allemand, puisqu'on ne sauroit en imaginer un assez dur, assez barbare, assez Gothique pour qu'ils ne s'en soient pas déjà emparés. Je suis presque sûr que tout sera prêt pour le temps où nous l'avons pensé, et j'ai pris quelques mesures indirectes pour la publication. Ne seroit-ce encore qu'un songe agréable? mieux

---

How often have I lamented that his powers should have wanted the influence of an unsullied reputation! His passions have consumed him; if he had known how to control them, he might have lived for a hundred years. Our aristocrats tore him to pieces, and they regret him; the death of a man who sustained public credit is a real loss to them.

I propose to set off for Paris between the 20th and 25th of May, and to leave it for London between the 10th and 15th of June, so that I shall arrive towards the middle of June; and, by way of an agreeable diversion to my thoughts, I shall at once set to work on Kirkerberg. We must give up the idea of inventing a German name for our letters, since it is impossible to imagine one so harsh, barbarous, and Gothic, as not to have been already appropriated. Every thing will be ready, I have little doubt, by the time we had anticipated, and I have indirectly taken some steps for the publication. What though it should still be but an agreeable dream? and yet an agreeable dream is better than a

vaudroit un joli songe qu'un mauvais réveil. Quoiqu'il en soit, je suis bien sûr qu'on ne perd rien pour attendre. L'intérêt ne diminue en aucune manière, et rien n'a paru qui doive décourager l'émulation de nos correspondans.

Letter LXXIX.

TO MADAME G——

Madam, Gray's Inn, May 20. 1791.

I am very much ashamed of not having written to you sooner; and I am ashamed, too, of making you an apology, because you are so used to such kind of apologies from me. The best apology I could make, would be to give you an account of the manner in which my time has been spent; but I shall spare you the pain of reading so uninteresting a diary, in which you would find me perpetually occupied in a way which, of all others, is least pleasant to me.

I am exceedingly obliged to you for the very interesting account you give me of Mirabeau's funeral. I sincerely regret his death. You certainly do not do him justice, when you suppose him destitute of all private virtues. I know that he was capable of very warm friendship, that he often exerted the greatest zeal, and made very considerable sacrifices

---

sad waking. However that may be, I am sure that nothing is lost by delay. The subject loses none of its interest, and our correspondents have no reason to be discouraged by any thing that has yet appeared.

to serve his friends. I know, too, that he has been very grossly calumniated in several instances which have come under my own immediate observation.[1]

You have before this time heard, and, I make no doubt, lamented, how the question respecting the abolition of the slave trade has been decided in our House of Commons.[2] Nothing can be more disgraceful to the nation than such a decision, after so long an inquiry too; and after that inquiry had shown the necessity of an immediate abolition in the strongest light possible, and had converted into well authenticated facts what had before been only matter of conjecture, and the supposed and probable consequences of the trade. I believe the history of mankind cannot furnish another instance of a nation, calmly, and after long deliberation, giving its sanction to continual robberies and murders, because it conceives them to contribute to its riches. We have but one consolation under this disgrace; it is a consolation, however, which is itself the source of another species of disgrace. It is, that our House of Commons is not a national assembly, and certainly does not speak the sense of the nation. It is remarkable, that, though the question was carried by a great majority, not one man who has any character for abilities spoke on the side of the majority, and all the members who are most eminent for their talents took a very active part on the side of the abolition. But elo-

1 See *antè*, p. 81.

2 On the 19th of April, 1791, Mr. Wilberforce's motion for leave to bring in a bill to prevent the further importation of slaves into the British colonies in the West Indies was lost in the House of Commons by a majority of 163 to 88.

quence, humanity, policy, reason, and justice were easily defeated by the most stupid prejudices. The question, however, is not (as the West India planters flatter themselves) now at rest. It will be resumed in a future session, and must before long be carried. The arguments urged in the last debate, though they could not convince the House of Commons, have produced a very great effect on that large portion of the public whose hearts are not hardened by opulence, nor their understandings corrupted by commercial and political prejudices. Even the arguments for the trade have contributed to increase the public horror of it. One member, an alderman of London, to prove the advantage of slavery to this country, told the House that it afforded a market for the refuse fish and corrupted food, which could be sold for no other description of persons. Undoubtedly, neither the trade, nor even slavery in the islands, can exist for many years longer; and yet it is dreadful to think what misery must be endured in the interval which is to elapse before they are abolished.

We have had violent debates in our House of Commons on the French revolution; and they have produced a total, and, as it should seem, an irreparable breach between Fox and Burke. Fox has gained much with the public by his conduct, and Burke has lost as much. It is astonishing how Burke's book is fallen; though the tenth edition is now publishing, its warmest admirers at its first appearance begin to be ashamed of their admiration. Paine's book, on the other hand, has made converts of a great many persons; which, I confess, appears to me as wonderful as the success of Burke's; for I do not understand how men can be convinced without arguments; and I find none in Paine, though I admit he has great merit. It is a book calculated, I should have thought, to strengthen preconceived opinion, but not to convert any one. However, the event shows that I was wrong. The impression which it has made in Ireland is, I am informed, hardly to be conceived. But the French revolution there has always been universally popular; and if the enthusiasm which it has kindled should any where break out in acts of violence, it will certainly be first in Ireland.

I write to you in very great haste, and, I fear, illegibly; but I would not let slip the only opportunity I may have of writing for some time. Pray let me hear from you, and as often as you can conveniently. I don't deserve it by my letters, but I do by my thoughts, which transport me perpetually in the midst of your family. Pray remember me very affectionately to all of them, particularly to my dear friend G——.

SAML. ROMILLY.

Letter LXXX.

FROM MR. TRAIL.

Paris, June 27. 1791.

Nothing can exceed the good order and tranquillity which have reigned at Paris ever since the King's elopement.[1] Some very seditious resolutions have been adopted and published by some of the inferior clubs, and some abominable libels have also been published against Lafayette and the municipality, but, it would seem, with very little effect. Profound silence was recommended to the people on the entrance of the Royal family; and it was in general observed. I stood in the Champs Elysées, on the edge of the road, from three till near eight, and I never saw more tranquillity or even indifference on any occasion. An officer passed us about half an hour before the King's arrival, and called out as he passed, "Chapeau sur tête!" This order was punctually observed. I heard of a young man, who lost his hat, being obliged to get behind, that nobody might appear uncovered. In all the conversation I heard, not a symptom of pity or sympathy appeared—nor much resentment. Ridicule, contempt, or great indifference, characterized all the observations that were made. When the Royal family got out of the carriage, three gardes du corps, who had acted as couriers, and were brought back tied on the coach-box, were for

[1] The King's flight from Paris took place on the night of the 20–21st of June, and he was brought back on the 25th.

some time in great danger of being put to death by the mob, and even by the National Guards. A deputation from the National Assembly arrived in time to save them: they are in prison. It is needless to give you an account of the King's being stopped. Every thing known about it has been published by the Assembly. It is certain that the King has repeatedly declared that he did not mean to quit the kingdom. When Lafayette's aide-de-camp presented him with the decrees the Assembly had passed immediately on the discovery of his flight, it is said both the King and Queen expressed themselves with much violence and resentment.

I have been much entertained in listening to the discussions in the groups formed in the Palais Royal and in the streets. I have heard very little violence against the King, a good deal against the Queen, but still more against those who assisted their escape. "Le Gros Cochon" is the most common appellation. They seem unwilling to believe that the guards about the Tuileries knew nothing of the elopement. A woman said, speaking of the Queen and Mad^e^. Elizabeth's escape, "S'il avoit été question de Mad^e^. d'Artois et de Mad^e^. de Provence, je les aurois cru échappées en bonnes Savoyardes par la cheminée." When the King was passing yesterday, a man by me said, "Voilà vingt-cinq millions perdus, pour un Louis gagné!" The day the King went off, it was a very common reflection that the nation would save thirty millions a year. I did then suppose that the general opinion was for a Republic; but I am now persuaded I was mistaken, for since, nobody talks of it — at least very few. All the schemes I have heard proposed, imply continuing the monarchical form of government. They do also all imply setting aside in effect, if not also in form, the present Sovereign. When the commissaries from the Assembly met the Royal family, the Queen said, "Eh bien, factieux, vous triomphez encore!" She asked Lafayette's aide-de-camp, who came up with her at Varennes, "En quel état est Paris?" "Dans la plus parfaite tranquillité; votre départ n'inspiroit que du mépris." The King, on his arrival, was, it is said, much intoxicated. A thousand other circumstances are repeatedly mentioned. I give you these, as the most likely to be true of all I have heard.

When the people were destroying all the insignia of royalty they could find on signs, &c., they came to the head of the King of England, a sign of one of the restaurateurs in the Palais Royal; when they were about to "faire main basse," an orator persuaded them that the King of England was a good man, and the only good king in Europe, and so saved his Majesty's head. I did not hear what arguments he employed.

After Pétion and Barnave got into the carriage with the Royal family, the Dauphin examined the legend on Barnave's buttons, one after another, and at last said, "Vivre libre, ou mourir partout, Maman."

Voltaire's funeral procession will probably be put off. They say here, "Le clergé a refusé d'enterrer Voltaire, et Voltaire a enterré le clergé."

LETTER LXXXI.

TO MADAME G——.

Madam, Gray's Inn, August 2. 1791.

Indeed it is not just that you should always wait to receive a letter from me, before you let me have that pleasure. You have many subjects to write on, while I have none that are worth saying any thing about. Every day furnishes materials for a volume in the land of wonders which you inhabit; but here every day passes exactly like that which went before it. I speak of London; for at Birmingham [1], that happy uniformity, which is the effect of peace and prosperity, has been dreadfully interrupted. It is very singular that all the persons who have most suffered from the outrages of the rioters, were persons particularly distinguished for their benevolence and charity, and who had most contributed to the prosperity of Birmingham by their industry. But all their virtues were of no avail in the eyes of men who had been deluded, by those who are very improperly called their superiors, into a belief that they intended to overturn the civil and ecclesiastical constitution of the country. I do not say this from conjecture, for I am just returned from Birmingham, where I have had occasion to inquire particularly into the causes and circumstances of the riots; and I am perfectly convinced that the persons

[1] The Riots at Birmingham took place on the 14th of July and following days.

who were the most active in destroying and burning the chapels and houses, are not by any means the most criminal. The celebration of the French Revolution was entirely forgot in the rage of the people against the dissenters. Several of those who have most suffered, were not at the dinner, and had never entertained any thoughts of going thither: and the only cry that was heard among the mob was, "Church and King for ever, and down with the Presbyterians!" I inclose Dr. Priestley's and another letter giving an account of the dinner, which may perhaps entertain you.

Pray have the charity to write to me soon, and send me good news of the health of your little girl, for Mr. Trail does not mention her so often as her mother.

I beg to be remembered very sincerely and affectionately to M. G——, to Mad^e^. D——, and to all your family.

Yours, &c.,

SAML. ROMILLY.

LETTER LXXXII.

TO M. DUMONT.

Dear Dumont, September 6. 1791.

I send you the conclusion of the letter on Lotteries [1], and another letter on Cruelty towards Animals. I believe I formerly read it to you; but I have since added to it, and I think improved it. It consists of scarcely any thing but description;

[1] See note, p. 415.

but the subject admits of nothing else. Men cannot be reasoned into humanity, and perhaps our readers will not be sorry to find that we do not ergotise for ever.

I have added several passages from you to the letter on Elections and some of my own, and on the whole I think it much better than it was. I have been working very hard since you left us. I hope you have done the same. I long to see some of your original letters. Remember that, as yet, since K. has been in England, you have done nothing but translate. Pray send me originals and translations as fast as you can. I can hardly reckon upon more than a month's leisure, if so much, and after that, adieu to K. Enable me to make the best use of my time. Never send me a larger packet than I now send you, lest K. should cost me more in MS. than he will ever repay me in print.

Yours affectionately,

S. R.

Letter LXXXIII.

FROM MR. GEORGE WILSON.[1]

Hôtel du Roi, au Carousel,
Wednesday night, Sept. 21. 1791.

Dear Romilly,

You have in the French papers probably more French news than I can give you. Since the

[1] The following account of Mr. Wilson and Mr. Trail is taken from a copy preserved by Sir Samuel Romilly of a letter written by him to Sir Jas. Mackintosh, in 1816:—

"Cabalva, Sept. 8. 1816.

"Whishaw told me, just before he left town, that you were desirous of knowing where I first became acquainted with our late excellent friend

completion of the constitution, the Assembly has been dull, and we have gone seldom: we were

---

George Wilson; and I intended immediately to have written to you, but the unusually early and late sittings of the Chancellor day after day for the last three weeks, left me not a moment that I could call my own, and it really has not been till I have got out of town that I have had an instant of leisure. My first acquaintance with Wilson was in the year 1784. The first circuit I went, which was in the spring of that year, I met Trail, who was then travelling it for the last time. Having gone round to every assize town for three successive circuits, without having a single brief, he gave it up in despair, as he afterwards relinquished the Chancery bar. He was a very remarkable instance of a man most eminently qualified to have attained the highest honours of the profession, but who, having no other recommendation than his great talents, was indeed respected, admired, and consulted continually; but it was only by those who were of the same rank in the profession with himself. No attorney ever discovered his merit; he never got any business, and the profession was to him only a source of expence and disappointment. By being continually in the same society during the three weeks or month that the circuit lasted, we became very well acquainted together; and he was so intimate with Wilson, that it was impossible to have formed a friendship with him, and not frequently to be in Wilson's society. In a short time I became as intimate with the one as with the other, and our friendship remained undiminished and uninterrupted for a moment till I lost both of them by death — Trail in 1809, and Wilson in the present year.

"You were yourself so well acquainted with Wilson, that it is not likely that I should be able to inform you of any incident of his life, or any ingredient in his character, which is not already known to you. Perhaps, however, you may not have had so many opportunities as myself of observing his great sensibility and warmth of affection. Under a cold and reserved exterior he had the warmest attachment to his friends, and the tenderest sympathy for the misfortunes of others, that I ever met with; and though there was something of austerity in his manner, he was singularly kind and even indulgent to all about him. You knew, and must have remarked, the clearness of his understanding, the soundness of his judgment, the propriety and perspicuity of his language, and the great extent of his learning as a lawyer, and the readiness with which he applied it. That with such qualifications so universally known, acknowledged, and brought into practice as they were by his being for many years the leader of the Norfolk circuit, he should never have been raised to a judicial station, or, I should rather say, should never have had such a situation offered to him, must be admitted to be matter of just reproach to those at whose disposal judicial offices are placed. If judgeships were elective, and the Bar — that is, the men best able to estimate the qualifications of a candidate — were the electors, he would, by their almost unanimous suffrages, have been raised to the Bench. But, in truth, it was his other admirable endowments which prevented justice being done to his professional merit. If he had en-

present when the King's letter[1] was read, and enjoyed the transport with which it was received by all parts of the *Salle*, except the *côté droit*, who hung their heads and were silent. The proposition for an amnesty was prodigiously applauded by the public tribunes; and the moment the reading was over, the people in them rushed to the door, tumbling over each other as if the house had been on fire, to tell the news all over Paris. At the Champ de Mars, on Sunday, the ceremony was very fine, and the people pleased and good-humoured, but without those transports which they say were shown at the Federation. The illuminations in the evening were very fine in the Champs

---

tertained political principles less liberal and less honourable to himself than he did, he would probably never have seen men, far his inferiors in learning and talents, raised over his head to those honours which of right should have been his. I say *probably;* for, from what I know of his disposition, I entertain much doubt whether he would, at any period of his life, have accepted the office of Judge, and whether the Ministers might not have had the credit of desiring to raise to the Bench, without regard to politics, a man whose administration of justice would have been one of the greatest public benefits they could have conferred on the country, and yet have enjoyed what they consider as the solid advantage of appointing to the office as determined a Tory as they could find amongst their most favoured friends.. He thought so modestly of himself, and was so devoid of ambition, and so contented with the quiet enjoyment of the society of the small but well-chosen circle of his professional and literary friends, that I believe he would have thought the highest honours and the greatest emoluments of the profession too dearly purchased by the sacrifices they would have cost him, and the painful duties to which they would have subjected him. It was not, as you know, till very late in life that he was promoted to the rank of King's Counsel. It was at the instance of Lord Ellenborough, whose private friendship he had long enjoyed, that that rank was conferred on him, and I know that it was with some hesitation and reluctance that he accepted it."

[1] Containing the King's acceptance of the Constitution, which had been presented to him by the Assembly a few days before. On the 29th of September the sittings of the Constituent Assembly terminated.

Elysées and the castle and garden of the Tuileries. All Paris was there, and the Royal family appeared in the evening, and were well received, though perhaps with less enthusiasm than Lafayette. On Monday, "Richard" was given at the *Italiens* to an immense house. The song, "O Richard, O mon Roi!" was not interrupted till the excessive applause of the Aristocrats provoked it, and the piece was heard throughout. A *billet* was thrown on the stage, which the audience desired to have read; but as soon as it began, "O Louis, O mon Roi!" they stopped it, and a tumult arose. After some time a *juge de paix* came on the stage and commanded silence in the name of the law, which to my surprise was immediately complied with. He said the *spectacle* must not be interrupted by this paper. If the verses were fit to be published, they should have them in the *Journal de Paris*, next day. The audience clapped, the piece went on, and the verses have not been published. Last night all the Royal family were at the Opera; the Boulevard and the house as full as they could hold, and the most enthusiastic applause without any alloy. One verse, "Régnez sur un peuple fidèle," was encored, and amazingly clapped; and the applause, as far as I could judge, was distributed to their Majesties very equally. They have been very popular ever since their enlargement, and the acceptation has fixed it for the present, though the people in the groups still express a distrust of the King, and some of the Queen. There is a story very current that the Queen has discouraged the Emperor from assisting the Princes, thinking that the King must be a cypher at all events, and that she is better under the present government than with the Princes as conquerors.

Another story is, that the King said lately to an officer of the National Guard, that he was afraid of being assassinated by his brothers. Perhaps these things are circulated to persuade the people that the King and Queen have an interest in and are attached to the constitution. It is of great importance that their situation should be made comfortable, and that the world should think it so; and the leading men and the bulk of the people seem sensible of this, and disposed to contribute to it. Bailly and Lafayette were in the next box to the King last night, and several leading men in other parts of the house. Lafayette is to command at Metz, and Bailly[1] does not resign till November. A letter from Monsieur and M. d'Artois to the King, accompanied with another from the Condés, was published yesterday by Calonne's printer, and is said to be authentic. It is, I think, ill written and injudicious. It treats all innovation on the old system as illegal and void, and does not hold another assembly or any mode of forming a constitution, and it is full of unpopular expressions about nobility; and the declaration of the Emperor and King of Prussia is given at the end, which seems to bind them to nothing; and the emigrants at Spa now say, that every thing is put off till the spring. Last week the invasion was fixed for the

[1] Bailly had held the situation of mayor of Paris since the 14th of July, 1789.

beginning of October. I was in hopes that the amnesty would have brought back the greater part of the emigrants, but this letter makes it impossible for the Princes at least. Three deputies have been chosen[1] to-day for Paris, one a goldsmith, and all good men as I hear. Except Brissot, and Garran de Coulon, and perhaps Mulot, I have not heard of any violent man being chosen for Paris, and we hear good accounts of the elections in the country. Perhaps the best way of extinguishing Brissot is to choose him. It made an end of Wilkes. There is a story that Thouret, Chapelier, Beaumetz, and Talleyrand are to be in the King's council, without office or salary. I hope it is not true. It would be an evasion of the law which makes them incapable of office. It would never be believed that they received no emolument; and besides ruining these men and hurting the government, it would throw a suspicion on the whole work of the constitution, which is at present universally popular. The Republicans seem to be a very small party, and their leaders men of no talent, and very unpopular in the Assembly. I have never heard any of them make a tolerable speech. The man with whom I am most pleased is D'André, and he is now clearly the leader of the Assembly. I have heard an excellent character of him in private life, and as a magistrate at Aix. He is going to set up as a grocer. I never saw a man do business better, or take his ground with more judgment. I have

[1] As members of the Legislative Assembly.

been sometimes at the '89 [1], but do not speak with sufficient ease to get on much there. The only man of any eminence that I have made a little acquaintance with is Chamfort, who is a man of parts, but too fond of talking and of systems. There is a new book of Volney's, called *Les Ruines, ou Méditations sur les Révolutions des Empires*, written chiefly before the revolution, containing reveries of all sorts in a bad form, with some good things here and there. I have read but little of it. Sutton [2] and Lens live in the house with us, and we are much with Windham, Mitford [3], and Douglas. Every body sends you compliments, and we hope to hear from you soon. Sutton has a note to-night from Lally, who has a letter from you to Trail, which we hope to get to-morrow morning. I must conclude, because it is very late; and I must rise early to go to the Assembly, where we expect a debate about the Colonies.

Yours sincerely,

G. Wilson.

Letter LXXXIV.

FROM MR. TRAIL.

Dear Romilly, Paris, Sept. 26. 1791.

I had the pleasure of your letter by Mr. Lally a few days ago. I was in hopes that between Ascough and Wilson you would have had a

[1] This was a club called the Club of 1789, established in May, 1790. See *Moniteur* for 1790, No. 135.

[2] Lord Manners.

[3] Lord Redesdale.

regular and circumstantial detail of what is passing; but, with the best dispositions, they have frequently delayed writing till the last moment, and have then been prevented by some unexpected occurrence. I believe, however, they have both written at least once; I am sure Wilson did last week.

Things continue pretty much in the same state. The satisfaction with the King's unequivocal and decided mode of accepting the constitution is still manifest among all ranks of people. For the present, suspicion seems to be asleep; and I think it is not impossible, by a continuance of the same open and frank conduct, to prevent it from being waked. Some hot-headed people and some speculative republicans are, or affect to be, alarmed at the reception the Royal family meet with wherever they appear, as if there was the most distant probability of the people relapsing into their ancient idolatry of the *Grand Monarque*. Last night the King illuminated the Tuileries and the Champs Elysées in return for the testimonies of affection he has received from the people. He went in grand cavalcade with all the family, preceded by his servants, and followed by Lafayette and the *état-major*, to the barrier to see the illuminations; he was well received by an immense concourse of people wherever he passed. There was no enthusiasm to alarm the anxious and timorous patriots; but there was a great deal of hearty good-humour and satisfaction in everybody's countenance. Although the weather was not so fine as on the preceding Sunday, there was a much greater assemblage of people in the Tuileries and Champs Elysées : perhaps that was occasioned by the illuminations being much more splendid. I never saw any thing so magnificent.

The National Assembly revoked on Saturday the decree of the 15th of May[1] in favour of the *gens de couleur*. I am sorry it was ever passed; and am rather inclined to think that it was wise, under all the circumstances, to revoke it. It was certainly understood in the colonies, and with some foundation, to be contrary to the decree or declaration of the 12th of October. It was very likely to occasion a separation of the colonies from the mother-country, as, at present, measures of vigour for its execution could not be pursued. That event, though in itself no great misfortune, would, however, have been considered in all the trading and manufacturing towns a great calamity, and have been imputed to the revolution. Besides, it is more consonant to the *grands principes* that the colonies should be permitted to decide on this matter themselves. Barnave has throughout the whole business of the colonies behaved with great artifice and *mauvaise foi;* he has also met with severe mortifications in consequence of his misbehaviour. He made a very great speech, I am told, on Friday. Douglas heard it, and was much pleased: so he is in general with the manner of doing business in the Assembly. Mitford is also a tolerable French Whig. I am sorry the decree of Saturday is declared constitutional; it would have been better

[1] Making persons of colour born of free parents eligible to all colonial and parochial assemblies.

to have revoked the decree of the 15th of May, and to have declared every thing relative to the colonies to be within the province of the ordinary legislature. The friends of the *gens de couleur* in the Assembly are numerous; but there is not among them a good head, unless it be the Duc de la Rochefoucauld, who has certainly an excellent understanding, but wants energy of manner. Your friend, Dupont, has always a crotchet on which he is *entêté* like a mule. I have not heard how there appeared to be a decided majority against the colonial committee, although on the *appel nominal* there was a majority of above one hundred the other way.

I have just glanced over Talleyrand's report on national education. I don't like either his general principles or his plan. I hope the Assembly won't enter far into the subject; they have not time, and of course they will do ill what they attempt. It is adjourned to the next legislature. It is very generally believed that the Queen is determined to abide by the constitution rather than run any more risks; and that she is satisfied, if the Count d'Artois were to succeed, the King would be a cypher, and the Kingdom would be governed by the Princes. The declaration of the Emperor and the King of Prussia made but little sensation here; it amounts to nothing, and can only be considered as a very civil refusal. The letter of the King's brothers makes none: it is said to be Calonne's workmanship; it is ill written, and worse conceived.

It is clear that, in the *fêtes nationales* which they

intend to institute, no religious ceremony whatever will be admitted. This may be done on a sound principle, which can offend nobody. The *fête* should be such as every French citizen can partake of without violence to his religious principles.

Bailly has offered his resignation as Mayor of Paris, and, at the request of the municipal body, has delayed it only till November. It is said he is fatigued; and he has lately been insulted by the people, and accused of forestalling corn, of which he is, most undoubtedly, perfectly innocent.

A great number of *Aristocrates* have lately quitted the kingdom. The letter of the Princes and the declaration of Pilnitz have, perhaps, persuaded them that a counter-revolution would be immediately attempted. They all appear so thoroughly mortified with the King's acceptation and subsequent conduct, that I have not the least doubt of his sincerity.

Sutton, Wilson, and Lens desire their compliments. Lens sets out to-morrow or Wednesday for London and Taunton.

Yours, &c.

JAMES TRAIL.

LETTER LXXXV.[1]

TO ———.

October, 1791.

The impatience which in your last letter you said you felt to know what had passed at the assizes at Warwick must have been already pretty well sa-

[1] The following letter is taken from a copy in the handwriting of Mr. Romilly.

tisfied by the accounts which have appeared in the newspapers. If your curiosity was excited by the expectation that, in the course of the trials, some discovery would be made of the first instigators of the riots, you must have been much disappointed; nothing of that kind appeared. The persons tried were all men in low situations of life, and no discovery of any importance came out on any of the trials. Twelve men were tried, and only four were convicted. One was acquitted because the meeting-house which he had burned had not been properly registered, and therefore did not come within the Act of Parliament. Against another the counsel who managed the prosecution declined to call evidence on account of his youth; and the other six were acquitted, although the evidence against them was so strong that no rational being could entertain the smallest doubt of their guilt. Two of these six, Rice and Whitehead, acted as the ringleaders of the rioters, and Rice had been twice tried at Worcester and twice acquitted, though his guilt was proved beyond all doubt. If these two men had been convicted, it was hoped that they might have made a discovery of their employers; and for this reason it is supposed that the gentlemen, who have christened themselves the friends of Church and King, were particularly anxious for their acquittal. They were indeed anxious for the acquittal of all of them; and a private subscription was made for the purpose of affording the rioters all the legal assistance they could have. Two counsel and an attorney were employed for each of them, and three counsel appeared for the only prisoner who could afford to retain counsel for himself; for the friends of Church and King extended their generosity indiscriminately to all who had risked their lives in so good a cause. The assistance, however, which their counsel could afford the prisoners was inconsiderable, when compared with that which they derived from the absurdity of the leading counsel for the crown, the very extraordinary incapacity of the judge, and the most profligate partiality in the jury. The counsel for the crown began, in opening the first prosecution, by telling the jury that the prisoner was to be considered as an object of commiseration, and that he acted under a delusion and a species of madness, and he represented his case as that of a man who, though mistaken, was sincere in his opinions; and all this of a fellow who was a notorious thief, and had been tried several times before at Warwick for robberies. An opening so injudicious might induce any one to think that government was not sincere in the prosecution, and that they wished merely the show of a trial, which should end in an acquittal. That, however, certainly was not the case, and any one who has been often a witness to the conduct of the leader of our circuit has a much easier way to account for it; as it is a very usual thing for him to state a case as strongly as possible against his own client, and to sacrifice the cause which he is entrusted with to what he thinks a stroke of wit or a display of eloquence; and this was the case at Warwick, where his only object was to utter a nonsensical dissertation on difference of opinion, and to paint the devastation done at London in 1780, and at Birmingham a month ago, in a style that would very well have suited the tragedy of Tom Thumb. The judge, who has, and not undeservedly, the character of being the very worst upon the bench, who is totally ignorant of law, and who is incapable of stating facts in a manner intelligible to the jury, summed up several of the plainest cases for conviction in the only way that could give the jury a pretence for acquittal. In one case, after stating the facts as strongly as *he* could to the jury, and telling them that they were proved by four witnesses, the veracity of whom was entirely unimpeached, who had no interest in the matter, and all of whom must be perjured, and must intend wrongfully to take away the life of their neighbour if he was innocent, he concluded with telling them that whichever way they found their verdict would be equally satisfactory to him. Two of the men who destroyed Dr. Priestley's house were convicted; and as the evidence against them was not at all stronger than what was given against several of those who were acquitted, it can be ascribed to nothing but to a speech which was made by Mr. Coke, another of the counsel for the crown, on opening the prosecution, in which he represented to the jury the scandal which their conduct in acquitting men accused of such offences, contrary to the plainest evidence, would bring on themselves and on the country. The jury, who, being most of them men of property in Birmingham, conceived themselves to be gentlemen, and who thought they might give false judgments and commit perjury without any reproach to their reputation, but that to suffer themselves to be told of what they had done without resenting it would bring an indelible stain on their honour, immediately took fire and complained to the judge; and afterwards one of them told a friend of mine that he thought they were bound, as gentlemen, to insist on Mr. Coke's making them satisfaction, or fighting them one after another. Mr. Burke's favourite spirit of chivalry, you see, is not quite extinguished; and when one finds so much of it still prevailing among the *noblesse* of Birmingham, one cannot be surprised that the doctrines of the National Assembly are with them so unpopular. The rage which prevails in Warwickshire against the Dissenters is not to be conceived by any one who has not been there. There is no story so incredible, no calumny so gross, as does not meet with implicit credit, and the most speedy propagation among the friends of Church and King; and the complete refutation of one calumny, instead of begetting distrust of the truth of another, only procures it a more easy reception. The appetite for defamation grows stronger as it has missed the prey, of which it thought itself secure. I heard one of these zealots declaring his utter detestation, not of Dissenters in general, but of those of Birmingham, founded, as he said, on the whole of their conduct, which he declared to have been scandalous and infamous beyond all example. These expressions were so strong, and were uttered with so much vehemence, that I thought I had now at last found the opportunity, which I had so often wished for before in vain, of hearing some specific charges which had been the pretext for the persecution; and I ventured to ask the gentleman what were the facts to which he alluded; but I am afraid my question, though certainly unintentionally, was expressed in such a way as betrayed more doubt than curiosity; for he told me, with great impatience, that it was to no purpose to talk with a person so prejudiced as I was. The sufferers by the riots, though several of them were in Warwick, thought it decent not to appear in court, and indeed they had no more business there than any other spectator; but I heard it observed by a warm Churchman, that not one of the Dissenters had dared to show his face in court during the trials. The prosecutions have all been conducted entirely by the Solicitor of the Treasury; and yet I have heard many persons say that the Dissenters were so malignant that they tried to get all the rioters hanged, and that they would not be satisfied unless they could hang half the town of Birmingham. The Dissenters had established a Sunday school at Warwick, and through mere charity had sent thither some children of poor persons who were of the Church of England. This diabolical conduct has produced several meetings of the Churchmen of Warwick; and, with a Rev. Mr. Daniel in the chair, they have voted this conduct to be a dangerous attack upon the rights of the Church, and have appointed a committee to watch over and protect the Church from invasion. In a word, the spirit that prevails against Dissenters now in Warwickshire, and, I believe, in some of the adjoining counties, is not unlike that which raged against the Catholics in the time of the famous Popish plot. A gentleman of good education, and who, on all other subjects, is certainly a sensible man, told me, as a story which he had heard from good authority, and to which he gave implicit credit, that, on the day after the revolutionary dinner, a hamper was brought to the hotel, and left there without direction; that, on being opened, it was found to be full of daggers, and that it has never since been sent for, and no one knows by whom it was brought.

At the time of the riots, a common cry among the mob was, "No philosophers — Church and King for ever!" and some persons painted up on their houses, "No philosophers!"

Two of the men who were convicted have been pardoned; one of them very soon after the trial, and without any application being made for him by the people of Birmingham. His pardon was a matter of great surprise to the Birmingham people, as he was a man of very bad character. It is said he has a brother at Windsor, who is in a mean way of life, but with whom the King has sometimes entered into conversation in his walks.

Dr. Parr is almost as unpopular at Birmingham as Dr. Priestley. The reason alleged for his unpopularity is, that, in a sermon which he lately preached in the town, he mentioned Dr. Priestley by name, spoke in praise of him, and recommended some of his sermons. Perhaps a more probable cause of his loss of popularity is, that he has had private quarrels with the heads of the church-and-king faction. But, whatever be the cause of it, the fact is certain, that he has the honour to be involved in the persecution of the Dissenters; and, himself an intolerant high churchman, he wonders to find himself an object of enmity to an intolerant high church mob.

> Ille fugit, per quæ fuerat loca sæpe secutus:
> Heu famulos fugit ipse suos! clamare libebat,
> Actæon ego sum! dominum cognoscite vestrum.

Letter LXXXVI.

FROM MADAME G——.

Paris, 1791.

Nous avons revu avec intérêt Mr. Smith, puisqu'il nous a donné de vos nouvelles avec détail, mais nous sommes extrêmement fachés d'avoir aussi peu profité de son séjour. Il paroît partir avec une assez triste opinion de notre Assemblée Législative [1]; il est sûr qu'elle a bien perdu son temps depuis qu'elle est assemblée, et que du bruit, du tumulte, des dénonciations, puis du tumulte et du bruit, sont les seuls résultats de ses séances. Les têtes exaltées,

---

Letter LXXXVI.

Paris, 1791.

We had much pleasure in seeing Mr. Smith again, for he gave us many particulars about you; but we are very sorry to have enjoyed so little of his society during his stay here. He appears to leave us with but a poor opinion of our Legislative Assembly [1]; and, certainly, from the first day of their meeting, they have only been wasting their time. Noise and tumult and recrimination, and then tumult and noise again, are the only results of their sittings. Hitherto the en-

---

[1] It had commenced its sittings on the 1st of October, 1791.

jusqu'à présent, y ont eu une grande influence. Le désir général de la nation actuellement est pourtant celui de la paix et du repos. Toutes les classes de la société sentent que les temps de révolution ne sont favorables ni aux affaires ni aux plaisirs; et depuis ceux qui ont besoin de gagner leur vie, jusqu'à ceux qui ne veulent la passer qu'à jouir, tous souhaitent également l'affermissement de l'ordre. Mais il y a quelques obstacles qui s'opposent à l'accomplissement de ce vœu général, et nous serons encore assez longtemps obligés de les combattre. Les émigrations sont dans ce moment plus nombreuses que jamais; on dit même qu'elles gagnent d'autres classes que celle de l'ancienne noblesse. Il est très-difficile de deviner les motifs qui peuvent engager à cette triste résolution, car les puissances étrangères paroissent assez peu disposées à venir nous attaquer, et nous nous berçons beaucoup de l'idée que nous n'avons rien à en craindre. On commence à s'effrayer de cette émigration, et l'on pense qu'il seroit prudent de prendre

---

thusiasts have had great influence among them, although the general wish of the nation now is for peace and quiet. All classes of society feel that times of revolution are not favourable either to business or pleasure; and from those who have their livelihood to gain, to those who live only to enjoy themselves, all are equally desirous for the establishment of order; but however general the wish, there are several obstacles to its accomplishment, against which we shall still have to struggle for a long time. Emigration is at this moment more frequent than ever; and it is even said that it is spreading to other classes besides that of the old *noblesse*. It is very difficult to conceive the motives for so sad a determination; for foreign powers seem little disposed to attack us, and we even buoy ourselves up with the belief that we have nothing to fear from them. People are beginning to be alarmed at this emigration, and to think that it would be prudent to take some steps to put a stop

quelque mesure pour l'arrêter. Cette idée fait des progrès dans l'Assemblée; je crois pourtant que ce seroit une sottise, et que les gens qu'on retiendroit par force seront toujours de dangereux et mauvais enfans pour leur patrie.

Mon mari a reçu de votre part, Monsieur, un livre intéressant, et qui a été lu ici avec avidité par quelques personnes. Il est flatteur pour nous de voir notre constitution défendue par des étrangers. Nous ne pouvons cependant nous dissimuler qu'elle s'est assez ressentie de notre caractère François, facilement exalté, et présomptueux. Nous avons voulu n'imiter personne, et nous n'avons point profité des leçons que nous offroient l'expérience des autres nations. Si nous nous déterminons au moins à nous laisser éclairer par notre propre expérience, et à reconnoître sans partialité les défauts de notre gouvernement qui nous blesseront, ce sera déjà beaucoup, et nous serons alors assez avancés.

Nous avons une petite fille qui a un an accompli,

---

to it. This notion gains ground in the Assembly; but I think that it would be an act of folly, for those who are retained in a country by force will always be dangerous and bad citizens.

My husband has received an interesting book from you, which has been read here by some with avidity. It is flattering to us to see our constitution defended by foreigners; but we cannot, at the same time, conceal from ourselves that it has a tinge of the French character, which so easily gives way to extravagance and presumption. We were determined not to imitate; we have, therefore, not profited by the lessons which the history of other nations supplied us with. If we resolve at least to submit to be guided by our own experience, and impartially acknowledge those faults of our own government which may be injurious to us, it will be a great point gained: we shall then have made some progress.

Our little girl, who is just a year old, begins to walk and to lisp a few

qui commence à marcher et à bégayer quelques mots : dans quelque temps nous lui verrons former des idées. Nous tâcherons d'être raisonnables, de suivre les conseils de notre *Emile*, et de ne pas gâter cette plante confiée à nos soins.

Nous avons du regret de n'avoir ni livres nouveaux, ni brochures intéressantes à remettre à M. Smith. Nous n'avons à vous envoyer que les assurances bien sincères de notre inviolable attachement.

Letter LXXXVII.

TO MADAME G——.

Madam, Lincoln's Inn, Dec. 6. 1791.

Indeed your letters do not need to be scarce to make them valuable. As for mine, I wonder you have the patience to read them. I write from a country which furnishes no event worth communicating to you. About myself, I have nothing to write; my life passes without any incidents in it, and one day of it exactly resembles the former. I have been passing the whole of the last summer in town, seeing nobody but my brother's family, (for, indeed, at that season, there is nobody here to see,)

---

words; in a little time we shall see her forming ideas. We shall endeavour to act with sense, to follow the advice of our *Emile*, and not to spoil this tender plant entrusted to our care.

We are sorry to have no new books or interesting pamphlets to send you by Mr. Smith. We can only send you the sincerest expression of our unalterable attachment.

and scarcely stirring out of my room, but to go to his house, or to take exercise. You may judge that such a life does not afford any adventures to relate. The most important transaction that has taken place in it for a long time, and one which, for a very powerful reason, I ought to communicate to you, is, that I have changed my chambers, and that your future letters are not to be addressed to Gray's Inn, but to *Lincoln's Inn, No. 2. New Square.* I have changed much for the better as a situation for business, but much for the worse as far as my own pleasure is concerned. Instead of having a very pleasant garden under my windows, I have nothing but houses before me, and I can't look any way without seeing barristers or attorneys. This is another sacrifice which I have made to a profession, which nothing but inevitable necessity forces me to submit to, which I every day feel more and more that I am unfit for, and which I dislike the more the more I meet with success in it.

We do not think at all more highly of the present national assembly here than you seem to do at Paris. Nothing could be more mischievous than the decree by which the last assembly disqualified themselves. If any one wished to bring popular elections into discredit, he could not do it more effectually than by letting the people elect their representatives, but forbidding them to elect those in whom they had most confidence, and of whose talents and virtues they had had experience. It is certain that hitherto very little ability has been shown in the assembly, either collectively or by any of its members; but I have no doubt that they will improve, and that much good may be expected from them. I remember having heard Mr. Fox say, that a parliament was so good a thing, however ill it might be constituted, that, if it were to consist of the first five hundred men who should be met passing in a certain street, at a certain hour, it would be better than to have none. I believe it better to be governed by a very bad national assembly than by a very good king. I cannot but persuade myself that there are men of great talents in the assembly who have not yet spoken. It was natural to suppose that the most superficial men would be the most in haste to speak. Men who are conscious of their own superiority are not so impatient to discover it; they wait for some occasion worthy of them, and willingly forego a little reputation, which they are sure of reaping at some time or other in the greatest abundance.

I have been exceedingly shocked at the insurrection at St. Domingo. It was natural to expect that it would be imputed to those who have exerted themselves in Europe on behalf of the negroes, because, if a bad cause be not defended by falsehood and calumny, it must remain without defence. The planters have, ever since it was first proposed to abolish the slave trade, that is, for above five years, predicted insurrections in the islands. Like the prophecies of Henry[1] IV.'s death, it was impossible that they should not at last be right. It is observable, however, that there has been no insurrection in any British island, in which alone it has

[1] Of France.

ever been prop
that, as there n
the present barb
without insurrecti
is no more reason t
Domingo to the gen
of the negroes, than t
any other event that
The true cause of this,
insurrections, is the cru
one cannot but feel the wa
one hears men imputing
caused by their own crimes,
who resist them.

I remain, &

END OF THE FIRST VOLUM

LONDON:
Printed by A. SPOTTISWOODE,
New-Street-Square.